Shaken Wisdom

Shaken Wisdom

IRONY AND MEANING IN POSTCOLONIAL
AFRICAN FICTION

Gloria Nne Onyeoziri

UNIVERSITY OF VIRGINIA PRESS   *Charlottesville and London*

THIS BOOK IS MADE POSSIBLE BY A COLLABORATIVE GRANT FROM
THE ANDREW W. MELLON FOUNDATION.

University of Virginia Press

Printed in the United States of America
on acid-free paper

First published 2011

9 8 7 6 5 4 3 2 1

Library of Congress Cataloging-in-Publication Data

Onyeoziri, Gloria Nne.
  Shaken wisdom : irony and meaning in postcolonial
African fiction / Gloria Nne Onyeoziri.
    p. cm.
  Includes bibliographical references and index.
  ISBN 978-0-8139-3186-9 (cloth : alk. paper)
  ISBN 978-0-8139-3187-6 (pbk. : alk. paper)
  ISBN 978-0-8139-3200-2 (e-book)
  1. Kourouma, Ahmadou—Criticism and
interpretation. 2. Achebe, Chinua—Criticism and
interpretation. 3. Beyala, Calixthe—Criticism and
interpretation. 4. African literature (French)—20th
century—History and criticism. 5. African
literature (English)—20th century—History and
criticism. 6. Irony in literature. 7. Meaning
(Philosophy) in literature. 8. Postcolonialism in
literature. I. Title.
PQ3989.2.K58Z77 2011
820.9'960904 dc23

                              2011022867

To my husband, Robert Miller, and my son,
Amarachi Miller, and in memory of my parents,
Jonathan and Martha Onyeoziri

CONTENTS

ACKNOWLEDGMENTS

I would like to thank a number of friends and colleagues who have contributed significantly to the conception and completion of this work: Victor Aire, my first professor of African Literature; Henry Schogt, who first taught me semantics; the late Frederick Ivor Case, who helped me as I struggled with the complexities of African and Caribbean studies; and Françoise Lionnet. At the University of British Columbia, Valerie Raoul has been for many years a mentor and friend; Ralph Sarkonak's careful reading of my manuscript and constant encouragement and advice have been invaluable. I also want to thank Cathie Brettschneider at the University of Virginia Press for her guidance as well as the conscientious anonymous readers.

This project was supported in its initial stages by a fellowship from the Institute for Advanced Study and Research in the African Humanities at Northwestern University. Some of the ideas contained in chapter 1 were presented at one of the institute's weekly seminars. Later I also received the support of a standard research grant from the Social Sciences and Humanities Research Council of Canada. I am particularly grateful to the various institutions that have made it possible for me as a non-sighted scholar to have access to texts: Ontario's Audio Library Services, the Micro-text Section of Robarts Library, and the Crane Library of the University of British Columbia, with special recognition of Paul Thiele, Eleanor Wellwood, and Clay Dixon.

My special gratitude to my husband, Robert Miller, who has always stood with me in scholarship and in life. Above all, I give thanks to God for His infinite grace.

Shaken Wisdom

African Ironies?

Irony can be a response to an oppressor convinced of his superior wisdom. It can suggest that its user's wisdom is superior. Irony can also hold the line on traditional wisdom shaken by disruptive events. Wisdom itself can be ironic, therefore shaken from the inside. Wisdom displayed as absolute truth, by an older generation, for example, for some homogeneous community, can in turn be displayed ironically by a younger generation anxious to affirm its own claim to knowledge, understanding, and freedom. Irony can be a tradition, but it can also subvert traditions or perhaps hide traditions in itself in order to remind us of them while seeming to speak and live free of traditional influences.

But if irony is an integral part of the way that meaning is produced and communicated in all kinds of situations of human verbal interaction, and often appears in literary texts as a representation of that role, what are the implications for a study that undertakes to foreground a specific discursive practice as *African*?

In her study of Elechi Amadi's *The Concubine*, Virginia Ola uses the notion of irony to defend the heroine's Africanity from "Eurocentric" feminist accusations of sexism: "Even the irony which informs the title, *The Concubine*, on which much of the suspense and complexity of the heroine's own position are predicated is denied its own crucial contribution to Amadi's stylistic achievement. [...] The situation of ethereal or other worldly concubinage is the dominant irony of the text, as well as the first act of rebellion and self-assertion on the heroine's part" (132). Why would irony form so basic an argument for an African heroine's self-assertion and so important a means of leading the reader to a more balanced understanding of African traditions and experience? Such is the seminal questioning that underlies the conception of the present study.

THE GOAL

The goal of this study is to consider the relationship, within the context of African literary discourse, between irony and meaning. What is the purpose of irony, and how does it work in its various forms as part of the process of communication? I am not assuming that all African literature is ironic. Nor am I undertaking a historical survey of irony in the vast and diverse corpus of African writing or of African literary criticism. Through an approach based to a large extent on pragmatics, the branch of linguistics that attempts to account for what utterances mean when they are used in actual situations, this study will show that from its presence in traditional communities, through the struggle to respond to a long history of disparagement of all things African, through the disillusionment with postindependence leadership, to the postcolonial questioning of cultural identity, the tendency to say things without saying them directly, the subterfuge of implicit meaning in speech, is an abundant, effective, and yet little understood feature of the codes and practices of African self-expression. Irony remains a subtle but powerful means for African women and men to undercut assumptions of their economic and social powerlessness by adding ironic subtexts to their words, just as marginalized individuals and communities ironically undercut the verbal dominance of their oppressors and detractors. This practice of irony will be shown to illuminate many insinuating and stealthy utterances that form a vital part of the texture of meaning conveyed through the literary works of Ahmadou Kourouma, Chinua Achebe, and Calixthe Beyala.

THEORETICAL CONSIDERATIONS: IRONIC DISCOURSE AND AFRICAN CULTURE

Is African literature simply one possible example among others of ironic discourse? Or is African literature in some way more ironic than other literatures, thereby meriting special attention? Or could it be that irony in African literature has not been adequately explored in studies of literary irony or in the criticism of African literature itself? Studies of irony in literature have tended to privilege examples taken from specific literary traditions, for example, the many references to nineteenth-century French literature in Philippe Hamon's *L'ironie littéraire* (Literary irony), Muecke's preference for English literature, and Knox's emphasis on fifteenth- to eighteenth-century English writers. Even Linda Hutcheon's *Irony's Edge*, though politically conscious and focused on postmodern theories, privileges European examples. Laura Rice's *Of Irony and Empire* (2007) is an exploration of the potential that irony offers as a means of understanding the effects of imperialism on Muslim Africa: "Throughout *Of Irony and Empire*, the trope of irony provides a lens that valorizes the dialectical, reciprocal, and empathetic open systems over closed system analyses. It asks how Muslim African self-representation is refracted through the detour of the other, and how Western self-representation is refracted through the mirror of other social imaginaries" (4).

There is no denying that Africans have been involved in transcultural and reciprocal relationships of irony for a long time. An ironic gaze, as Rice demonstrates, has long been directed toward African societies while Africans themselves have often been denied even the possession of a "sense of irony." The trope of irony thus lends itself to the opening up, destabilization, and deconstruction of the imaginary essences, doxa, and fixed categories that have defined and continue to define the relationship between Africans and other peoples. My assumption in response to this relationship is that irony has no fixed point of origin: it did not begin with the gaze of the Other, nor can it be found in some primordial state not already taken up in a struggle for identity. The importance that I attach to the study of the rhetorical structures, style, semantics, and pragmatics of irony in several African writers' works is best understood in relation to this passionate though often elusive search for a voice that functions with humor, wit, wisdom, and rebellious freedom; a voice that is not first and foremost the imaginary construction of an imperial conqueror.

The absence of examples drawn from African literary texts in the theorization of ironic meaning and pragmatics has created a serious disconnect between theory and application. This is bound to be more acutely felt when one brings in the problem of African authors who have never benefitted as did Gustave Flaubert, Jonathan Swift, and Henry James from being the source of examples of what it actually means to utter ironic words and thoughts. Yet, as Juliana Makuchi Nfah-Abbenyi has so aptly pointed out, African women's fiction "can be read as 'fictionalized theory' or a 'theorized fiction.' We have seen in the works of these women writers 'indigenous' theory that is autonomous and self-determining, the theory often being embedded in the polymorphous and heterogeneous nature of the texts themselves" (149). There is every reason to think that a similar reasoning would apply to African writers who, though employing irony and working through autonomous and self-determining forms of discourse, have been left out of the theorization of irony.

In what sense, though, might African fiction be particularly ironic, more likely than other cultural traditions to turn to irony as a means of expressing its most pressing thoughts, questions, and beliefs? While much of the textual analysis to be found in this book does imply some explanatory links between history and literature, I am not taking lightly the complexity of the question of African identity itself. Notions of a common African cultural experience will tend to implicate two related political agendas. As Steven Howe points out:

> Since it is often difficult, if not impossible, especially in the United States, to identify Afro-American cultural traits as deriving from *particular* African peoples, it has become politically important for some intellectuals to emphasize that distinctions between those peoples were essentially insignificant, so that descent from a generalized "Africa" becomes more meaningful. This concern evidently coincides with that of people within Africa itself who want to emphasize elements of cultural unity or shared tradition, for their own quite different political motives of strengthening support for continental political unification. (103)

Any attempt to suggest a common origin of African cultures collides with a modern tendency to disparage diffusionist models in general: "In the postwar world, [. . .] the 'New Archaeology' largely dispensed with diffusionism, stressing instead the overwhelming influence of particular environments on historical development" (117).[1]

The study of the notion of "signifin(g)" by Henry Louis Gates, Jr., in his book *The Signifying Monkey* (1988), arguably constitutes one of the most sustained theoretical efforts to explain an African American cultural practice comparable to irony,[2] to trace out its presence in African American literary discourse, and to suggest a tentatively diffusionist model whereby similar cultural practices in Africa—especially among the Yoruba—can hardly be explained as mere coincidence. Gates stops short of open diffusionism when he says: "The Signifying Monkey, it seems, is distinctly Afro-American. Nevertheless, the central place of both figures [Esu and the Signifying Monkey] is determined by their curious tendency to reflect on the uses of formal language" (xxi). Both the undefined and highly controversial presence of Africa in the hyphenated term "African-American" and Gates's unwillingness to explain this "curious" common tendency leave us faced with a sense of ambiguity and potential but unconfirmed connections. If the curious tendency were coincidental or reflective of some universal human trait, what would be the point of discussing the Yoruba mythological figure Esu in a work on the theory of African American literary criticism?

The central concern of this book is not to prove the existence of a type of irony that would have to be viewed as distinctly African or that would imply an overarching unity of culture within the continent or throughout the diaspora. Although the very use of the term "Africa" can never be totally devoid of an underlying notion of cultural identity, my concern is to show connections in irony and ironic meaning among authors of a number of different places, times, and ethnic origins within a broad framework of African experience. This will involve their approach to language, their "double-voiced" verbal stance as reflected through narrative, the sociopolitical environment in which that language is employed and deployed, and the traditional verbal context, in the sense of multigenerational practices, surrounding their engagement with language, culture, and the various incarnations of Otherness they confront.

In discussing popular black music, another cultural form that carries its own quotient of ironic intentions, Paul Gilroy (1993) remarks that "the syncretic complexity of black expressive cultures alone supplies powerful reasons for resisting the idea that an untouched, pristine Africanity resides inside these forms, working a powerful magic of alterity in order to trigger repeatedly the perception of absolute identity" (101). It is important to realize that while Gilroy challenges the notion of "pristine Africanity," he also relies heavily on the conviction that a broad spectrum of cultural and implicitly discursive practices is continuously being born out of equally complex historical processes. That is why he goes on to emphasize the need to comprehend "the reproduction of cultural traditions not in the unproblematic transmission of a fixed essence through time but in the breaks and interruptions which suggest that the invocation of tradition may itself be a distinct, though covert, response to the destabilizing flux of the post-contemporary world" (101). This is not the only time Gilroy has recourse to an analysis based on historical causality. Links are also made to the plantation economy (75) and the "terror associated with the notion of 'race'" (51).

But it is particularly interesting that the invocation of African tradition is seen as a covert response, since covert purposes in the use of language are often central to irony. Could the irony that permeates many African literary works reflect the covert struggle of a tradition to continue affirming itself in the face of its own growing self-denial, a search for a place somewhere between pristine Africanity and no Africanity at all? There is no simple answer to this question, since covert discourse can also be subversive. It can affirm or deny the authority of tradition or confront contradictory traditions and question both, all the while hiding within its own covert positions. Gilroy himself is attempting to preserve, under the guise of black culture, a dynamic notion of African culture in the context of a geopolitical chronotope of diaspora. When he does discretely refer to "common sensibilities" of "black cultures in different parts of the world," he includes "both those residually inherited from Africa and those generated from the special bitterness of new world racial slavery" (81).

HISTORICAL CONTEXT: IRONIC DISCOURSE FROM THE ANTI-COLONIAL TO THE POSTCOLONIAL

Reflection on Gilroy's notion of covert responses to historical change and their connection to irony leads us to reconsider the historical relationship between African societies and the presence of ironic meaning in literary discourse. The context of modern African literature in its early stages coincides with the period of colonial rule. Many of the works of that period reflect an irony that would have to be analyzed in terms of anticolonial struggle. But even an intensely ironic work such as Mongo Beti's *Le pauvre Christ de Bomba* (1956; *The Poor Christ of Bomba* [2005]) requires a carefully adapted analysis involving far more than reading the text as straightforward opposition to a dominant political and cultural regime.

The first-person narrator of *Le pauvre Christ de Bomba* is Denis, an adolescent altar boy who is accompanying the Reverend Father Drumont on an extensive visit to the Tala area. The priest wants to see how faithful the faithful are and the extent to which they may be returning to traditional cultural practices at the expense of Church teachings. Denis notes his experiences and thoughts in a personal journal. On one occasion, Father Drumont meets a young man named Gaston who claims to be a good Christian: he lives with his mother while trying to save enough money to get married and firmly denies having a concubine, even in the face of Father Drumont's apparently ironic skepticism, "Are you sure [you don't have a concubine]? pressed the Father, laughing softly" (52). The Father finally congratulates Gaston: "Stay as you are, for who knows, perhaps it's because of you that great misfortune has not already befallen this country?" The reader has no sure way of knowing whether Drumont's skepticism has in fact been overcome or whether the hyperbolic terms of his praise for Gaston reflect an undertone of irony (through which Drumont is hedging his bets). Denis comments further: "We left, and as we went Matthew sang the praises of Gaston, who is a relative of his. It's odd: why should there be men like Gaston who both believe in God and sincerely practise their religion, and others who think only of vice, like those who are dancing now in defiance of the Father's prohibition?" (53). By naively following the Father in a wholesale condemnation of African cultural traditions, and by accepting at face value Gaston's claim to purity, Denis would be making use of an ironic intention that would have to come from an anticolonialist voice speaking through him and behind him. Yet his mere insistence on the fact that the one praising Gaston is a relative suggests his at least peripheral awareness of the shaky ground on which this devout Christian's claim stands, while the question Denis asks himself tells us that he wonders at the arbitrary nature of the choices that are being made around him, even as he seems to present those choices as clear-cut and obvious. If the Reverend Father is so right, why is it so easy to ignore him? How can we explain the fact that Denis can display such apparent naïveté and at the same time an implicit insight through reflection?

Oswald Ducrot (210–11) insists on the distinction between irony and negation as two forms of polyphony that are apparently similar because they are both based on the telescoping of two antagonistic viewpoints. Negation displays two antagonistic utterance-agents and identifies the speaker with only one of them, whereas irony, according to Laurent Perrin (174–75), pushes one utterance-agent to center stage and leads us to identify the speaker with that single agent who pretends to support a viewpoint that he or she is implicitly discrediting as unworthy of credence.[3] Polyphonic irony, as Perrin understands it, is founded on a paradox created at a pragmatic level. One viewpoint is imputed to an utterance-agent with whom the speaker pretends to identify at the level of the meaning of the utterance, but a second and not necessarily concurrent viewpoint could reasonably be attributed to that speaker in a particular situation. In *Le pauvre Christ de Bomba*, this identification of the implied author with the speaker—Denis writing in his diary—is often aleatory. Denis is sometimes the speaker and sometimes the utterance-agent. Another utterance-agent as narrator represents Denis as having a limited ironic vision that sometimes coincides with his own and sometimes falls short of it in scope and depth.

How can we explain this difference in relation to the alienation of colonial-period African authors who had to insist on their own identity as Africans while putting into question numerous dominant and widely accepted stereotypes surrounding that identity? Richard Bjornson explains that

> On one level, Beti's early novels are addressed to Europeans. In a humorously ironic fashion, he informs [Europeans] about the harsh reality behind stereotypically benevolent images of colonial society, and he appeals to their sense of truth and justice. On another level, these works speak to and for Africans, revealing the mechanism of a system that distorts their lives and drawing attention to the conditioning process that predisposes them to regard such distortion as normal. On both levels, he is prodding readers into a critical consciousness that would enable them to comprehend colonialist oppression as it occurs in the real world beyond the pages of his novels. (92)

In Bjornson's interpretation, one of the targets of this double intention on Mongo Beti's part is Denis himself as a speaking subject. He himself sees no irony in what he is reporting of the Reverend Father's discourse and thinking because he "lacks the critical consciousness to interpret the full significance of what he is reporting"; he "exemplifies the gullibility of a colonized subject who willingly acquiesces in his own subjugation" (101).

But is it likely that Mongo Beti, in wanting to awaken the consciousness of Africans, would deny his own narrator any semblance of ironic intelligence? The notion of irony in African literary discourse, as is often the case in African oral traditions as well, is constantly shifting and circulating between different levels of narration, voices, and viewpoints. The notion of shifting ironic viewpoints will lead us to question such interpretations as Bjornson's, which associate irony with an essentially univocal polemical agenda.

Following a subtle and detailed analysis of Drumont's oratory before the people of Tala, Charles-Lucien Bouaka notes that, paradoxically, the priest's pathos and powerful imagery are met with coldness and indifference by his African audience (18): as suggested by the novel's title, the Christlike dedication and sacrifice of the missionary become more

intensely ironic as the grandeur of Drumont's personal passion and heroism is more starkly juxtaposed to the people's reaction. The unstated assumption behind Bouaka's analysis is that the irony of misplaced pathos
is engineered by the novelist through the writing of Denis: "Dominated
by the lucidity of a journal recorded day by day [by Denis], the writing we
are analyzing [. . .] seems, with this search for clarity, to aim at situating
the character of the preacher himself in a sharper light" (19).[4]

Le pauvre Christ de Bomba was Mongo Beti's second novel, published when he was twenty-four years old, and when most African nations had yet to achieve independence. That there was something ironic
about the book was almost undeniable, though where that irony re-
sided and how it worked are still not a subject of universal agreement.
On the one hand, Odile Tobner, Mongo Beti's wife and collaborator,
believes that the book's irony "resides not in the words of the characters themselves but in the very structure of the novel" (12). Bouaka, on
the other hand, for whom "humour, irony and satire are consubstantial
to the [first] two novels" of Mongo Beti, stresses the style and form of
Drumont's discourse, as it is mediated by Denis, as the vehicle of the
author's ironic intentions.

As historical and political circumstances changed over several decades, and as Mongo Beti's protagonists also changed, from the "naive" adolescents of the early novels to the rebel heroes of the novels of
the 1970s, to the inquiring journalist of his final novels, *Trop de soleil
tue l'amour* (Too much sun kills love) (1999) and *Branle-bas en noir et
blanc* (Commotion in black and white) (2000),[5] Mongo Beti continues
to use irony, through ever shrewder fictional voices, to level criticism
at a shifting target figured and reconfigured as the enemies of Cameroonians' (and Africans') hopes and aspirations. He joins a growing
number of voices in postcolonial African fiction that have contributed
to a type of writing sometimes referred to as the "roman de la désillusion" (see Onyeoziri 2003). Like political fables in which an imaginary
but lifelike dictator presides over a violent subculture of tyranny, many
works of this period may be read in rhetorical or pragmatic terms as almost more sarcastic than ironic: despite great subtlety in many folds of
their garments, these texts leave little doubt as to the target or political
implications of their narratives.[6] Some of the works that have contributed to the construction of this narrative form are Yambo Ouologuem's
Devoir de violence (1968; *Bound to Violence* [1983]), Henri Lopes's *Le
pleurer-rire* (1982; *The Laughing Cry* [1987]), Wole Soyinka's *The Interpreters* (1965), Ousmane Sembène's *Le dernier de l'empire* (1981; *The*

Last of the Empire [1984]), and Aminata Sow Fall's *L'ex-père de la nation* (The ex-father of the nation) (1987).

Pierre Fandio, in an illuminating comparative essay on Mongo Beti and Kourouma, cites a number of such authors. He includes earlier works of both Mongo Beti and Kourouma, such as Mongo Beti's *Perpétue et l'habitude du malheur* (1974; *Perpetua and the Habit of Unhappiness* [1978]) and Kourouma's *Les soleils des indépendances* (1970; *The Suns of Independence* [1997]), works that "depict unabashedly bloody dictators who, in the days after the independence of African states, seized power, transformed their countries into gulags and their fellow citizens into perpetual convicts" (116).[7]

Fandio suggests that although Mongo Beti and Kourouma represent two very divergent and sometimes even opposing political and literary destinies, one as the target of the "foudres de l'establishment" and one as the "moderate" often rewarded with fame and prestigious prizes, the two authors' critical vision converged in their nearly contemporaneous novels, Mongo Beti's *Trop de soleil tue l'amour* and Kourouma's *En attendant le vote des bêtes sauvages* (1998; *Waiting for the Vote of the Wild Animals* [2001]).

The "heroes" of the two works are subjected to ritual punishments by narrators who metaphorically challenge their phallic supremacy by leaving them enmeshed in open-ended and incomplete stories. Fandio comments: "There is thus no longer any doubt that the exclusion and marginalisation that their 'heroes' are subjected to at the paratextual and utterance-act levels are part of a deliberate and conscious strategy" (121).[8] The "chiefs" of these two novels "exercise an illusory power the vacuity of which they themselves are not always aware" (122). While this transition from the the despot, with his dreadful power, to the puppet dictator reflects the collapse of despotic support systems related to the end of the Cold War, the books do not bode well either, in Fandio's view, for any burgeoning democratization: "The 'independence' of the chief in relation to the auxiliaries of power such as the police, the 'cooperation technique' and political parties (in power and in opposition) leads to a decay of power itself and of the fragmented centres of decision-making that are thus divided into little groups independent of an inexistent central power" (134).[9] The promise of Mongo Beti's and Kourouma's novels is not as much in the political landscape itself as in what Fandio sees as the "renewal of the perception of power in African fiction" (135). On a broader scale of comparison, one might suggest that African literary discourse has reached, by the beginning of the twenty-first century, a point at which irony is more urgently needed than sarcasm. The once obvious objects of irony are less visible and their "power" and intentions more ambivalent, more awkwardly enmeshed in their own words and word games. At the same time, the less obvious targets of critique, the "groupuscules" of Fandio's analysis, have multiplied and fragmented.

This fragmentation of the problems and actors faced by African societies is not, however, limited to the admittedly innovative texts of Mongo Beti and Kourouma. As early as 1987, Achebe's *Anthills of the Savannah* contained many of the elements of fragmentation and ambivalence at the levels of utterance and narration. The resources of verbal irony are not the sudden creation of some post–Cold War consciousness that popped up ex nihilo but relate to cultural communities and practices that exist and change over time. The voices that speak for those communities are not universal, unequivocal, or all-encompassing but contested and contestable claims to voice and to the power to shape perceptions. The corpus of this study thus includes three authors (Ahmadou Kourouma, Chinua Achebe, and Calixthe Beyala) who reflect a changing view of the power and meaning of ironic discourse as well as of the societies they represent. Achebe, like Kourouma, represents the changing character of power in African political and social life. Irony is needed to critique that power without simplifying or stultifying it. Both writers use proverbs as a means to remind us of the origins of their sly analyses of power. Beyala's irony not only critiques the historical exclusion of African women's voices and writing from both political and literary discourse but also shifts our focus toward the postcolonial, the diasporic, and the transcultural.

As this is not a historical survey of irony in African literature, but a study of the relationship between meaning and irony in discourse associated with African culture, no claim is made to any final conclusion about what is fundamentally African or fundamentally ironic. But the three authors studied are divergent enough in origin, language, and perspective to offer us a way of strengthening our understanding of the forms and spaces of ironic meaning that continue to reside in many African communities in postcolonial times.

POSTCOLONIAL REASSESSMENTS: IRONY AS MIMICRY AND IDENTITY

In his attempt to prove that obscenity and the grotesque are not limited to nonofficial cultures as Bakhtin claimed but "are intrinsic to all systems of domination and to the means by which those systems are confirmed or deconstructed" (102), Achille Mbembe insists that "[t]he postcolony is characterized by a distinctive style of political improvisation, by a tendency to excess and lack of proportion, as well as by distinctive ways identities are multiplied, transformed, and put into circulation." But since these multiplied identities also imply a need for control through violent means, Mbembe compares the "postcolony" to a "stage on which are played out the wider problems of subjection and its corollary, discipline" (103). He illustrates his reference to multiplied and transformed identities through two African novelists associated with ironic and/or satirical and politically subversive writing: Sony Labou Tansi (*La vie et demie* [1979; *Life and a Half* (2011)] and *Les yeux du volcan* [The eyes of the volcano] [1988]) and Ahmadou Kourouma (*En attendant le vote des bêtes sauvages* [1998]). Both Labou Tansi and Kourouma have used the fictional representation of multiple voices to display, ridicule, and mimic both colonial and postcolonial oppressors. But mimicry is not always seen as ironic imitation alone, and it is not always placed under the sign of self-emancipating agency. For Albert Memmi, the colonized's attempt to mimic the colonizer was always doomed to failure, as the shibboleth of difference was inevitably detected and derided as "simiesque" by the intended object of imitation: the only person who could be truly designated as the object of irony in that case was the imitator who bears the responsibility of his or her failure to attain complete assimilation. For Homi K. Bhabha, not only is mimicry bound to always be partial; its incompleteness is a part of its conception from the beginning as the way the colonizer constructs the colonial Other: "colonial mimicry is the desire for a reformed, recognizable Other, *as a subject of difference that is almost the same, but not quite*" (86). Bhabha's mimicry leaves no place for the colonized to write back to the originator of his or her "partial" being: "The desire to emerge as 'authentic' through mimicry—through a process of writing and repetition—is the final irony of partial representation" (88). There was little room in the colonizer's construction of the Other for "présence africaine" behind the mask of mimicry, as Bhabha suggests in referring to Aimé Césaire's *Discours sur le colonialisme* (1955; *Discourse on Colonialism* [2001]).

While both Mbembe's multiple identities and Bhabha's notion of mimicry suggest possible relationships between the concrete realities of African postcolonial societies and the potential for ironic intention in all forms of discourse, lacking in both cases is any convincing explanation of why writers such as Kourouma, Achebe, and Beyala would want or need to use irony and how they use it. That none of these writers could be expected to be pure and absolute practitioners of a single voice of resistance to all forms of tyranny and injustice goes without saying. But to deny them agency as speaking subjects on the grounds that they can only disrupt dominant discourse with a partial and ambivalent expression that can "conceal no presence or identity behind its mask" (Bhabha 88) amounts to what Mbembe calls "assigning Africa to a special unreality such that the continent becomes the very figure of what is null, abolished, and in its essence, in opposition to what is: the very expression of that nothing whose special feature is to be nothing at all" (4). But the works of political satire such as *En attendant le vote des bêtes sauvages* that Mbembe mentions as examples of texts of multiple identities are also stories of the regime of violence that disciplines such multiplicity. Rejecting the Bakhtinian opposition between the official and the nonofficial, Mbembe insists that the "emphasis should be on the logic of 'conviviality', on the dynamics of domesticity and familiarity, inscribing the dominant and dominated within the same *episteme*" (110).

The problem, then, resides in the location of irony. If irony is to help us understand the predicament of many postcolonial African writers while still suggesting why they might be considered African writers in the first place, that is, in some way connected to traditions of discourse and community, it cannot be only as a meta-critical afterthought on how the empty mimic must be an "ironic" figure. Nor can it be only the mask of an imagined culture of resistance whose double voice encodes its opposition to forms of authority in which it has no kind of investment. Rather the multiple and constantly changing meanings associated with ironic discourse need to be understood within the framework of communication and of the communities where that communication takes place.

WHAT IS IRONIC DISCOURSE?

While recognizing that irony "by the very simplicity of its definition becomes curiously indefinable" (1), Claire Colebrook provides some historical background for the concept's definition. She starts with Plato's Socratic dialogues in which "*eironeia* is no longer lying or deceit but a complex rhetorical practice whereby one can say one thing—such as Socrates' claim to be ignorant—but mean quite another, as

when Socrates exposes the supposedly wise as lacking in all insight"
(2). She goes on to point out that in the dominant viewpoint of the
Latin rhetorical tradition from Quintilian through to the Renais-
sance, "*ironia* was not considered to be the full-scale mode of Socratic existence that it was for nineteenth-century writers. *Ironia* was
a trope or figure of speech, an artful way of using language" (7). The
philosophical scope of irony expanded through the eighteenth and
nineteenth centuries to include a sense of loss separating reality and
illusion associated with Romanticism, tragic irony that contrasted individual aspirations and the hardness of fate, and a cosmic irony that
in Hegelian thinking marked the distance between the individual and
the collective in human history. But, as Colebrook explains, twentieth-century material on irony in both philosophy and literary theory
tends to bring us back to verbal irony: "Irony is possible when language is used in ways that run *against* our norms; it thereby brings
our norms into focus" (41). Preference for an irony anchored in the
shared verbal practice of a community is reflected in Wayne Booth's
focus on "stable irony" as a form of double meaning that can be interpreted through reference to fixed social and cultural conventions.
Focusing on stable irony does not, however, eliminate the political
ambivalence that the use of irony entails: "Irony is both questioning
and elitist, both disruptive of norms and constructive of higher ideals.
On the one hand, irony challenges any ready-made consensus or community, allowing the social whole and everyday language to be questioned. On the other hand, the position of this questioning and ironic
viewpoint is necessarily hierarchical, claiming a point of view beyond
the social whole and above ordinary speech and assumptions" (Colebrook 153). A postmodern interpretation of this ambivalence leads to
a questioning of all communication that ultimately grounds itself in
an intended meaning: "If there is nothing other than signification,
with no subjects who signify or world to be signified, then we would
be left with a world of 'saying', without any possibility of underlying
truth or ultimate sense. Such a world would be radically ironic, for
no speech act could be legitimated, justified or grounded" (153). All
of these historical faces of irony are potentially relevant to African
fiction. Since our concern is with the possible meanings attached to
ironic expression in several novels by Achebe, Kourouma, and Beyala, our study will have to account for verbal irony: a large portion of
these novels is devoted to the representation of African speech situations and communities. It will also need to account for various forms

of situational irony that relate to the ambivalent interpretation of historical experience, since the unity or disunity of "African culture" is a constant struggle for and against the notion of a historical African identity. Despite the inclusion of most conventional forms of irony in this study, one overarching definition of irony would be self-defeating for an examination of its relationship to meaning in African literary discourse. Such a definition would oblige us to assume that any author considered to be African would tend to use irony in accordance with an underlying master plan or within a prefabricated framework. What we might risk doing, however, in order to glimpse a larger picture in an extremely intricate field of possibilities, is to review the principal positions surrounding the relationship between being ironical and what one means to say. We can then suggest what these positions may or may not have to offer in our attempt to understand irony as it accompanies, generates, or uses meaning through African fiction.

While the predominant view among rhetoricians and semanticists is that irony is not adequately explained by the trope of antiphrasis (saying the opposite of what one means), there is also considerable emphasis given to co-textual and contextual indices that lead the hearer of an utterance to suspect that the speaker's intended meaning does not perfectly match his or her apparent or explicit statement.[10] This imperfect correspondence leaves room for the idea that ironic discourse seeks to say what cannot be said, or at least what cannot be said otherwise. If said otherwise, that is, not ironically, the utterance act would accomplish some purpose but not *its* purpose: to say something without saying it. Catherine Kerbrat-Orecchioni suggests that in ironic language, the hidden message becomes the denotative meaning, what is actually being communicated, whereas the apparent meaning becomes the connotation ("L'ironie comme trope" 122). From this reversal the possibility arises that the "cover" message itself could take on a significant new role as a moving or enlightening form: a dancer, backing up from her spectator as if to draw attention to herself but leading our line of vision to a fire behind her that she seems not to notice.

Alain Berrendonner will argue that the purpose of such a saying and not saying is not primarily aesthetic but argumentative and ultimately defensive. The ironic speaker leads us toward certain conclusions while putting in place an escape route in the event of censure by attributing any conclusion drawn to the hearer's interpretations and assumptions. Assigning irony an argumentative function places it in the field of pragmatics, the study of the relationship between the meaning of an utterance and its communicative purpose. In the context of African fiction and its possible communicative functions, Berrondonner's defensive interpretation of irony could account for many of the postcolonial political relationships that have arisen from the tyranny of censure and self-censure (Mbembe's "discipline," for example), but it cannot account for aggressive, threatening, and subversive functions of irony, available for the use of oppressors and their victims alike. Laurent Perrin's emphasis on raillery, implicitly ridiculing another's discourse, as he incorporates Wilson and Sperber's concept of mention (the idea of reproducing a part of another discourse in order to put it on display and implicitly question or mock it), becomes a crucial complement to the idea of irony as an argumentative practice. We see the abundance of raillery, not only in earlier works of anticolonial ironists such as Mongo Beti, Ferdinand Oyono, and Wole Soyinka, but equally in recent works of Calixthe Beyala, Ahmadou Kourouma, and Boubacar Boris Diop. How does one make people the target of ridicule, reproach, or even accusation without their recognizing themselves, at least in the immediate, as a target? At the same time, room needs to be made in our understanding of irony for the interpreter, who at some point could notice the fire behind the dancer's feet and bring a "hidden" message ever so briefly into view: the fire is extinguished the moment it is focused on because it was only burning—that is, only ironic—as long as the dancer seemed not to notice that to which she was leading our gaze.

Irony as related to meaning is spoken in context, as changing historical conditions imply changing concerns. Like Bhabha's "inappropriate" mimicry, it is also out of place, because in speaking to what it does not say, it opens the door to shifting perspectives. The voices that convey the shifting perspectives on what is masking the truth in order to deceive, and what is masking the truth in order to reveal the truth, cannot be named with a fixed identity in time and place, nor in age and gender, but are constantly working at identifying themselves as ironically African through traditions, predicaments, tyrannies, and liberations. The pragmatic argument that irony does not simply mean the opposite of what is said but means more by constructing a fictional context in which something unsaid can finally be addressed is not a final answer to the question of what irony is. It is, however, a profoundly helpful explanation of why and how voices that identify themselves as African ironically are African.

WHY ACHEBE, KOUROUMA, AND BEYALA?

While it would be impossible to study enough African authors to claim to represent any universal and exhaustive account of irony in African fiction, it was important to offer some degree of geographic, linguistic, and gender diversity. The choice of Achebe, Kourouma, and Beyala includes former British, French, and German colonies, West and Central Africa, men and women. At the same time, the three authors also offer some historical affinities. They all experienced some form of displacement from their native countries, and all insisted on maintaining firm contacts with them. They are also well known and widely read authors both within Africa and throughout the world.

I have not chosen to discuss texts written by African authors from the early postindependence period to the present, from Chinua Achebe's *Arrow of God* (1964) to Calixthe Beyala's *Les arbres en parlent encore* (The trees are still talking about it) (2002), because of any assumed epistemic divide between colonial and postcolonial consciousness. My purpose is to show that the forms and strategies of African literary discourse are embedded in an experience that continues to live out the implications and consequences of colonialism within the context of a postcolonial wondering/wandering about the selfhood of African nation-states and Africanity itself. The historical and cultural contexts behind the uses of irony that can be observed in my corpus, while still quite diverse, are often related to common problems such as the impact of the European colonization of African countries since the late nineteenth century, the racialization of social and cultural relationships, the place of Africa in a contemporary globalized world, the oppressive character of many postindependence regimes, and the evolution of patriarchy under colonial rule and beyond. Many of the texts referred to make extensive use of proverbs and other traditional forms of discursive practice, such as the *veillée*, or wake, mentioned in both *Les arbres en parlent encore* and Ahmadou Kourouma's *En attendant le vote des bêtes sauvages*. They also offer extensive meta-commentary on traditional culture. The ironic discourse that ultimately surfaces as the reader strives to understand and process the meanings of the text is in all cases strangely suggestive of a changing but persistent tangle of African tradition. I prefer the term *persistent* to Gilroy's "residual" because *persistent* implies an ongoing process of cultural rhetoric, inventiveness, and self-affirmation, while *residual* suggests a more archaeological view of a cultural element that remains present without the power to change anything, despite the dynamic quality attributed to the new hybrid culture containing that so-called residue.

A PRAGMATIC APPROACH: IRONY IN ACTION

The explanation of how the historical conditions of contemporary African literature have led to a particular ironic function is the subject of the first chapter of this book. That ironic function is facilitated by various persisting traditional potentialities as well as by the language of the texts studied. In order to elucidate that function, I address the question of the ways in which discourse produces meaning through irony as illustrated by Chinua Achebe's verbal, especially lexical and semantic, nuances as he represents the language of political oppression in *Anthills of the Savannah* (1987).

As discussed in chapter 2, while irony is intimately tied to language, its interpretation cannot be accomplished with reference to poetic figurativity alone. Irony serves a practical communicative purpose the analysis of which can be understood only in the pragmatic framework of the way language is used to accomplish particular practical purposes.

In introducing a collective work on the problem of distinguishing between semantics and pragmatics, Zoltán Szabó echoes a distinction made by Charles Morris in 1938. Semantics is concerned with "the formal relations of signs to objects to which the signs are applicable" (Morris 6), and pragmatics with "the relation of signs to interpreters" (Szabó 1). Szabó later restates this distinction in the light of Grice's theory of implicature: "Semantics is concerned with what is said, pragmatics with what is implicated, and utterance interpretation—the process whereby the addressee ascertains what the speaker meant—has typically both a semantic and a pragmatic component" (3). Although Szabó refers to this view as "traditional" and questions its assumptions, he also recognizes that the distinction itself "has yet to be adequately articulated" (7).

A more radical critique of conceptions of semantics that fail to separate the formal study of meaning from considerations of utterance and speaker intention can be found in the same volume, in Nathan Salmon's essay "Two Conceptions of Semantics": "To conceive of semantics as concerned with speaker assertion [...] is not merely to blur the distinction between semantics and pragmatics. It is to *misidentify* semantics altogether" (321). While arguing against the confusion of pragmatics and semantics, he illustrates with remarkable saliency how closely the two areas are related:

> What we represent with the symbols we produce need not be the very
> same as what the symbols themselves represent. We are constrained
> by the symbols' system of representation—by their semantics—but we
> are not enslaved by it. Frequently and routinely in fact what we repre-
> sent by means of a symbol deviates from the symbol's semantics. Most
> obviously this occurs with sentences we utter, whereby we routinely as-
> sert something beyond what the sentence itself semantically expresses.
> Irony, sarcasm and figurative language may be cases in point. (323)

My discussion of various linguistic and rhetorical approaches to irony
will show that the same debate occurs in the analysis of irony. Where
does one draw the line between conceptual meaning and meaning assumed or produced by the speaker? It is my contention that the very
place that irony occupies in the field of language—as a form of meaning that intentionally subverts the language it uses—precludes its being
studied without reference to both linguistic meaning and intentional
utterance. The blurring of the distinction between semantics and pragmatics is a part of the problem of exploring irony in literary discourse
and even more so literary discourse related to highly charged and problematic traditions such as African literatures that have arisen out of
multiple sociocultural and political struggles.

This necessary transition from semantics to pragmatics is already
suggested by the overt political intent of *Anthills*, but Kourouma's
Monnè, outrages et defies (1990; *Monnew* [1993]) and *En attendant le
vote des bêtes sauvages* offer a striking display of irony in practice at
multiple levels of language use. In chapter 3, we begin to see why the
political message needs to be ironical because it is spoken at one and
the same time about, by, and to the hyperbolic leader/betrayer of the
postcolonial African state. Koyaga of *En attendant le vote des bêtes sauvages* and Djigui of *Monnè, outrages et défis* are subtle and magnificent
masters of irony, and yet Kourouma reaches through multiple layers
of history and tradition to find ironic questions and questioners able
to complete, reproduce, and reverse the irony of the tyrant, reminding
him that his tyranny as an oppressor of his own people is ultimately a
repression of the self when viewed by a polyphonic speaker who represents Africa as if from within.

Kourouma's reliance on traditional verbal practices in his evocation
of the sociopolitical work of irony suggests that while his novels are situated in a postcolonial and even postmodern context, denying the verbal authority of the past while struggling with the conditions of its continued presence, his irony cannot be neatly separated from a persistent

African tradition of speech acts. The proverb has been studied exten-
sively, and its importance in African traditional society can hardly be
ignored. Yet if its traditional social function had significant pragmatic
elements that went beyond signification in a strict Saussurian sense,
and if, as I will demonstrate, irony in African culture constitutes a pre-
condition to effective social and political interaction, there is a serious
gap in our understanding of proverbs because they have not been explained as potential ironic acts of discourse. Although *Arrow of God*,
the primary text of chapter 4, predates both *Anthills* and Kourouma's
two texts discussed above,[11] an ironic reading of some of the traditional
Igbo proverbs incorporated into this early postcolonial novel allows us
to dismantle the "frozen" isolation often attributed, according to Mudimbe, to African oral traditions[12] and to show that their pragmatic potentialities are directly related to practical problems of expression and
self-expression comparable to those found in Kourouma's postmodern
narrative. Proverbial irony implies that ironic intention is not always
directly attributable to an individual speaker, though that speaker can
also use the occasion to put in his or her two cents' worth, but may
reflect intergenerational and collective values threatened by changing
conditions.

   Both the complexity of utterance responsibility, referring to the utterance-agent, in the pragmatics of irony demonstrated by Kourouma's
texts and the problem of tradition contained in Achebe's proverbial irony
imply an underlying problem related to the ironic voice. Who can allow
themselves to speak ironically, and on behalf of what community do they
speak? This line of questioning parallels Mudimbe's analysis of the relationship between African ethnography, the work of colonial missionar-
ies, and "the new African discourse" on anthropological studies of Africa:
"Who is speaking? From which context? In what grids and in what sense
are the questions pertinent?" (64). The ironic voice represented in African
fiction may not be asking easily identifiable questions that would allow
us direct access to the kind of *episteme* that Mudimbe discusses. These
questions do reflect an important pragmatic challenge to received wisdom and knowledge from both within and without the discourses that
have assumed the authority to represent African tradition. Often male
and patriarchal, these discourses are invested with ideological rigor, as in
Kwame Nkrumah's pan-Africanism, with authoritative cultural knowledge, as in Jomo Kenyatta's *Facing Mount Kenya* (1965), or with apparent
financial opulence, like the El Hadji of Ousmane Sembène's *Xala* (1974).
It is for this reason that the rise of African women's writing in general and

the controversial and iconoclastic career of Calixthe Beyala in particular have challenged our notions of African traditional culture while installing an African woman's claim to voice within the problematic space of ironic expression and understanding. This challenge to patriarchy is the subject of chapter 5. The African woman ironist who emerges through the voice and narrative of characters like Ève-Marie of *Amours sauvages* (Savage passions) (1999) and Édène of *Les arbres en parlent encore* seems to be locked in an open-ended but potentially creative struggle with lingering colonial and patriarchal legacies. Western feminist readings of African women's writing and of Beyala in particular have not emphasized irony and its potential role in the self-expression and self-realization of African women. Mildred Mortimer, for example, in introducing Beyala as a second-generation African woman novelist aggressively attacking "African patriarchy," states that "[t]he Cameroonian novelist responds to patriarchy's silencing of African women with language that is violent and sometimes crude. Her female protagonists react to physical violence against women—battering and rape—with castration and murder" (117). Although Mortimer's study does not involve *Amours sauvages*, the representation in that novel of violence against women and the women's response to it illustrates the importance of irony in the overall strategy of resistance to patriarchy, prejudice, and colonialism that Beyala has been seeking to develop in her writing. The topos of "murder" in *Amours sauvages* is highly charged with ironic undertones. In a context of African diasporic life, the perpetrator of the murder of the anonymous victim (Mlle Personne) is a white man, Jean-Pierre Pierre, even though, ironically, the African community realizes that it is likely to be accused of the crime from the moment the body is discovered. At the same time, the narrator-writer Ève-Marie, faced with the abusive behavior of Jean-Pierre Pierre, places an imaginary plot aimed at killing him at the center of her nascent writing career. By absorbing the murder theme into the process of writing a novel about her community, Ève-Marie effectively subverts the stereotypes of violence surrounding her community and ironically suggests the need to paint a broader picture in order to more fully understand the true underlying violence that affects women's lives from an African woman's perspective. As reflected in the title *Amours sauvages* (Savage passions), which maliciously juxtaposes the notion of passion with "savagery," one of the most familiar stereotypes of Africanity, violence itself becomes an ironic trope for the gap between African women's self-representation and their representation by and through others.

Time will tell to what extent the study of irony in the collective narratives of African peoples and the texts of contemporary African writers may change our understanding of irony in general, or of the way it can be analyzed as a factor in the use of natural languages. But at present, there is some urgency to the need to understand better the dynamics and agency of African civilization, a civilization that is neither a "frozen" past nor a doomed present fraught with disease, underdevelopment, insecurity, and "failed states," but one that continues to have the ability to think and speak for itself. African irony may be a door ajar through which that self-expression and self-understanding will better reveal itself.

CHAPTER ONE

From Rhetoric to Semantics

An old woman does not say everything that she knows.

—Igbo proverb

Under what circumstances does a literary discourse need to be ironic? Since written texts and representations of orality are often interdependent in the context of African fiction, irony helps interlocutors express two apparently contradictory facts: their sense of community and their unease with one another. As a reinterpretation of an oral discursive practice, the written text may be born out of a traumatic and divisive cultural rupture. In Cheikh Hamidou Kane's novel *L'Aventure ambiguë* (1961; *Ambiguous Adventure* [1972]), the words of the dowager princess known as the Grande Royale, addressed to a communal gathering, reflect the dynamics of such a rupture: "The [French colonial] school in which I would place our children will kill in them what today we love and rightly conserve with care. Perhaps the very memory of us will die in them" (42).[1] This possible death of memory is, in a sense, realized by Kane's book itself, which remembers the culture of the protagonist's people through the kind of purified French literary writing that the Grande Royale's children (*nos enfants*) were sent to acquire at the expense of their own identities. In an Anglophone novel of the same period, Chinua Achebe's *Arrow of God* (1964), the priest Ezeulu sends one of his sons to learn about European culture in the face of a changing world that he recognizes without accepting: "'The world is changing,' [Ezeulu] told [his son]. 'I do not like it. But I am like the bird Enekenti-oba. When his friends asked him why he was always on the wing he replied: 'Men of today have learnt to shoot without missing and so I have learnt to fly without perching.' I want one of my sons to join these people and be my eye there. If there is nothing in it you will come back. But if there is something there you will bring home my share'" (45–46). Of course the share Oduche brings home is ironically his "mission" of putting a sacred python into a box in order to prove his commitment to the "Christian" principles he has been taught. This abomination, as it is seen by the people of Umuaro, is an early sign of Ezeulu's fall from grace in the traditional community, of his defiance of that community, and of the demise of his priestly role, that demise being a symbol of growing disunity. At the root of the abomination is the introduction of the written text (especially the Bible) and the imperatives of cultural transformation that it was used to impose. Achebe's writing itself can be seen as an attempt to bear truthful witness to the meaning of traditional Igbo culture through an active engagement with the literary production of colonial writers as interpreters of African society. As Alain Ricard remarks, "Chinua Achebe's itinerary as a writer inscribes itself in literature written in English as an anti-novel on Africa: he wants to show that Joseph Conrad in *Heart of Darkness* (1902) and Joyce Cary in *Mister Johnson* (1939) have hardly tapped into Africa's literary potential" (239).[2] Ruptures within traditional cultural communities and between generations can thus be understood as sources of uneasiness, making irony a necessary tool of discretion and subterfuge, but they also form the basis for the situational irony of the producer of African fiction. Writers "represent" their culture as rooted in oral traditions. Their tools become their malaise, and that malaise encourages them to look for ever deeper and more powerful tools in the cultural memory that they seek to reinstate.

The need for irony can be understood in terms of a traditional family gathering, for example, called to discuss a problem in the family. The participants have to respect certain conventions regulating the way in which they communicate with one another. Yet the people know that they have gathered because these problems have arisen following a breakdown of, or a threat to, the very culture that has formed the basis for those conventions. The meeting is held as if everyone were functioning according to a shared cultural code, and the way people speak is determined or controlled by that code. Yet the people gathered together are aware of the fact that the social and political foundations of their speaking community have been shaken and undermined by historical ruptures. There is a need for an ironic language using verbal conventions of a shared culture in order to imply that the basis of those conventions has broken down.

Linda Hutcheon, in *Irony's Edge: The Theory and Politics of Irony*, mentions the fact that, despite the political risks of its being misunderstood or misappropriated, irony has recently come to be seen as an appropriate means of expression "for those with 'divided allegiance' (Sollors 1986) that comes from their difference from the dominant norms of race, ethnicity, gender or sexual choice." But she also recognizes that "there is far from agreement on the value of ironic signifying, especially among those for whom a firm and stable racial subject position is seen as a political necessity, if not an existential reality" (31). Such a "firm and stable racial subject position," however strong its political necessity may be, is never obvious or assured, whether in the context of an African diaspora struggling to build connections with an ancestral homeland or of postcolonial continental African communities attempting to speak of a traditional culture lived as real on a daily basis but resembling more and more, as time goes on, a constructed product of memory.

This is one of the reasons for the need for an ironic code reflecting this double use of conventions and the expression of the loss of what those conventions are based on. Such irony is different from anticolonial irony, as it can be found in earlier works of Mongo Beti such as *Le pauvre Christ de Bomba* (1956) and in Ferdinand Oyono's *Une vie de boy* (1956; *Houseboy* [1991]). Mongo Beti sought to subvert the conqueror's language in order to show the colonized African's awareness of the oppression going on around him and at the same time reveal that the power of the Other is founded on the lies of imperialism, according to which such power is absolute and does not suffer from any human weakness.

Any theory of irony in African literary discourse will have to take into account the ironic function of speaking to and through the Other as well as speaking to and through the other (*la confrérie*) who is part of one's own community. In other words, at some point there may be an interface of these two functions, a use of irony for the imperialist Other and a use of irony for oneself or for one's community. The eruption of the imperialist Other into the universe of African society is directly related to the need for irony to find expression within communities: at an early stage, authors needed to couch their critique of imperialism in irony in order to escape censure and satisfy their European publishers, readers, and critics; even when the need for such subterfuge became less urgent, it remained important to show the Other that his or her claim to superiority lacked solid foundations.

The need to speak ironically to European audiences does not preclude the strong possibility that there was a connection between the
use of irony in African languages and orality as a means of communication within a community. It was important for people to use irony so
that they could function as a community, for the purposes of humor,
linguistic elegance, and subtlety.[3] This is because irony allows people to
communicate within and through a complex network of relationships.
Written literary discourse implies a lone voice, even if it is dialogic or
polyphonic in its construction, the lone voice of a writer who writes in
a kind of private tranquillity. The writer may invoke other voices, and
may place irony in various strategic loci of the form and substance of
the expression and within the forms and substance of the content, to
borrow Hjelmselv's terms, throughout the narrative. This can be seen
as a literary procedure used by the private individual speaker in order
to represent a communal world. Any effective theory of the semantics
of irony has to take into account these different uses and roles of irony
both as an important device and as a verbal tool in the use of community discourse and in the context of an oral culture.

After examining various occurrences of irony in the works of three
Ivorian authors—Dadié, Kourouma, and Adiaffi—Germain Kouassi
comes to the conclusion that it is primarily what he calls "irony by dramatisation" that reflects "the persistence of African speech" and constitutes "an unequivocal witness to the African verbal art generally
celebrated in the moonlit story-telling wakes where the attitudes and
ways of being and doing of beings and things are staged in order to be
mocked" (387).[4]

Even without the rupture arising from the European assault on Africa and all the other ruptures that accompanied it,[5] there has been
from precolonial times an intimate relationship between orality and
irony in African discourse. The distance that practice creates between
the speaker and the subject/object of discourse is a part of the linguistic and rhetorical competence needed for its production and reception. It is difficult to retrace that connection in a study concerned
with irony functioning after the rupture, even though the pre-rupture
is always a putative construct. But we could also talk of traces or re-
currences of a relationship between orality and irony, as it is manifest
in the works of many African writers, men and women alike, especially in proverbs and other wise sayings that are incorporated into
their texts as well as in some art forms that are suggested as means of
expressing irony.

The irony in Ahmadou Kourouma's *En attendant le vote des bêtes sauvages* and *Allah n'est pas obligé* (2000; *Allah Is Not Obliged* [2007]) is mostly centered on rupture within the African communities represented. At the same time, the analyst and interpreter of these works is conscious of the fact that it is difficult to follow Kourouma's discourse because he has recourse to hyperbole and depictions of extreme violence. In these novels, Kourouma is perhaps influenced by Sony Labou Tansi (a Congolese author who was known for biting satire and iconoclastic social and political images) and seems to be attracted to ridiculous and grotesque extremes in his ironic depiction of the abuse of power. But how else could one effectively express the extreme sufferings and violence inflicted on Africans through the slave trade, colonialism, neocolonialism, dictatorships, and, in recent years, cultural and economic globalization? Specific examples will trace irony back to the problem of a relationship between orality and ironic discourse, not necessarily in terms of some original African community of oral speech, but in terms of the malaise of that original community being represented as a convention, almost as a stereotype, and consequently acting out its rupture as the breaking down of its foundations.

In *En attendant le vote des bêtes sauvages*, irony is presented first and foremost as a problem of linguistic mediation determined by the nature of colonial contacts and interactions.[6] Irony is reintegrated into the search for a literary genre that the "polyphonic narrator" calls *les donsomanas* (purification rituals involving hunters) in which, instead of mediating or mediated irony, one observes a shifting multiple ironic perspective as, for example, in the references to *les hommes nus* (naked savages) in the opening pages of the novel. One wonders if this is not a parody or satire of colonial discourses, anthropologists' view of precolonial, "primitive" Africans before the intervention of the European *mission civilisatrice*. At the same time, the apparently parodic expression of such a view seems designed to inscribe irony into the way in which people use conventional culture. Even if one could interpret the whole idea of *les hommes nus* as a form of lost innocence, authenticity, or identity, it is still only the double meaning of irony that can permit an author to represent innocence, authenticity, or identity without either accepting or denying it (reminiscent of Schlegel's theory of romantic irony). The possible parodying of the idea of *les hommes nus* is neither a total denial of a state of being that was precolonial, entirely different from what is now known, nor an endorsement of a naive belief in that innocence or authenticity. The very existence of that state of being, as well as any implicit idea of a functioning precolonial community—a collective foundation that had nothing in particular to do with Europe—is neither totally affirmed nor totally denied.

On the one hand, the whole issue of precolonial African culture and history lends itself to anthropological mythologizing. On the other hand, this very denial is part of the denial of African history, also a central and actively pursued imperialist ideology, which claimed—and still claims in word and in action—that Africa had no past, no particular structure or form, was just a primeval chaos, until the arrival and intervention of Europeans. Hélène d'Almeida-Topor explains that "the image of a pre-colonial Sub-Saharan Africa living in chaos, without any real political organizations and without States has long had considerable resonance in France, as in other Western countries" (31).[7] Christopher Miller points out that in Africanist discourse "[t]he time before was 'pure anteriority' and cannot be described; it was 'vast and monotonous' in its stagnation; it was different from our time, therefore it did not exist" (247–48). The opposing group of paternalistic European anthropologists such as Leo Frobenius, who affirmed that African culture was very profound and sophisticated, created a countermythology of an idealized African civilization.[8] There was no middle ground for African creative writers between these two forms of mythologizing, except the assumption of an ironical stance. Tim Cox views irony, in the comparable context of the postmodern slavery narrative, as a means of undercutting "schemes of group identity formation prominent in the authors' contemporary cultural situations" (137). The narrative strategies he describes "undercut their apparent intent to supply answers to central and persisting questions of identity." Kourouma is also attempting to undercut an implicit assumption of absolute truth but at the same time is driven, as are many contemporary African authors, by the practical necessity of truth telling as an urgent response to present violence and to a persistent form of past (colonial) violence against the selfhood of African people. Irony, seen in this light, appears, paradoxically, as a subtler labyrinth of utterance-based undercutting than what Cox describes as a starker and more direct elocutionary act.

But is there an ideal balance between the "primeval chaos" of Africa before the arrival or intervention of Europeans and a glorious and idealized African culture and civilization? The subtle use of language in much African fiction points to the fact that there must have been a middle ground, a functioning society that, like all other societies, had its problems. The only way of showing this is to be ironical about the two forms of mythologizing. In their creative literary works—Kourouma's *En attendant le vote des bêtes sauvages* is a recent example, while Yambo Ouologuem's *Le Devoir de violence* (1968) shows that this problem is not entirely new—African creative writers refute the idea of an absolute binary opposition between the two periods in the history of African experience through the use of hyperbole, which is a strong signal of the presence of irony while at the same time constituting the very material ironized. This is because hyperbole had a place in traditional epic and legend, as in, for example, D. T. Niane's *Soundjata* (1960), in which the legendary founder of the Mali empire is presented as capable of uprooting a baobab tree with his own hands. In order to deflate unfounded claims, hyperbole is used as both one of the traditional and literary practices being ironized and a signal of irony. These writers play on conventions because in the twentieth- and twenty-first-century novel, the convention that hyperbole is a signal of irony is bound to be functioning, yet hyperbole is part of the stuff of legends, particularly legends in oral societies.

As my comments on Chinua Achebe's discourse will demonstrate, the understanding of verbal irony has to be attained through the structure of telling—the very act of *prise de parole*. In this case, a slightly modified version of Roman Jakobson's model of the functions of communication is needed. Instead of being a linear model going from sender to intended receiver, ironic communication is more of a circle, diverting the line of discourse so that the sender, the intended receiver, and the object are all constantly shifting, switching places as the circle moves, coinciding and diverging, sometimes alternatively, sometimes simultaneously. In *En attendant le vote des bêtes sauvages*, this shifting movement of irony is connected with the relationship between the role of the *sèrè* and that of the *koroduwa*. At the beginning of the novel, the first speaker, Bingo, defines these roles: the *sèrè*, who is Bingo himself, "is a minstrel, a bard who recounts the exploits of the hunters and praises their heroes" (3).[9] The responder, or *koroduwa*, "is an initiate in the purificatory stage, the catharthic stage. Tiekura is a *koroduwa*, and, like all *koroduwa*, he plays the buffoon, the clown, the jester. He does anything he wants, and nothing he does goes unpardoned" (3).[10] The *sèrè* and his *koroduwa* work together in performing the *récit purificatoire* known as a *donsomana*.

This change of voice is marked in the text by a constant shifting from *il* to *vous* in addressing the hunter-dictator Koyaga and in switching constantly from first- to second- and to third-person narrative, as a kind of interpolation of free indirect speech. The shifting can also be seen as a social and discursive deixis,[11] given that an intention or hidden political agenda often lies masked behind the ironic discourse. In this linguistic gymnastics, the reader needs to be able to recognize the switch, since there is no initial indication that one or the other has taken over. This is characteristic of oral speech situations. Even the other characters' relationship with the dictator Koyaga is not simple, given the constant switching from Koyaga to Maclédio—the latter being a representation of the continued functioning of the griot in the modernized form of the "propagandist," the Minister of Information. The reader observes Maclédio's audience expanding from Koyaga, though he is at the same time Koyaga's mouthpiece, to the Master Hunters attending the *donsomana*, to the people of Koyaga's country, and to the world outside, including the European. The final level is that of the readers who have to learn to think like spectators in order to understand what is going on, since they are represented as watching the spectacle and not just reading a text.

The central question surrounding the possibility of this research and underlying the inquiry into the functioning of irony in texts such as *En attendant le vote des bêtes sauvages* needs to be: Is there an African literary discourse? What would it consist of if African literature is based on a relationship between orality and irony? For example, the semantics of the proverb at a micro-discursive level (see Onyeoziri 1993) holds at least part of the answer to the question of what African literary discourse might consist of. In this work, my primary interest is to examine closely the different ways in which irony as a rhetorical concept functions and signifies in the African novels under discussion. A work of art is ironical because it is based on language, having its own sets of accepted signs and conventions already developed within the tradition of that particular art or genre, which is why this study investigates the aesthetic dimensions of irony. When does the artist, as it were, subtly play the bars of the musical notes off key? One could claim that without the aesthetic effect, there would not be a political effect either, to quote Toril Moi, who also emphasizes the need for the feminist's awareness of the implied aesthetics of political approaches to art: "aesthetic value judgments are historically relative and [. . .] they are deeply imbricated in political values" (85). The urgency and magnitude of African writers' experience and commitment are such that they are called upon to be critical as well as creative. I continually examine the implied irony, the victim, object, or target of the ironic utterance as well as its import. Due to the textual uncertainty that irony sometimes creates, the ironic discourse of a politically engaged writer sometimes turns around to reveal contradictions within his or her level of consciousness.

As I read and reflect on the practice of irony in African literary discourse, I often see a watched discourse that has learned in turn to watch others or the Other. African novels have demonstrated, since the colonial period, a remarkable tendency to ironize. Authors, in speaking *for* those who are constantly represented as not having understood or who do not possess the discursive subtlety of colonizing Europe, put forth their subtlest and most complex discursive forms,[12] exemplified in *irony*, as a principle, an answer, and a heritage. Since the beginning of postcolonial times, African novels have often demonstrated the effectiveness of this mode of signifying that Henry Louis Gates, Jr., calls "the trope of tropes" in the interrogation of different types of discourse. A particularly striking example of signifying in African literature appears in a recent work of the Senegalese novelist Boris Boubakar Diop, *Le cavalier et son ombre* (The horseman and his shadow). An artist has been commissioned to execute a sculpture of "the national hero" whom he has never seen. When asked how he was able to accomplish this, he answers: "It's not difficult, it was enough for me to think of any old low-life bastard. We all know some low-life bastards and I had one of them constantly in mind in doing this work. There you have my artistic method" (127–28).[13] The artist's method itself becomes a trope of representation that ironically transforms the national, the monumental, and the celebratory into a mode of subversive political satire.

This is not to suggest that every discourse is to be interpreted ironically simply because the reader observes a certain dissonance between the signifier and the signified, or even because of the presence of hyperbolic and euphemistic utterances or expressions. According to Muecke, a satisfactory definition of irony must be broad enough to describe a wide range of phenomena and yet precise enough to distinguish irony from other figures of speech that it resembles or with which it overlaps, such as sarcasm, pun, and satire (1969: 14).

A rhetorical definition of literary irony attempts to delineate the dynamic intersubjectivity between author and reader. Wayne Booth describes the process whereby readers reconstruct what he calls "stable irony." Stable ironies are "deliberately created by human beings to be heard or read and understood with some precision by other human beings" (5). They build on "meanings different from those on the surface," but "once a reconstruction of meaning has been made, the reader is not

then invited to undermine it with further demolitions and reconstruc-
tions" (6). Their interpretation can be satisfactorily completed within
a definable discursive and referential context (6). Referring to a sentence from Samuel Butler's *Erewhon* in which the narrator says, "as luck
would have it, Providence was on my side," Booth asserts that the equation of "luck" and "Providence" is bound to be read as an ironic joke.
Though the context leading to this interpretation is complex, "the end
results are nearly certain." Booth adds: "Any reader who fails to see
some sort of joke about how belief in luck and belief in Providence both
relate and clash has missed the ironic point" (19).

In the reconstruction of meaning that stable irony invites, the reader
cannot help noticing some incongruity between the words and the expressions in which they are used. In order to arrive at an intelligent
interpretation, the reader must make a decision in the context regarding the author's knowledge and belief. The interpreter can then choose
a new meaning or cluster of meanings that seems more pertinent or
plausible, even though it might still involve other related figures, such
as paradox.

Hutcheon questions the possibility of stable irony, given the cultural
specificity of the communities in which the process Booth describes
can operate successfully (97). She also questions the recourse to the author's "knowledge and belief" as the basis of the decision to understand
an utterance ironically: "The ironist is not the only performer or participant and, therefore, the responsibility for ironic communication (or
its failure) is a shared one" (123). We need to see how Hutcheon comes
to doubt the existence of stable irony in order to see how the interpretation of the speaker-receiver relationship should influence our understanding of irony in African literary discourse. Hutcheon insists that
the "complex process of relating, differentiating, and combining said
and unsaid meanings—and doing so with some evaluative edge" is a
"culturally shaped process" (89). She reasons that if the conditions for
the successful transmission of ironic meaning involve shared cultural
knowledge and values, it must be the intersection of two or more communities that creates irony and not irony that creates a relationship of
understanding: "No theorist of irony would dispute the existence of a
special relationship in ironic discourse between the ironist and the interpreter; but for most, it is irony itself that is said to *create* that relationship. I want to turn that around here, and argue instead that it
is the community that comes first and that, in fact, *enables* the irony
to happen" (89). Irony cannot be "stabilized" through the relationship

between the ironist and the interpreter only but rather through "the culture, language, and social context in which both participants interact with each other and with the text itself" (91). For Hutcheon, the "discursive communities" that are potentially involved in this relationship are so numerous, diverse, and complex that the sharing needed "will inevitably always be partial, incomplete, fragmentary" (92), but the limited sharing that does take place is sufficient for producing and understanding irony.

The intended or potential audience of an African ironist is made up of discursive communities that are, if anything, even more complex than those suggested by Hutcheon. Not only are there audiences within audiences, but at times the ironist may destabilize a discursive community's own self-understanding. This problem appears with striking effect in chapter 12 of Achebe's *Anthills of the Savannah* (152–61). The novel recounts the struggles of several citizens of the fictional state of Kangan who strive to resist the growing oppression of a military dictatorship. One of these characters is Ikem Osodi, the editor of a national newspaper recently suspended from his position for expressing dissident opinions. Ikem has been invited to give a lecture to university students in the aftermath of his suspension. The entire passage can be seen as a meditation on audience and voice that culminates in a multilayered ironic utterance.

Throughout the chapter, the narrator insists on the audience's reaction to each of Ikem's statements. These reactions range from complacent and complicit approval, when the listeners feel that Ikem has affirmed their own sense of righteousness, to uncomfortable "mixed, cautious applause" (158), when their position is questioned. A reference to an earlier speaking engagement at the Bassa Rotary Club (154–55) is inserted into the narrative in order to show the contrast between the students' reaction and a straightforwardly hostile reaction to Ikem's accusations: "The rotund geniality of his hosts was instantly shattered and distorted into sharp-pointed shapes of aggressiveness" (155). In the case of the university lecture, Ikem is facing an audience that generally shares, or at least thinks it shares, his values and beliefs. But Ikem reflects from the beginning of his speech on the irony underlying his real intention: "No doubt [his lecture] had the right revolutionary ring to it and Ikem smiled inwardly at the impending *coup d'état* he would stage against this audience and its stereotype notions of struggle, as indeed of everything else" (153). Ikem's motives are further explained:

> By nature he is never on the same side as his audience. Whatever his
> audience is, he must try not to be. If they fancy themselves radical, he

fancies himself conservative; if they propound right-wing tenets he unleashes revolution! It is not that he has ever sat down to reason it out and plan it; it just seems to happen that way. But he is aware of it—after the event so to say, and can even offer some kind of explanation if asked to do so: namely that whatever you are is never enough; you must find a way to accept something however small from the other to make you whole and save you from the mortal sin of righteousness and extremism. (154)

Through a process of questioning, hyperbole, mockery, and satire, the speech brings the students to the realization that they are not the audience that they imagined themselves to be: there are no peasants present (not even any proxies sent in by peasants); there are no market women. There might be a few workers, but who are workers? They "go on strike when outdated and outrageous colonial privileges [. . .] are threatened" (157), while their leaders "quote Fanon on the sin of betraying the revolution" without realizing that "revolutions are betrayed just as much by stupidity, incompetence, impatience and precipitate action as by doing nothing at all" (158). The confusion of his audience is reflected in the "mixed, cautious applause" that follows. When Ikem arrives at the final category of audience, the student, he uses ironic preterition (claiming not to say what you actually intend to say) in order to set his predominantly student audience up for his ultimate attack: "I should really be careful here as I am quite anxious to get home safely tonight" (160). In fact, he is anything but careful when he cites a case in which students on National Service protest being sent to a "remote rural station" by burning down a maternity block built by peasants. The students in Ikem's audience begin to see themselves as other than what they had imagined: "[t]he laughter had died all of a sudden." He concludes by reassuring the students of their potential identity as leaders: "'You must develop the habit of scepticism, not swallow every piece of superstition you are told by witch doctors and professors. [. . .] When you rid yourselves of these things your potentiality for assisting and directing this nation will be quadrupled.' Tremendous applause. Surprisingly?" (160–61) The return to approval and the narrator's possibly ironic question suggest that Ikem has achieved ambiguous success in communicating with his audience, questioning the students and yet leaving them room to believe in themselves. If they were truly reflecting in the way Ikem asks them to reflect, why is the applause tremendous? Is the narrator (or Ikem himself) less than fully surprised because the audience is predictable in the ease with which it returns to complacency? The chapter is

framed by two comments from the chairman of the meeting that raise
further questions surrounding the success of Ikem's discourse. First,
"Mr Osodi's concept of struggle [is] too individualistic and adventur-
istic" (161) and, second, writers need to "move to the higher responsibility of proffering prescriptions." Although Ikem is able to reestablish
his position with a clever pun—"Writers don't give prescriptions. [. . .]
They give headaches"—these comments and the audience's approval
of them—"some applause" and "Applause"—lead us to suspect that
Ikem's discourse has overlapped only temporarily and partially with
the discursive community to whom he has been speaking. Irony was
a means of finding common ground between Ikem and his listeners:
that the discourse of revolutionary change has come to represent the
avoidance of change, that it has become a facade behind which parasitic
classes were now hiding. But the students and their professors and leaders remain determined to see themselves through Ikem's eyes as if he
were one of them and not an outsider questioning them. The resulting
irony for the reader is that the common ground of discourse that allows
Ikem to speak to his listeners as part of a shared discourse is necessarily shaken by their failure to recognize how partial and ambiguous that
commonality is.

The ambiguity created by this chapter of *Anthills of the Savannah*
as to the covert intention of any identifiable ironist leads us to won-
der if we have not crossed Booth's "formidable chasm" from stable to
unstable ironies "in which the truth asserted or implied is that no stable reconstruction can be made out of the ruins revealed through the
irony" (240). Booth distinguishes between "local" or "limited" unstable
ironies, in which the reader is "kept off balance" by leaving doubts as
to the author's intentions in specific utterances but still maintains "a
strong political or moral message" (250), and infinite instabilities, in
which the ironic intent seems to be the negation of all meaning. One
centerpiece of Booth's discussion of infinitely unstable irony is Samuel
Beckett's *The Unnameable*. Booth criticizes those who conclude from
Beckett's discourse that "the only meaning is that there is no meaning,
and any reconstruction of an irony is as vulnerable to destruction as
any other" (259). According to Booth, such interpretation, paradoxically, cannot account for the positive emotional and intellectual value
that such interpreters derive from reading and discussing Beckett. In
contrast, as Laura Rice points out, instability itself can carry a powerful
political charge in the climate of late imperialism. Unstable ironies underline the fact that discourses are in competition with each other: "We

have entered the era of unstable ironies in which transcendent meaning has become one discursive regime among others" (8). Rice also has
instability in mind when she refers to the potentially liberating force of
irony: "Irony is strongly associated with freedom because of its liberating potentials—not the least of which is laughter. Irony is apotropaic;
through mockery, it helps the oppressed resist internalizing the evils of
injustice" (13).

Although it would be possible to speak of African authors whose
irony might be interpreted as infinitely unstable, including Yambo
Ouologuem, Sony Labou Tansi, and Boubacar Boris Diop, Achebe's
portrayal of Ikem's lecture offers some insight into a historically and
culturally contextualized explanation of unstable irony. None of the
concerns that Ikem raises, in relation to African societies—the exclusion of the voices of the peasant classes and of market women
from the conversations of those privileged classes (including university students) who claim to want social progress, the corruption and
selfishness of both workers and their union leaders, elitism and eth-
nocentrism on the part of university students—is ultimately denied
as a problem by the ironic form and structure of this passage. What
seems to disappear in the infinite negation of Ikem's encounter with
his audience(s) is the possibility of an authentic voice being heard
within the social and political structures of the postcolonial state. The
old man who gave Ikem the story of political struggle with which he
opened his lecture, and who is now being held in prison because storytellers "threaten all champions of control,"[14] as well as the absent
peasants and market women, without being offered as token symbols
of "Fanonian orthodoxy," do offer some form of localization, or con-
textualization, to the potentially endless irony deriving from the fact
that speakers and audiences alike are unable to free themselves from
the contradictions and hypocrisies of their own position. I would argue that irony in postcolonial African fiction is not grounded in total dependency on oral tradition and popular culture but moves forward critically in relation to multiple discourse communities with, in
the background, the memory of a complex configuration of partially
silenced audiences: political prisoners who have disappeared, rural
women and traders, innocent victims of violence.

Muecke (1969: 19) gives three formal criteria for (all?) irony that offer a more mutable context of interpretation. These criteria will help us
better unravel the difficulties encountered in this contextualized form
of unstable irony:

1. Irony involves a hierarchy of perspectives.

2. Irony is a "double-layered or two-storey phenomenon. At the lower level is a situation as it appears to the victim of the irony (where there is a victim) or as it is deceptively presented by the ironist (where there is an ironist). . . . At the upper level is the situation as it appears to the observer or the ironist. The upper level need not be *presented* by the ironist; it needs only to be evoked by him or be present in the mind of the observer." This second criterion, seemingly in contrast to the hierarchy of perspectives, holds that "there is always some kind of opposition between the two levels that may take the form of contradiction, incongruity, or incompatibility. What is said may be contradicted by what is meant [. . .]; what the victim thinks may be contradicted by what the observer knows" (Muecke 1969: 19–20).

3. For the third criterion Muecke may have in mind Aristotle's *Ethics* which distinguishes two extremes that diverge from the meaning of truth: *alazoneia* or vainglorious self-assertiveness on the one hand and self-depreciating dissimulation of one's knowledge and abilities on the other hand (see Muecke 1970: 15). The first one is often associated with confident unawareness which, as Muecke points out, implies an unavoidable assumption (or presumption) that leaves one open to moral or intellectual censure. The victim is "the person whose 'confident unawareness' has directly involved him in an ironic situation" (Muecke 1969: 34).

One of Muecke's examples for this analysis is Henry James's sentence "It was a period when writers besought the deep blue sea 'to roll'" (1969: 17). The hierarchy of perspectives is based on the historian's superior awareness of the unoriginal and predictable use of language he sees in the authors to whom he refers. At the lower level is the apparent belief in the poetic value of certain expressions shared by authors of the "period" described; at the upper level, the sense of cliché and unfounded hyperbole shared by a later, more reasonable literate generation. The generation on the receiving end is shown to be guilty of *alazoneia* through the implied verbal modesty of the ironist's generation.

This three-part formal analysis is distinct from the category that is called the "object of irony," which "may be a person (including the ironist himself), an attitude, a belief, a social custom or institution, a philosophical system, a religion, even a whole civilization, even life itself" (Muecke 1969: 34). Each of these can be an object of irony in a literary work. Our analysis of Kourouma's *Monnè, outrages et défis* will be an exploration of the scope that the object of irony may assume. As the French begin to conquer the kingdoms surrounding that of the protagonist, King Djigui, one neighboring ruler commits suicide just as the colonial troops enter his fortress: the king "still had the strength to sit up and kill himself with his own hand, to honor the solemn oath he had made, 'As long as I live the Nazarenes will never enter Sikasso!'" (11).[15] In this example, the object of irony is not only the dying king himself but also his word as a sacred speech act as well as the cultural and religious context in which that speech act was conventionally pronounced and understood.

Since it is not easy to determine whether the king of Sikasso was aware of his statement's irony, the previous example also illustrates the delicate difference between verbal irony and situational irony. The former is usually linked with ironic remarks or utterances, while the second has to do with tragic, comic, or melodramatic situations. The distinctive feature operative in the two is that of intentionality. The ironist, who may be the implied author, the narrator, or one of the characters, consciously chooses the vocabulary and/or the style of his or her discourse in a particular ironic remark. A character in the work, out of confident unawareness or self-assertiveness (Muecke 1969: 20), makes a statement that invites a corrective "intellectual judgment" (1969: 22). According to Muecke, verbal irony implies that the ironist is someone consciously and intentionally employing a technique. Situational irony does not necessarily imply an ironist except perhaps as a pseudo-victim. It is often a question of coincidence, a state of affairs, the outcome of events or of a decision that is felt or seen as ironic (Muecke 1970: 8).

Muecke, uncomfortable with the implicit assumption that verbal irony necessarily involves the use of language or voice, prefers the locution *being ironical*, since "an ironic situation in a novel or play, a film, or a painting is the realization of an artist's intentional techniques and strategies" (paraphrased in Ramazani 4). Ramazani goes on to suggest that for Muecke, "there exists between art and the world a symbiotic hermeneutic whereby ironic situations in fiction mirror those in life and art teaches us to more readily identify ironic occurrences in life" (4). Muecke seems to have arrived at a terminological impasse in trying to incorporate intentionality as the main feature distinguishing *instrumental irony*, another term he uses in place of *verbal irony*, from the representation of ironic situations.

Catherine Kerbrat-Orecchioni, in her article "Problèmes de l'ironie," attempts to delineate the difference between verbal and referential, or situational, irony. Referential irony, she says, is a contradiction between two contiguous facts, whereas verbal irony is a contradiction between two semantic levels attached to the same signifier or signifying sequence (17). As far as she is concerned, both the ironic observation of reality and the description of an ironic situation remain distinct from verbal irony. The most important element in her definition and categorization of irony is the reminder that we should not lose sight of the imaginary nature of the referent in literary fiction. "When we speak of 'referential' irony, we mean that the referent is, already, a semiotic object" (15).[16] Kerbrat-Orecchioni's insistence on the semiotic and constructed nature of the literary referent is very important to note in the case of Achebe's *Anthills of the Savannah*, for example, in which one-to-one correspondence to reality would be misleading. In this case, the representation of *power-let-loose* and its consequent workings in dictatorship and repression as well as the various attempts to bring about transformation have no obvious one-to-one correlation with specific events in Nigeria or elsewhere. It is the suggested meaning that constitutes the "true" meaning in an ironic discourse, and this is the meaning that the interpreter *must* arrive at in order to understand the utterance and its coherence in the apparently contradictory sequence of events (Kerbrat-Orecchioni 20).

But verbal irony in its semantic function must be able to answer the following questions with some precision: Is the intended meaning truly the opposite of the literal meaning? How does its semantic dualism compare with that of other figures and modes? What is the relationship between its manifest and its implicit contents? How great is the distance between these two contents?

The following passage from Achebe's *Anthills of the Savannah* will allow us to gauge the helpfulness of the semantic analysis of irony in our attempt to answer these questions and at the same time to understand the ironic intentions and levels of meaning that play out in African literary discourse. Another major character, a friend of Ikem Osogo's, is Chris Oriko, who is also an old friend of the dictator and his Minister of Information. Chris is the narrator of the first chapter. The reader gradually begins to perceive the depths of Chris's disaffection with the regime of his now powerful friend through the irony embedded in his voice. Chris uses a cabinet meeting in which members discuss the possibility of perpetuating the President's hold on power to frame his growing malaise in relation to the President, his fellow ministers, and his own role:

> At this point [the President] is boldly interrupted by the Commissioner
> for Justice and Attorney-General and then by everybody else with
> an assortment of protests. Actually it is His Excellency's well-chosen
> words that signalled the brave interruption, for despite the vigour in
> his voice the words themselves had sounded the *All Clear* and told us it
> was all right now to commence our protestations. So we began to crawl
> out into the open again. In his precise manner the Attorney-General
> says: "Your Excellency, let us not flaunt the wishes of the people."
> "Flout, you mean," I said.
> "The people?" asked His Excellency, ignoring my piece of pedantry.
> (4–5)

In irony, instead of the contextually motivated first meaning or denotation of a figure, we have a coherent literal meaning whose symbolic import is suggested by the situation described by the text. The ironist has recourse to the pun, or double meaning of the word "flaunt." The word's meaning is split into relevant segments so that the ironist can take advantage of the potential semantic correlations of a lexical item, depending on the role it plays in the lexical system of the language. In this passage, semantic inversion involves not only two semantic levels attached to each signifier but also a relationship arising from the partial resemblance and the partial synonymy of the words *flaunt* and *flout*.[17]

In order to understand how the irony works semantically, the following questions are pertinent: Why does the narrator suggestively offer the word *flout* to "rectify" the Attorney General's chosen word *flaunt*? Might there be any semantic relationship between these two words that is worth investigating? Is the narrator simply correcting a possible mispronunciation that could create some confusion or suggest linguistic deficiencies on the part of some stereotypical political figure? Why does the Attorney General not withdraw his ambiguous word, and why does the President, the apparent intended receiver of the lexical item or items, suddenly become interested in the verbal environment (the co-text) of the lexical item? He repeats *inquiringly*: "The people?" Why does he apparently prefer to activate the first or the denotative meaning of *flaunt* in the context while seeming to ignore the two meanings of *flaunt*—two levels of meaning that involve some kind of contradiction?

An interpreter of the passage might not (or should not) ignore the overstatement, hyperbole being a strong signal of the presence of irony, in the Attorney General's utterance addressed to the interested

President: "You are condemned to be a life-time President!" At this point, the interpreter identifies the interest these two words (*flaunt* and *flout*) might have suggested to the power-seeking President.

The divergent and convergent meanings of the two words suggest that the President could indirectly *flaunt*, in the sense of "flutter or wave proudly," the said wishes of the people, namely, to keep him on as a president for life, while ostensibly pretending to *flout* it. The semiotic signs surrounding the utterance of these two words, as well as the pragmatic innuendos in the attitude of the two speakers, the Attorney General and Chris, should be noticed. The validity of the new interpretation can be confirmed or otherwise put into question by the unfolding of the narrative. In this case, the two potential functional correlations of the word *flaunt* might remain ambiguous to certain readers until the appearance, several chapters later, of the old man of Abazon's narrative account of the manipulations involved in the question of the referendum—Chris's role in it, fellow resister Ikem's attitude toward the whole issue, and the position of the people of Abazon—at which point the reader realizes that Chris's offer of the word *flout*, the second meaning of the word *flaunt*, was intended to point in that direction. He, Chris, says *flout* but does not think *flout* and does not want the reader to understand *flout*. Following Kerbrat-Orecchioni's model of verbal irony, Chris's intended ironic meaning is that the President's real concern is not to ignore the wishes of the people as the Attorney General has obsequiously suggested but to convince himself that the people's will is a trophy he can confidently wave. At the same time, the President's ruse could backfire: while trying to profit from the polysemic function of the word, he may be revealing his attempted manipulation of the people as disclosed later in the novel. The President wanted to play the ironist in the context, but his game reveals itself to be a lie rather than irony; as the French would say, "À tout malin un malin et demi." The subtlety and level of sophistication of the irony in African discourse in general, oral and literary, and particularly in Achebe's discourse, make it difficult to dismiss, as does Oumar Sougou, the importance of this passage by considering it to be simply a reflection of the Cabinet's mediocrity. Sougou maintains that "the sterile language of the General, coupled with the semantic misuse of the word *flaunt* by the Attorney-General, which Chris ironically 'rectifies' as '*flout*', connote a linguistic deficiency which is indicative of the Cabinet's mediocrity" (43). The reader might be initially deceived into thinking that it is a semantic misuse or malapropism, but he or she needs to work further in order to follow the irony. The characters may use certain seemingly inappropriate words for ironic effect, but it would hardly be due to any linguistic ignorance and/or incompetence on the narrator's part. A careful reader versed in African discourse and its subtleties will observe that the author's linguistic and rhetorical competence underlies the whole text. Ezenwa-Ohaeto remarks that the "image of power [in the myth from one of Kangan's communities] rampaging 'naked' also illustrates the necessity for a conscious control of power" (24). Those in power, in their political ambitions and excesses, would rather hide under the umbrella of being yoked with lifetime leadership by the people, indirectly flaunting the wish of the people while ostensibly pretending to flout it. By having the President declare that "he would still do things properly and constitutionally no matter the provocation" while at the same time indirectly planning and organizing the murder of his critics (143), Achebe adopts one of the most powerful devices for teaching and correcting those in authority. By means of this artistically crafted ironic mode, he effectively identifies the responsibility of being in power and at the same time attempts to "redirect power to its possible progressive objectives" (24) aimed at constructive change and transformation for the good of the nation.

On the question of the signals that lead the interpreter/analyst to read a text or interpret a message as ironic, Jonathan Culler says that "when we propose that a text means something other than what it appears to be saying we introduce, as hermeneutic devices which are supposed to lead us to the truth of the text, models which are based on our expectations about the text and the world" (157). This touches on the question of how we understand a text. Ramazani (27) quotes Beda Allemann, who says that "in order to understand a text, we must have always already understood it" (392). In other words, how can we possibly interpret a text correctly as ironic unless we have always recognized it as ironic? Wayne Booth's *The Rhetoric of Irony* is "about how we manage to share ironies and why we often do not" (ix). One might well ask how ironic communications ever get transmitted successfully in spite of their inherent ambiguity if the decoding of irony is such an extremely aleatory process, just like any other trope, according to Kerbrat-Orecchioni. The very value of verbal irony lies in the reader's recognition of the way in which it problematizes a more direct form of communication. And according to Ramazani, given that no text is ironic in itself, "the recuperation of verbal irony depends on those signals whereby the ironist suggests that his mask is designed to be seen through" (27). Such signals comprise the context, "the whole of the textual and extra-textual factors that induce an ironic reading," all the intrinsic and extrinsic clues, the internal contradictions, and, according to Muecke, "what the author says or implies over and above what he seems to be saying" (1969: 58). These internal and extratextual markers of irony include "a contradiction of facts or of opinions," "a logical contradiction," "a discordant telling in speaking," "any discrepancy between what is said and the language in which it is expressed," and "any discrepancy between what is ostensibly said and what is revealed of the author's real character" (1969: 58–59).

In the case of the lexemes *flaunt* and *flout* in *Anthills of the Savannah* and their place in the larger drift of the text, the whole page where these ambiguous words appear is full of negative statements that pile up on top of one another as the Cabinet's discussion of the President's implicit desire to legitimize his absolute authority continues:

> "Yes, Your Excellency," replied the Attorney-General boldly. "The people have spoken. Their desire is manifest. You are condemned to serve them for life." Loud applause and shouts of "Hear! Hear!" Many voices in contest for the floor.
>
> "I am no lawyer," says His Excellency, his slightly raised tone breaking up a hand to hand tussle among the voices, "only a simple soldier. But a soldier must keep his word."
>
> "But you, I beg pardon, I mean Your Excellency, cannot break a word you never even said. The nonsense about one hundred per cent was only the machination of a newspaper editor who in my judgement is a self-seeking saboteur."
>
> "No obligation, Your Excellency, to keep faith with heretics," boomed the Reverend Professor Okong's voice. (5)[18]

Every sentence has so many negatives that they cancel one another out—at least that seems to be the case—so that each element is seemingly contradictory. This series fits into a yet larger wave of contradictions. Thus, when readers reconstruct the text, they analyze each element separately from the hierarchy of perspectives and meanings, and so this becomes an ongoing pattern of expression. But as we examine carefully the implications and implicit meanings of the choice of a particular word—its co-text and context—we recognize the relationship between the text and the language as well as the different levels of meaning or signifying. In this context, the word *flaunt* is chosen by a speaker who may or may not be aware of the implications of the lexical item. But another listener, who is *not* the intended receiver of the word, offers another word, *flout*, well aware that the two words overlap in a significant way for the intended receiver and utters it in the hearing of both the sender and the intended receiver in order perhaps to clarify what the first speaker meant or means, or perhaps to imply an urgent need for precision. This second speaker (or, rather, intruder) is the Commissioner for Information, who, as the President says, "owns all the words in [the country]" (7). He is conscious of all the ironic implications deriving from the tension between the two meanings of the word *flaunt*, and by virtue of his role in the context as observer-ironist-narrator, he wants to activate the first meaning of the word *flaunt*—"display oneself ostentatiously or impudently"—so that nobody thinks of the other meaning, which would falsely be to the President's credit. Immediately, the President plays the ironist himself by pretending not to have heard or understood the importance and the implications of the Commissioner's word. At the same time, the President inquiringly confirms with the first speaker, the Attorney General, the people's mandate for him to be a "life-time President." At this point, Chris's word *flout* becomes even more important to the President because he can get his way by means of *chleuasme*, or false modesty, in a manner that borders on lying. He pushes the false modesty further to a ridiculous mocking point, with "I am no lawyer; . . . only a simple soldier" (5) and, again, "When we turn affairs of state back to you and return to the barracks" (4). The text offers a second proof of the irony built into these two overlapping words in the old man of Abazon's narrative, through which readers learn that the "Big Chief" had said that he was being forced by the people to be a lifetime President, thus realizing the two meanings of the word *flaunt* at the same time, "display oneself ostentatiously or impudently" and "treat or behave with disdain." The negative pointers and the way these words and their meanings cancel each other out signal the presence of irony. It is part of the artist-novelist's commitment to revealing through the aesthetics of the text the way in which politics is played in this imaginary but representative African context.

In addition to this double language of the ironist, who could be at different moments the original ironist, the observer, or the victim, and the prevalent contradictions between the lexical items used, these are not just words serving as verbal ornamentation; they are not employed or suggested innocently. But one wonders what hermeneutic models come into play when irony in words, sentences, and expressions is interpreted in relation to the connotative meanings. Where autonomy is yet to be won, where power hierarchies inherited from the colonizer

have remained more or less intact, where in the face of government corruption and state repression national independence has proved something of a farce—the struggle for selfhood is much more than the subject of self-reflexive irony. In a postcolonial context, self-legitimization
depends both on discursive play and on day-to-day *lived* resistance, a
struggle for meanings that is *in* the world as well as on paper.

When African writers employ irony because of repressive political
situations that have limited their freedom of speech from the colonial
era to the present through neocolonialism, or political situations that
involve some danger implicit in any artistic representation of the world,
or simply because of the subtlety and efficaciousness of double language, there is a tendency to see irony as a form of subterfuge, a way of
escaping blame or defeat. But Vladimir Jankélévich believed that irony,
quite to the contrary, not only attacks a certain target—a person, an attitude, even a whole civilization—but also forces that target out into the
open, revealing the true structure of its contradiction, mode of thinking, and acting (10). For African writers, the most pressing question is
one of continuity: a heritage, a link between their oral and written creative discursive practices, often aimed at either bringing out the best
from their interlocutor or otherwise leaving the detractor confused and
humiliated.

There is also the aesthetic dimension to consider: How could irony
as an excuse or refuge also serve as an artistic device for enhancing the
value, quality, and complexity of a work of art?

This entire project on the semantics of irony in African literary discourse is founded on my intuition that a detailed, sometimes technical,
largely linguistic inquiry into the actual semantic structure of an ironic
literary text could help us see exactly what type of communicational
and artistic strategies are in fact being deployed and how that deploy-
ment relates to pragmatic strategies within given social, cultural, and
political contexts.

As Holger Erling, editor of *Critical Approaches to "Anthills of the Savannah,"* rightly observes, "[m]ost African authors have in one way or
another been influenced by Achebe's writings" and have received from
him a "model to deal with language and politics." *Anthills* "comprises
the sum total of Achebe's political and literary thinking" (1). These two
important elements of Achebe's writing are tied together with the artistic device of irony. This device is most effectively located in *Anthills
of the Savannah* at the level of the lexical items and utterances in a way
that strongly differentiates the device of irony from mere subterfuge

(see Gagiano 204). In this subtly crafted political fable in which he brings together in his analysis, through the use of synecdoche and metonymy, a certain number of conditions related to contemporary African societies, Achebe demonstrates more than ever his "balanced and ironic sense of history" (Gagiano 276). He does not minimize his concerns and preoccupations with the issues of change or transformation and power in African nations at the end of the twentieth century. (Ezenwa Ohaeto and Gagiano, among many others, examine in detail the issues of power and change in *Anthills*.) But Achebe still casts a critical and ironic glance at the reminders of colonization, neocolonialism, and decolonization. "New modes of thought, new patterns of discourse," as Erling says, an essential "mode of signifying," to quote Henry Louis Gates, Jr., are found in this work. Hence the need to develop an approach that bridges traditional rhetorical approaches to irony, more recent explorations in the verbal, signifying practice of irony, and the discourse of African authors who are seeking, paradoxically, to "be themselves" in new ways.

The old woman who does not say everything she knows is not a silent or absent voice. She has had to choose between the said and the unsaid, the explicit and the implicit, accusation and insinuation. Her dignity lies in her decision to be ironic and in her knowledge of what irony can and cannot do.

CHAPTER TWO

Interpreting Irony

The millipede that is stepped on keeps quiet while
its aggressor is the one to complain.

—Igbo proverb

A translator undertaking an English version of Calixthe Beyala's *Amours sauvages* might hesitate in translating the name that the narrator-protagonist Ève-Marie gives to the young woman whose strangled body is found on the doorstep of her apartment: Should "Mlle Personne" be translated as "Miss Somebody" or "Miss Nobody"? With her characters' names ranging from Plethora to Opportune des Saintes-Guinnées, Beyala is a powerful practitioner of onomastic irony. The young victim's name is ostensibly based on the fact that *nobody* knows who she is: "A young woman was sprawled out on the floor. Nobody had ever seen her in the neighbourhood, nobody had crossed her path, and that is why I nicknamed her Miss Nobody" (61).[1] But she is also nobody because her assassin and in general a violent society have robbed her of her personal identity. At the same time, the scandal of her namelessness also makes her Miss Person in that she represents the right of personhood and personal integrity that an unjust and oppressive society denies all the marginalized individuals portrayed in *Amours sauvages*. Ève-Marie's initial and apparently innocent act of naming prepares the reader for an ironic interpretation through the potential double sense of the word *personne* and through the narrative incongruity between the carnival-like atmosphere surrounding the discovery of the body and the narrator's growing anxiety in relation to the implications of the body's presence in her world.

In precisely what way can irony help us interpret the socially conscious anxiety that underlies Ève-Marie's apparently matter-of-fact attitude toward the young woman's dead body? David Kaufer, in an attempt to relate irony to meaning, suggests that "[t]he judgment of irony usually turns on the juxtaposition of certain interpretations of a sentence, text or situation with incompatible ones" (453). Kaufer's explanation coincides with this study's concerns with the semantic interpretation of ironic utterances. Where and how is the irony inserted? Noticeably absent, however, in Kaufer's explanation, at least at this point, are the individual word and the utterance—a segment of language assumed by a speaker—although Kaufer's conception of irony does implicitly account for some consideration of *utterance* meaning. Thus, for example, he will say that sarcasm, which he defines as a *tone* of utterance, may be enhanced by irony that "rhetorically" allows a speaker "to achieve emphasis through negation" (453), whether that negation functions as false contradiction, pretended denunciation or praise, victimization of outsiders, or "elaborate equivocations to appease audiences who harbour incompatible beliefs" (454).

Kaufer goes on to insist that, despite these practical ambiguities that irony may exploit and even contribute to, "it is important *not* to confuse irony with the indiscriminate use of ambiguity," since virtually all sentences of a natural language "are filled with ambiguities" (454). A linguistic ambiguity becomes ironic, according to Kaufer, only when it is consciously and artistically produced and therefore requires an element of aesthetic judgment for successful interpretation. There is in fact an implicit aesthetic value woven into ironic utterances in African traditional proverbs. They are "the palm oil with which words are eaten!" Or to quote another Igbo meta-proverb: "Only a foolish person asks that a proverb be explained to him."

Kaufer makes a distinction between ironic phenomena—irony in conversation, in tragedy, in comedy, for example—and an ironic form of interpretation. This distinction suggests as its goal a means of explaining the *designata* of irony (i.e., what ironic utterances are trying to say) as a general form of meaning and corresponds closely with the main interest of this chapter: how ironic utterances are interpreted in the context of African literary discourse. Thus it will be necessary to consider briefly what Kaufer understands by the term *interpretive form*.

First of all, interpretive form is based on binary oppositions, or "pairings of objects or concepts where one element of the pair is incompatible with the other" (456). But these binary oppositions are not necessarily based on logical incompatibility, which, in any case, would not account for irony of situation, but rather on "a more general form of aesthetic opposition." Binary oppositions may be realized through a great variety of oppositional structures. A speaker may make a statement that contradicts a previous one or use suppressed negation in the form of a set of apparently compatible items that have a hidden difference the receiver has to decipher; or he or she may make a statement inconsistent with known characteristics. Some oppositions are based less on logic than on conventional analogies, such as war and peace or love and hate.

But what is the function of these oppositions? According to Kaufer, "ironic interpretation allows a speaker (and an auditor as well if the irony is successfully communicated) to 'take a perspective' on the situation at hand vis-à-vis opposing meanings" (459) by implicitly revealing his or her own choice as to which pole of the binary opposition should be activated in the given context. This taking of perspective is what Kaufer refers to as "the irony model of meaning," which he opposes to "standard semantic theories" that rule out perspective as a semantic property and limit such properties strictly to statement-meaning.

In the case of Mlle Personne, an opposition between "nobody" and "somebody" is one of cultural values, opposing the assumption that an unidentified murdered woman is destined to eternal nonexistence and insignificance to the nagging suspicion on Ève-Marie's part that Mlle Personne's body poses a concrete and meaningful question for the community that has found her. In discussing the religious significance of family ties in African traditional religions, John Mbiti remarks that "[u]nless a person has close relatives to remember him when he has physically died, then he is nobody and simply vanishes out of human existence like a flame when it is extinguished" (25). The narrator and characters of *Amours sauvages* are faced with the concrete reality of a postcolonial Parisian neighborhood where such a vanishing is commonplace. They experience collective malaise and loss, further compounded by the anxiety that, as immigrants and especially as Africans, they are likely to be blamed for the murder.

A standard semantic interpretation would eliminate the opposition from the outset with reference to the co-text: the statement that *nobody* had ever seen her. But a hidden difference between this apparent suppression of ambiguity and a potential ironic form of interpretation arises immediately from the fact that the subject of the explanatory utterance "nobody" is not the woman herself but an anonymous and nonexistent public witness. Mlle Personne herself is not the nobody, according the narrator's explanation, but rather the victim of this no-body's awareness or lack thereof. The cultural context of Ève-Marie's uprooted and marginalized community is needed in order to move from this suggestive discrepancy in her explanation of Mlle Personne's new name to an ironic interpretation.

Hannele Kohvakka has suggested a model based on a *Textlinguistik* approach, which is designed to help us grasp the intratextual contradictions that demonstrate the presence of irony. At the lexematic level, "unexpected expressions and lexical connections occur" (241), whereas at the textual level, "contradictions can be explained through the analysis of the logical structure of the text" (244). Kohvakka presents the various levels at which contradictions may occur: "lexical knowledge," "text (logical construction of argumentation and elaboration of themes)," "context (situation, speaker, hearer, world knowledge)," and "value system (always in the background)" (244). Although, according to Kohvakka, all these levels may play a role in the signaling of irony, they do not all have to function for the interpretation of a given ironic text or utterance to succeed: "Irony can constitute itself in a way that is exclusively context bound, exclusively co-text bound, or both context and co-text bound" (250). Kohvakka posits several types of contradiction that signal irony and that correspond to textual levels. The base level—the one furthest from the form of the utterance—involves "knowledge of the world." In our discussion of Mlle Personne, for example, this would include an awareness of the African community's shaky standing as racial and cultural outsiders within French society as well as the spiritual implications in some African traditions of aberrant anonymity in death (see Mbiti). The co-textual level concerns logical-textual expectations. This involves the assumptions and questions that the discovery of an anonymous dead body imposes on the finder. This is followed by the level of thematic contradiction, including the universality of violence as opposed to the stereotypical connection of violence with the black community. The semantic-syntactic level involves nonlogical connections such as the grammatical subject status of the name "Personne" in Ève-Marie's explanation of how she named the body. Finally, the lexematic level reveals grammatical, lexical, and stylistic contradictions of expectations: this is the level of what Kohvakka calls the "ironic target utterance." Thus, as an example of an ironic utterance, Ève-Marie's choice of the name Mlle Personne reflects the irony of a white woman anonymously murdered (we later learn by a white man) in the midst of a largely black community. She is nobody since nobody knows her, though she is somebody—otherwise her body would not have created the malaise that it did. All of this begins with the lexical double meaning of the word *personne* as "nobody" and "somebody" but is fully deployed through syntax, narrative context, and the socio-political situation.

As it accounts for both the style and the conceptual basis of a text's structure, Kohvakka's model may be useful at the methodological level. But it does not address clearly the micro-semantic level, where different meaning traits within the same lexeme may lead to ironic contradiction. Nor does it account specifically for the figurative aspect of irony. Catherine Kerbrat-Orecchioni and Alain Berrendonner have devoted considerable discussion to these issues.

In her article "L'ironie comme trope," Catherine Kerbrat-Orecchioni, while sharing Kaufer's implicit opinion that some form of pragmatics is a necessary component of the analysis of irony, places more emphasis on semes or meaning traits involved in particular segments of text and discourse. In this study on the semantics of irony, irony is not limited to its tropological dimension, a limitation that would, according to Kerbrat-Orecchioni, reduce its scope to *verbal irony* (thereby excluding situational irony) and to the word or syntagm. Limiting the scope of the study to the syntagm would in turn exclude "the dimension arising from *macro-structures*, which puts its stamp on the whole text and which characterizes the global discursive attitude of its speaker" (8). Perrin (98) criticizes Kerbrat-Orecchioni's approach for subordinating the speaker's "global discursive attitude" to an initial rhetorical effect of antiphrasis.

The type of analysis that Kerbrat-Orecchioni suggests does offer one advantage: it attempts to define the particular relationship between two meanings that characterizes irony and its subtlety as opposed to other figures such as metaphor. Irony can function as a trope only in absentia, that is to say, it must conform to the following conditions:

1. The existence of only one *signifier* to which
2. are attached two semantic and/or pragmatic levels
3. whose relationship is hierarchical
4. in the following way: showing a reversal of the usual hierarchy—the literal sense (first, obvious, part of the language) is connoted; whereas the derived sense (second, latent, more or less new) is denoted (9).

Achebe's *Arrow of God* is a text highly charged with irony both in the relationships it represents and in the subtle distinctions of its language. Ezeulu is the high priest of Ulu, the principal deity of the village of Umuaro. When Ezeulu is detained for an extended period by the co-lonial officer Winterbottom, in connection with a conflict between Umuaro and a neighboring village, Ezeulu blames people within his own community for betraying him, thereby compromising his sacred status. In response, he intentionally delays the priestly approval of the eating of new yam, thereby placing his community in peril. Paradoxi-cally, he both asserts and undermines the authority of Ulu as traditional religious beliefs are gradually giving way to the advance of Western re-ligion. The narrative ends with Ezeulu's tragic descent into madness, following the sudden death of his favorite son, Obika. Early in *Arrow of God*, the narrator reflects on a central problem of the priest Ezeulu's story, which relates to the meaning of the word *power*:

> Whenever Ezeulu considered the immensity of his power over the year and the crops and, therefore, over the people he wondered if it was real. It was true he named the day for the feast of the Pumpkin Leaves and for the New Yam feast; but he did not choose. He was merely a watch-man. His power was no more than the power of a child over a goat that was said to be his. As long as the goat was alive it could be his; he would find it food and take care of it. But the day it was slaughtered he would know soon enough who the real owner was. (3)

There are at least two divergent sememes, or clusters of meaning traits, activated for the word *power* in this passage. The first contains the notion of control over other human beings and in fact over an entire community. This cluster also contains the notions of "absolutism" and "arbitrariness." The second cluster contains an ability to act in deter-mining the well-being of others but adds the semes "temporary," "pro-visional," and "conditional." The first sememe places the agent of power at the top of the decision-making process, while the second makes the agent of power subject to the power of another. It would be difficult to identify the two sememes as opposites in any rigorously logical sense, yet the intuitive opposition leaves room for irony to infiltrate the rela-tionship between the narrator who makes the foregoing assessment of the priest's lived reality and Ezeulu's own consciousness as represented in the form of free indirect discourse: "No! The Chief Priest of Ulu was more than that, must be more than that [. . .] Ezeulu was stung to anger by this as though his enemy had spoken it" (3). By saying "as though his enemy had spoken it," the narrator reveals an internal irony based on the double meaning of *power* combined with a figurative ("as though") representation of the source of the opposing viewpoint. Since the entire passage is characterized by free indirect discourse, the "enemy" who comes between Ezeulu's imaginary absolute authority and his subordination is as much his own voice as the representation of a member of the community—such as his rivals Nwaka and the priest of Idemili. The irony may reside in the fact not so much that someone questions Ezeulu's definition of his own power but that he does not have the power to detach the voice of his "enemy" from his own. An absolute antonymic opposition would hardly lend itself to such an intricate interweaving of perspectives.

Irony may even be based on a difference in meaning that does not involve opposition: "I'm a genius" does not mean "I'm an imbecile." Moreover, many uses of the word *irony*, according to Kerbrat-Orecchioni, apply simply to a wry attitude toward some situation that is somehow in itself contradictory, and this brings us back to situational irony and, for Kerbrat-Orecchioni, the need to combine semantics with pragmatics (10).

It is therefore important to emphasize from the outset that the problem of irony is connected with interpretation and plays on the linguistic as well as rhetorical competence of the intended receiver. Without encyclopedic knowledge of Igbo language, history, and culture, Achebe's readers may understand narrative events and even ideas yet pass over ironies embedded in the implications of apparently straightforward statements. The didactic overtones of *Anthills of the Savannah*, a work that, as Oumar Sougou rightly observes, "probes into the world of power" (35) through dialogues, symbols, images, and structures are best seen in the novel's irony, carefully and not incidentally woven into lexical items, syntagms, and utterances entailing insinuated as well as "transferred" meanings. In examining the various areas in which irony as a literary tool, consciously employed by an artist, can be studied semantically at the level of the word, the utterance, and sentence meanings, I shall also examine them in the light of the functioning of irony at the semiotic level, bearing in mind that the latter level involves the narrative structure. In analyzing and interpreting some chosen passages from the novels under discussion, I shall maintain a distinction between irony and the other figures and rhetorical devices that abound in African fiction, tropes such as metaphor, metonymy, and synecdoche, as well as other devices, including sarcasm and satire, that do not

seem to be as reflexive and instructional as clear ironic utterances and
in which, in the words of Margaret Rose, "the author's statements are
only directed outwards to the world of the reader" (13).

Kourouma's *Monnè, outrages et défis* is the story of Djigui, a fictional
Malinké ruler whose remarkable reign begins before the French colonial conquest and continues through the colonial period. He is at different times and in different circumstances a resistor, a victim, a collaborator, an exploiter, and a critic of the colonial regime. His prestige as a
monarch, though often ironically undermined by his compromises and
his willingness to oppress his own people in order to maintain some
semblance of authority, is shored up by the support of griots, advis-
ers, and courtiers, including the scepter bearer Fadoua. Fadoua's death
in the latter stages of the narrative could be seen as preparing the way
for Djigui's final fall from grace and ritual death. Following Fadoua's
burial, a strange portent descends on Djigui's royal palace, the Bolloda:

> The evening of the burial, whereas no threat of rain justified it, the
> opaque night thickened to the point where only the owls powerful in
> flight could cut through it. We were not surprised to see them come but
> didn't expect there to be so many. It was by hundreds that the grand
> dukes invaded the Bolloda, hooting, howling and hollering late into
> the night. From our huts we were convinced that in their own way they
> organized the funeral services of the defunct, who was surely chief of
> the brotherhood of the soul-eaters, those sorcerers who disguise them-
> selves as owls to destroy the vital principle of the victims who are of-
> fered to them. (175)[2]

The reader has to resolve the contradiction of the defunct Fadoua being
a member of a brotherhood of owls and of both Fadoua and his "broth-
ers" being sorcerers. The solution to these contradictions is mythical
rather than purely metaphorical in the sense that the narrator attributes the common traits of brotherhood and sorcery to the two parties
on the basis of collective conviction, supposition, and shared beliefs:
the defunct was *surely* chief of the brotherhood. At the same time, the
narrator's reference to owls as "the grand dukes" (denoting a variety of
owl) produces a metaphorical semantic contradiction at the level of its
connotation. But whereas the humanizing trait may be explained by
the subsequent evocation of a supernatural brotherhood, the nobility
suggested by the comparison to grand dukes requires further interpretation. The owls are compared to nobility because the inhabitants of
the Bolloda are mystified and intimidated by the defunct man's influence, which extends beyond the grave and reduces their own status and

authority, especially the status and authority of the king. The ambiguity that persists is nevertheless potentially ironical because the narrator's sincerity in presenting this mythic metaphor is dependent on his modalization of the information as something of which he and others "were convinced" at a particularly stressful and disturbing moment in the history of the kingdom of Soba.

How can we explain the intimate relationship in this passage between the metaphorical elements needed for interpretation, the narrator's ironic suggestiveness, and the role of the passage in the overall argumentative strategy of *Monnè, outrages et défis* that leads to an ambiguous assessment of Djigui's legacy?

Given the importance of distinguishing between irony and other rhetorical figures—metaphor, hyperbole, litotes, paradox, for example—as well as showing its link with them, Alain Berrendonner prefers to consider irony as an object of linguistic study under the general notions of meta-communication, argumentation, and norms. Berrendonner dissects the traditional definition of irony as a "figure by which one wishes to have understood the opposite of what one says" (175).[3] He goes on to argue that this commonplace rhetorical idea or cliché of irony supposes the presence of a logical contradiction within the global signification of an utterance. In Berrendonner's view, the most decisive objection to the traditional definition of irony should be its inability to differentiate irony from other forms of contradiction with nothing ironic in them. It is easy to assert that every figure of speech, every trope, is fundamentally based on the identification of an internal contradiction in the utterance. In the case of metaphor, for example, Berrendonner aptly remarks that as soon as one undertakes to analyze a basic metaphorical utterance, such as "This actress bellows" [Cette actrice mugit] (178), one will recognize a particular case of explicit contradiction established between two co-predicates (*actrice—mugir*), one human, the other nonhuman. Berrendonner demonstrates that "the conjoined attribution of two properties to the same object produces a contradiction" (178).[4] Substitutions made possible by reference to similarities between the actress's loud voice and some bovine noise will constitute a logically valid interpretation. Metaphor, like irony, is amphibologic (that is, ambiguous or equivocal in the way it is worded): the howling from the actress is likened to the cow's *minauder*. At the same time, one wonders which of the two conflicting terms is the improper one, the modalized metaphor: the solution could go both ways. The contradiction has two interpretative solutions and so remains ambiguous. The situation of interpretative ambiguity thus created does not necessarily constitute an ironical contradiction.

In the case of the owls in Kourouma's passage, the problem of semantic contradiction and the resulting ambiguity cannot be easily detached from a certain degree of ironic suggestiveness. There will always be at some level an inherent contradiction between viewing owls as birds and viewing them as human beings in disguise. If irony is excluded from our interpretation of the passage, the combination of the denotative seme "owls" and the connotative seme "human beings of high nobility" becomes more or less incidental. The equation of the owls and the soul-eaters becomes an ethnographic observation of a traditional religious belief. But if the owl is also a metaphor for a secret brotherhood, and if that brotherhood was secretly helping to hold together Djigui's partly imaginary royal authority,[5] then the narrator's purpose in establishing this equation is to suggest that the possibility, in the minds of Djigui and his followers, of a clandestine brotherhood involving Fadoua was a creative act of explanation that drew on traditional myths without necessarily affirming their "reality." If it seems ironic that people believe owls to represent human spirits, the idea that such a representation is purely anthropological, devoid of figurative ambiguity, is equally subject to irony.

In Achebe's *Arrow of God*, is Ezeulu's description of his eldest son, Edogo, and his half brother, Okeke Onenyi, ironic? After a discussion of the unexplained coldness between Ezeulu and Okeke, involving a communal voice lost in speculation and ambivalence, Ezeulu is quoted as once having said, "Those two? [. . .] a derelict mortar and rotten palm nuts" (148). Neither the referential interpretation nor the argumentative intent leaves much room for doubt. Ezeulu implies that Edogo and his uncle are comparable in their unjustified claims to specialized skill, with the incumbent social and economic value. Neither is useful, and their irritating alliance is even more useless since the palm nuts that would normally be crushed in the mortar but cannot be, due to the mortar's defects, are not even worth processing in the first place. Is Ezeulu's metaphor ironical? Ezeulu does not seem to be interested in the many possible arguments that the community voice tries to reconstruct or imagine concerning the rights and wrongs of his relationship with his half brother. Yet the stakes of his conflict do include some fundamental aspects of his sacred office. The legitimacy of Ezeulu's title to the priesthood as well as his perceived inequality with his father, due the fact that, according to some people, his father's unbounded priestly powers had been split between him and his half brother (see page 147), could be at stake in this "cold war," at least if he were to recognize its foundations. Rather than position Ezeulu defensively in an argument, the metaphor of the useless vessel for a useless product constitutes an attempt to offhandedly dismiss his half brother's argument itself as irrelevant. But in that Ezeulu's use of the metaphor is reported by a vox populi narrator who has gone to such great lengths to explain the possibly deeper implications of both his brother's magic and his son's silent defiance, it is ultimately not possible to eliminate fully the potential of an ironic voice behind the metaphor of uselessness. The contradiction cannot be resolved without the attribution of double uselessness being cast in a subtly defensive light.

The examples from Beyala, Achebe and Kourouma, despite the particular problems of interpretation that they raise, do seem to support Berrendonner's claim that the presence of a contradiction within the meaning of an utterance is not a sufficient defining property of irony (182). Contradiction is a sign of a figurative mechanism in a speech act of any kind. As soon as a number of rhetorical phenomena that are not peculiar to the functioning of irony as a figure can be eliminated, the problem of irony becomes one of a search for its specificity (Berrendonner 182). How is irony distinguished from other figures of speech? What are the distinctive properties or traits of irony? In order to address these questions, Berrendonner first examines irony as an argumentative ambiguity designed within meta-communication to persuade and possibly convince the intended receiver. He examines the theory of argumentation from different angles in relation to ironic functioning (182).

Berrendonner states that what makes a proposition *susceptible* to antiphrastic and ironic use is the possession of an argumentative value (183). By argumentative value, he means every pair of propositions that permits us to define two classes of utterance—one positive, one negative. The argumentative value of a proposition is determined by its belonging to one or the other of these two classes, which are normally disjoined: the same proposition cannot be used to argue in the same instant in one sense and also in the contrary or opposite sense (185). This would go against a fundamental law of discursive coherence and natural moral constraint that it carries. Irony appears to be precisely like a violation of this law of coherence, and a contradiction is perceived in relation to the argumentative value of the utterance. Such a violation is perceived in the fact that in presenting an argument, the speaker also presents its contrary. In the ensuing argumentative contradiction, the intersection between the two classes of argument ceases to be empty.

This definition of argumentation might explain why, in what follows, Berrendonner revisits some other classical figures of speech, reminding us that some metaphors can be qualified as ironic, while others cannot, and yet all metaphors involve a contradiction (185–86). According to him, this is simply because a good number of metaphorical utterances have no particular function in argumentation, which is a sine qua non of ironic utterance, and so have no definite value in this regard. The utterance that contains the metaphoric contradiction does not have the role of carrying the argument to a conclusion and of making the stated value judgment triumph over its contrary; there is nothing ironical about the contradiction it contains. It is simply a matter of referential incoherence and may be a descriptive one. But it also happens that the metaphor becomes the instrument of irony in the utterance, because in that case, it "fulfills the argumentative function and the contradiction which creates it thus conjoins two incompatible argumentative values, especially in animal metaphors" (186).[6] Is the statement "he is ruminating on a theorem" ["il rumine un théorème," as on pages 85 and 187] praise or mockery?

Édène, the narrator of Beyala's *Les arbres en parlent encore*, begins her eleventh *veillée*, or wake, with a generalized hyperbole that affects both nature and society:

> At the sixth moon, says Édène, the ears of corn turn so yellow that they make the thoughts of men look clear. The waters rest; the snakes forget to bite; the birds do not build their nests; the parents stop giving orders and their children can break whatever they lay their hands on.
>
> And that sixth moon back then, we were bedazzled. It was so intense that most of us wouldn't even open our eyes. If my memory serves me well, this happened when Michel Ange de Montparnasse decided to leave us: "I must serve the French Republic!" he told us. (233)[7]

The argument in this case is that the departure of Michel Ange was a shock to the Issogo community because he had become a beloved adopted son. The seasonal backdrop of the sixth moon was a time of quiet, even to the point of relaxation, such that people were profoundly unprepared for a new cosmic event like the departure of the white man who had given everyone life and joy. The hyperbolic argument of Michel Ange's traumatizing decision is doubled with the hyperbolic sense of public duty and loyalty to the mother country that Michel Ange is quoted as expressing. His integration into the Issogo community cannot be flatly denied, since that would also deny the openness, tolerance, and hospitality of the community that is tied to the conclusion that Michel Ange's departure did constitute a disruption. Édène's father underlines the sober reality of such a conclusion by reminding Michel Ange of his matrimonial commitment to the Issogo woman Esprit de Vie. The hyperbolic bedazzlement is thus not contrary to the argument it seems to support but appears too extreme for the practical conclusion to which it leads, namely, that Michel Ange's departure was a quasi-cosmic loss to the community. But we later learn that Michel Ange does not respect his commitment to Esprit de Vie when he returns as the French commandant with his "proper" French wife. He accepts Esprit de Vie as a servant at best and at worst as something associated with domestic animals. We also learn that the advantages of the French regime over the former German one are presented throughout the narrative as doubtful and that Michel Ange's relationship with both the Issogo and the colonized people he is to govern will sour and even sink into ridicule as the narrative of his term of office unfolds. The underlying counterargument is that Michel Ange's disruption of the life of the Issogo has more to do with an ongoing alienation of the community through the disruptive and destructive effect of colonial domination than it has to do with an imagined loss of a heroic adopted son. The latter becomes an ironizing myth.

Berrendonner asks why reinforcing a judgment by means of modifiers of intensity makes it easier to understand that the contrary is intended. He goes on to explain that the phenomenon is understandable if we recognize that irony is a process that superposes on a given argumentative value the contrary value, considered to be more in conformity with the speaker's intentions. The argumentative effect of hyperbole is to form arguments that exceed the conclusion for which they are used in the first place (187). The argument is often too strong to be honest and pushes the decoder of the utterance to think again.

A very simple question in *Arrow of God* shows how, in Achebe's representation of traditional argumentative rhetoric, irony functions as the juxtaposition of an implicitly provocative argument to the stated or expected arguments of the other. Provoked by the preaching of the mission school to which Ezeulu sent him, his young son Oduche has scandalized the whole community by imprisoning the sacred python. Speaking to Oduche's mother, Ugoye, Ezeulu admits his responsibility in causing the crisis but then insists that she must know where her son is. She replies, "Is he my son now?" (59). The narrator coyly comments: "He ignored her question" (60). Besides subverting any stereotype of African women's submissiveness to patriarchy, this sentence demonstrates the principle of mention, the principle that irony is produced by implicitly referring to the discourse of someone else, in that Ugoye is referring to previous utterances that she implicitly attributes to her husband. Her reference may concern a specific utterance, but more importantly, it evokes a discursive practice in Ezeulu's past through which he has continuously asserted his right to determine his children's fate without the responsibility of consulting the children's mothers. It is even possible that Ezeulu was not usually required to voice this utterance since it was embedded in the common discourse of the community. Ugoye's question, as a speech act combining the deixis of the possessive pronoun *my* and that of the adverb *now*, implies another time when he was *your* child, according to a previous utterance act. This implied previous utterance act is reproduced less through the questioning of the change in ownership than through false naïveté combined with raillery as she pretends to show surprise. Her question, while challenging the wisdom and justice of the designated patriarchal utterance, also challenges the justice of a world in which responsibility comes back to women and mothers who were not granted a voice in the decisions that provoked the problem in the first place. Irony is generated by the feigned surprise as a form of raillery, the holding up of the target's discourse, and the referential or situational irony of a patriarchal society that fails to see its own dependency on women's wisdom and good sense, of which she shows herself by her own verbal skill to be a worthy example.

Understanding irony as the superposition of two contradictory argumentative values (see Berrendonner 190–91) allows us to understand the duality of ironic functioning that is peculiar to certain terms. This duality comes from the fact that the same term can simultaneously carry two argumentative values, which can appear to be quite compatible, one deduced from the other. This means that the same term can be the object of an antiphrasis based on each of these two values, thus taking up two different ironic meanings. Berrendonner also uses the same argumentative ambivalence (192) to explain how, in spite of an apparent absence of any contradiction in the utterance, such expressions or facts are still perceived to be ironical. (e.g., "'I'm one of your greatest admirers,' 'Your kindness overwhelms me,' backhanded compliments, compliments that switch at will to blame"[8]). He affirms that even if the elements of irony are present in these utterances, antiphrasis seems to be missing.

Insisting on the argumentative value of ironic contradiction, Berrendonner explores the "how," or the functioning of ironic interpretation. By what systematic mechanism does an utterance assume, ambiguously, two contradictory argumentative values (196)? In order to arrive at what it means in the first place to argue, he undertakes to define the concepts of argument and conclusion. But it is under the rubric of "Irony as a fact of meta-communication" that Berrendonner's contribution to the theorization of irony should be most appreciated. His discussion of Wilson and Sperber's article "Les ironies comme mention" (already worked on by other linguists, including Kerbrat-Orecchioni) helps us understand both how irony functions and how it is interpreted. According to Wilson and Sperber, irony can be defined as a case of mention. "To ironize would thus be to produce an utterance, by using it, not as an instrument (to speak of reality), but as mention/echo in order to speak of itself as an utterance, and to signify the distance one takes from it. Seen that way, irony would be related to *reported speech*" (Berrendonner 197).[9] That echo may or may not be attributed to particular individuals, and the object of the mention may not be obvious but merely suggested. According to Wilson and Sperber, all ironies, even those that may not be typical, can be described as implicit mentions of other statements. These mentions are interpreted as the echo of an utterance or of a thought whose author means to underline *their* incorrectness or their "lack of exactitude or pertinence" (Wilson and Sperber 409).[10]

For Berrendonner, this helps explain the argumentative functioning of irony: the double play involved, the enunciative duplicity that the classical rhetorics of ethics have never failed to underline. The double play refers to a double level of utterance acts. In this sense, when someone is ironizing, he or she is making a statement (utterance act) E^1 about another utterance act $E°$ anterior to it or an implicit one that the speaker is trying to put down (Berrendonner 198). The utterance act E^1 treats $E°$ like reported speech, like the stating of a content that itself refers back to another or an earlier, inappropriate, utterance act. Irony is thus a spoken mimicry, capable of speaking at one and the same time of the world and of itself (Berrendonner 211). It is an utterance act E^1 that comes out at the same time as an affirmation of a proposition p and as a pejorative qualification of another utterance act $E°$, about the same content and mentioned as an echo of it.

When Édène, the narrator of *Les arbres en parlent encore*, employs auto-referential irony at the beginning of most of her six wakes, and especially at the start of the first wake, she can be seen as using mention in a way that is not only rhetorically creative but also grounded in reflection on the historical and cultural conditions that make her irony possible: "A confession written in a foreign language is always a lie. It is in the language of Baudelaire that we lie. One will prefer to tell what is easy to express, and will leave out one fact or another out of laziness, not wanting to go to the dictionary. It's understood that this story told in our dialect would not have had the same tone. Our existence was anything but spectacular. But my emotions in sharing these memories with you are sincere and intense" (11).[11] The argumentative paradox of this statement resides in the fact that Édène asks her readers to accept as sincere the emotions she shares with them in telling a story that she admits is a lie. Is it possible to lie with sincere emotion? The paradox is further exacerbated by the ambiguity of the statement "It is in the language of Baudelaire that we lie." Does this mean that the use of French betrays the true cultural value and meaning of Eton narrative or that the telling in a foreign language provides a convenient cover for deception or self-deception? This paradox can be better understood through the analytical distinction and relationship between utterance and utterance act. What Édène admits is that the utterance act she is undertaking is itself falsified by the cost of transcultural communication. This is a cost that implicates not only herself as a speaker but also the reading audience for whose sake the lie has become a necessity. In saying that the utterance is a lie, she puts into question both the telling and the hearing as a representation of family, culture, and society. This, however, is itself rendered ambiguous by the narrator's claim to sincerity. The result is that while the truth-value of the utterance—the whole narrative—is subject to caution if not mistrust, the utterance act ultimately stands as a witness to its own validity because we have been told the cultural implications of its performance. Thus the confession itself, by inscribing ironic distance in relation to the message, establishes a defensive argumentative posture that is reinforced by an allusion to the supposed superiority of colonizers and their language. Berrendonner insists that "to produce irony is to contradict one's own utterance while accomplishing it" (216).[12] In an ironic utterance, two meaning values contradict each other—what the utterance says or states is the contrary of what the utterance act says—and this produces argumentative paradox.

Examining the common assumption that irony is fundamentally concerned with railing and mockery and that as a result always has a target or a victim, Berrendonner asserts that this assumption metaphorically equates irony to polemics through the use of the cliché of the arrow and its target (224). A polemic-based conception implies a tropological vision, making irony a case of the semantic transfer of a proper sense to a figurative sense that would be contrary to it. Laurent Perrin (8–9), like Berrendonner, underlines the inadequacy of a definition of irony as antiphrasis but also believes that the pragmatic function of irony is closer to raillery or mockery than a defensive posture in argument. While Berrendonner's model is effective in explaining the precarious position of the African author as ironist, the notion of raillery is unavoidable in explaining the relationship between verbal irony and the problem of the polyphonic narrative voice and shifting multiple perspectives.

Berrendonner nevertheless maintains that irony has a fundamentally defensive function. It forestalls sanction resulting from the way institutional norms function, with their laws about conformity and nonconformity of verbal behavior (228). As an argumentative paradox, irony allows the speaker to argue without running the risk of consequent sanctions (239). In using irony, one marks one's own discourse as argument, arguing on two levels—the utterance level and the level of the utterance act—in such a way that each one both implies and disproves the other. In this process, irony becomes a means of escaping or avoiding the rule of coherence in communication. Irony escapes this restriction and thus extends the speaker's possibilities of self-expression while allowing him or her to escape sanction. In relation to African culture, though, we have seen the need for irony to be shared, sometimes even by those it seeks to criticize. The failure to grasp irony as the utterance act's goal constitutes a serious lack of social and linguistic competence. An understanding of this expectation is needed for an effective reading of ironic African texts since argumentative defensiveness also involves a call to the receiver to participate successfully in an act of shared understanding.

For Berrendonner, irony is a trick allowing the ironist to both unmask and forestall any normative constraints. Irony is "the ultimate refuge of the liberty of the individual" (239). The idea of a refuge of human freedom is very applicable to postcolonial African fiction, given the historical background of this literature as well as its present climate. But as further analysis of texts drawn from African novels will demonstrate, his categorical conclusion ("It matters little whether irony is moral or not. The essential [. . .] is that it is a fundamentally defensive manoeuvre"[13]) fails to account for the political use of irony as an arm by potentially oppressed or dominated people. Irony often constitutes a strong, though indirect and subtle, attack that can disarm or even humiliate an oppressor. Ironic words or utterances, whether sarcastic, satiric or allegorical, can be so subversive, albeit subtle and refined, that the ironist is feared even by a powerful adversary. Irony is a very strong *arme de combat* for many African writers, so much so that ironic discourse has contributed to movements of social and political liberation, just as Ferdinand Oyono's unmasking of the colonial master's and mistress's apparent moral superiority in *Une vie de boy* became a classic of anticolonial rhetoric.[14] Through analyses of texts involving political protest, social critique, and African feminist thought, I argue that irony is equally offensive and defensive. Irony in African fiction often has an object of critism, and yet, and this is perhaps the deepest cultural paradox, it sometimes offers at its center a sense of the pleasure of the text and of the word, because of its beauty and subtlety. An even more troubling paradox will be seen in the fact that irony can be written within a tradition that it at once defends, teaches, and subverts.

Like the proverbial millipede, which would seem totally powerless to challenge its aggressor but in its apparent silence and withdrawal causes the aggressor to think of himself or herself as a target, the ironist of African literary discourse could be conceived as revealing the eloquence and power of the unsaid as well as the discomfort of many potential targets.

CHAPTER THREE

Pragmatics and Ahmadou Kourouma's (Post)colonial State

Rather than the dry tree that is expected to fall,
it is the green tree that crashes.

—Igbo proverb

Ahmadou Kourouma is perhaps the ideal author to consider as we turn toward pragmatics. Though his first novel, *Les soleils des indépendances* (1970), radically undermined the assumptions of stylistic heterodoxy in the use of the French language by African writers,[1] his life and career were by no means dominated by stylistic debates. A practical person, a soldier, a dissident in exile, an actuary who left a gap of twenty years between his first novel and his second (*Monnè, outrages et défis*), Kourouma consistently sought to use the language of fiction to address issues of social and political oppression. He was arguably one of the most powerful voices raised in the critique of governance in postcolonial Africa. His irony is thus a locus of meaning and of doing: how irony works, why it is necessary, and how it seeks to act on the reader's worldview necessarily come together in our analysis of two of Kourouma's great postcolonial narratives, *Monnè, outrages et défis* and *En attendant le vote des bêtes sauvages*.

By focusing on what Edgar Lapp (1992, 12)[2] refers to as "verbal irony," we will be able to read a number of ironic utterances as they are represented in Kourouma's fiction as the kind of verbal practice to which our previous discussions of semantics, interpretation, and argumentation have pointed.[3] This broader view of discursive practice will complement the argumentative analysis of irony proposed by Berrendonner and show how, in the context of African literature, irony is defensive as well as offensive, artistic as well as political, and subversive as well as traditional.

Viewing irony not as a "linguistic form" but as a "specific way of dealing with language (and not language alone)" (12), Lapp bases his inquiry on a series of questions (13–14) that can be applied to Kourouma's representation of ironic communication in the context of Koyaga's trial in *En attendant le vote des bêtes sauvages*:

1. What factors, other than purely linguistic ones, are involved in the production of an ironic expression?

2. In what way is the intended ironic meaning (*eigentliche Bedeutung*) derived from the literal meaning?

3. How can ironic expression be distinguished from other forms of indirect communication?

4. What is the communicative function of ironic expressions?

5. Can irony in general be adequately described through linguistic methods or does it demand an interdisciplinary approach and, if so, what sort of interdisciplinarity would be needed to study irony in African literary discourse?

Immediately after the introduction of the *donsomana*, or purifying ritual, of Koyaga, whom Bingo, the *sèrè* (master of ceremonies), refers to as one who will remain "with Ramses II and Sundyata, [. . .] one of the three greatest hunters of humankind" (3),[4] Tiécoura, the *koroduwa*, or responder, is invited to contribute his "grain of salt" (4).[5] Tiécoura gives the *donsomana* his own interpretation: "President, General, Dictator Koyaga, we are going to sing and dance your *donsomana* during five festive *sumu*. We shall tell the truth. The truth about your dictatorship. The truth about your parents and your collaborators. All the truth about your filthy tricks and your bullshit; we shall denounce your lies, your numerous crimes and assassinations" (4).[6] He is, as will be the consistent pattern throughout the book, abruptly called to order by Bingo, the *sèrè*: "Stop insulting a great and righteous man of honor like Koyaga, the father of our nation. If you don't malediction and misfortune will pursue you and destroy you. So stop it! Stop it!" (4).[7]

In one sense, linguistic factors already manifest in these two utterances are sufficient to indicate the presence of ironic intentions. The *koroduwa*'s utterance contradicts the *sèrè*'s initial honorific form of address while the *koroduwa* is speaking as a participant in the same ritual process. Even the *koroduwa*'s initial apostrophe suggests the same deferential attitude toward Koyaga. While Tiécoura's claim to a discourse of truth may shock the spectator/reader, what is more significant is that he claims that this truth telling is part of the overall collective process of the *donsomana*: "We are going to sing and dance your *donsomana*. . . . We shall tell the truth." While this surprising claim may suggest irony as paradox, it is in fact the *sèrè*'s reproach of Tiécoura that clearly creates an implied ironic meaning, because the former attacks Tiécoura on the grounds of his situation and not of the meaning of his utterance. This criticism of the *koroduwa*'s verbal and gestural behavior rather than his claim to truth has specific implications. The possibility that Tiécoura is in fact on a track leading to the truth suggests that the *sèrè* himself may share his views while needing to avoid an open admission of this concurrence because of the official nature of his role. If this is the case, the honorific titles he uses in his response ("grand homme d'honneur et de bien," "notre père de la nation") may themselves take on ironic proportions through one of two routes: hyperbole or mention (making them clichés of sycophancy).[8]

Both the *koroduwa*'s and *sèrè*'s roles may be interpreted as forms of raillery. Perrin (1996) argues that antiphrasis is rarely a direct source of ironic expression but rather an indirect and secondary semantic operation following in the wake of an act of raillery: "Irony cannot be reduced to a simple inversion of the signification of words and sentences since it consists primarily of making fun of someone by seeming to support him/her and by trying to convince us precisely of what is literally expressed" (91).[9] The statement that is thus displayed and its implicit original author are irreparably disqualified in that the ironic speaker has through a pejorative representation disqualified in a definitive way what is supposedly communicated (102). In this sense, the "blasphemy" of Tiécoura constitutes a hyperbolic background of ridicule designed to foreground the ironic raillery of the *sèrè*, who, in pretending to "rein in" the excesses of the *koroduwa*, simultaneously discredits the official discourse of tyranny on which Koyaga depends for his survival. Gbanou (2006), in documenting Koyaga's resemblance to the Togolese dictator Étienne Éyadéma, compares Kourouma's text both to official propaganda extolling Éyadéma and to unofficial anti-Éyadéma satires. He concludes that Kourouma's writing "is situated in the following test: how to order itself between two polarities of the same subject, maintained respectively by a State rhetoric that buries legends and by a rhetoric of contestation inclined to making a pathological portrait of its object" (62–63).[10]

In order to apply this irony that falls between official and subversive rhetoric to Lapp's questions, the factors behind the ironic expression

include the *donsomana* as a cultural code that assigns official or subversive roles to various speakers and suggests the purpose of the ritual
as one of penal or corrective purification. A political subtext involving
reference to totalitarian leadership constitutes a second nonlinguistic
factor in the sense that speaking to a head of state requires terms of respect. Finally, textual ambiguity is produced by the introduction of the
donsomana into the novel's structure. Readers, searching for a recognizable narrative voice, sense the irony of a speaking community that
seems to ignore them and to carry on its own dialogue outside of their
expectations, though the written text itself seems to welcome them and
invite them to witness the "cultural spectacle" of the *donsomana*. Justin
Bisanswa describes Kourouma's multiple-voiced structure as "a narration of surprising developments" (23). He further describes the effect
of this type of storytelling: "the most immediate effect of these mirror
games is to put the reader in an unstable posture. One is never sure in
which story one finds oneself: that of the character or that of the narrator" (23–24).[11] All of these effects are directly related to the creation of
ironic distance between the reader and the text but tend as well to posit
determined "readers of the novel" who are looking for a linear and coherent narrative behind the textual games they encounter. To the extent
that readers seek to understand as much as possible the *donsomana* on
its own terms, a further ironic distance is created by the cultural barriers to understanding that arise from the apparently contradictory behavior and utterances of the principal actors.

Lapp's second question, as to how ironic meaning may be derived
from literal meaning, is particularly difficult to answer for two reasons.
On the one hand, all meaning is absorbed into the process of ritual purification: parallel series of epithets and hyperboles stand in opposition
to each other as if in their rightful place since they are spoken by the
actor designated for that purpose. On the other hand, a more shadowy
and enigmatic irony may be derived from the question as to why Koyaga, at the stage in his career when he seems to be the undisputed master of the postcolonial African state, would choose to undergo a ritual
purification at the hands of fellow hunters.

If, then, the ironic expression established by the opposing epithets
addressed to Koyaga is absorbed into a ritual whose ultimate purpose is
unclear to us, we can say that the entire discourse of the *donsomana* is
a form of indirect communication. It implies a secret verbal exchange,
understandable only to the initiate, to which we are made witnesses
from the outside. In other words, we are not designated as the intended

receivers of any of the messages being sent, yet we indirectly witness the whole event. In what sense is this indirect communication ironic in a way that could be distinguished from other forms of communication such as deception—pretending to be unaware of the truly intended receiver's presence in order to manipulate him or her—or intentional histrionics? The irony in this case resides in the complicity of the reader who knows that he or she is being drawn into a game of deception and yet continues to imagine himself or herself to be an innocent outsider.[12]

If the reader's complicity is what distinguishes this use of the *donsomana* as an ironic expression, then the communicative function of such expression must be understood in pragmatic terms, that is, in terms of the study of language in relation to its users (Mey 5). It is not primarily the representation of a historically or politically ironic situation but the cultivation of an attitude and of a public eye capable of ironic judgment. It is an initiation for the noninitiate, not in that it can make us Koyaga's peers as hunters but in that it enables us to judge Koyaga as if we knew him as well as the culture for which he stands.

This state of affairs helps us trace out at least some of the fields of study that are necessary to describe the ironic function of African literary discourse. The bridge between structural semantics and pragmatics is based on the way in which potentially ironic terms are embedded in the "ritual" use their speakers make of them. Cultural analysis provides the only link between the text and the imagined cultural event of the *donsomana*. Finally, historical knowledge of the various types of totalitarian regimes in postcolonial Africa makes it possible to account for the representational power of the novel within the bounds of its pragmatic function. A discussion of Kourouma's earlier work, especially *Monnè, outrages et défis*, will enable us to show how historical context is related to a pragmatic interpretation of verbal irony.

In *Les soleils des indépendances*), Kourouma's message is communicated through the dislocation of the French language and the presence of the Malinké language. Kourouma "takes over the French language, [...] interprets it in Malinké, in order to render the language Malinké, by suppressing linguistic boundaries, to the great surprise of the reader" (Gassama 23).[13] In *Monnè, outrages et défis*, Kourouma touches on the linguistic and historical reality of *la Francophonie* through indirect discourse. Stereotypical ideas of Africa are both demythicized and subverted through speech characterized by multiple ironic narrative voices. This context functions at three levels of ironic expression identified by Philippe Hamon (98): a discrepancy between two parts

of the same utterance, between two different utterances, or between
the speaker and his or her utterance. After identifying the principal
speaking actants—the collective narrator who uses the pronoun "we,"
the griot-narrator, and the autodiegetic narrator-king—I will point out
the discrepancies between their discursive practices and those of other
speakers.

African literature has often been produced in a context of social and
political malaise. In the 1950s, it addressed a colonial public; during
the early years of independence, the struggle surrounded the problem
of acculturation; since the 1970s, it has expressed disillusionment in
the wake of the misadventures of national cultures. Among the most
revolutionary texts of the latter period (in both theme and style) are
arguably Yambo Ouologuem's *Le devoir de violence* (1968), Ngugi wa
Thiong'o's *Petals of Blood* (1977), and Kourouma's *Les soleils des indépendances* (1970). The works of disenchantment of the 1970s, representing the evils of established centers of power, such as national bour-
geoisies, for example,[14] as well as various class interests that clash at the
discursive level, reproduce a multiplicity of conflicting points of view.
Monnè, outrages et défis (1990) offers the example of Soumaré, a representative of the new category of bourgeois cadres who enjoyed forms of
subaltern power under the colonial administration. They are the best
fed, the best paid, and the best placed, during a period of remote-con-
trol decolonization, to take over from the colonizers.

The multiple narrative voices of the story often turn to satire, parody,
and a humorous and yet biting irony in responding to the discourse
of various hegemonic powers, both African and European. In *Monnè,
outrages et defies*, the narrator implicitly establishes, through a collective proverbial voice, parallels between the misdeeds of the king and
those of the French colonial officers with whom he is dealing.

According to the new historicists, influenced by post-structuralists,
a historical novel should emphasize the role of representation and discourse in social life: "The new historicists were particularly interested in
how such collective representational systems work in the reproduction
and contestation of social power" (Ryan 129). History is conceived as a
space where several discourses and systems arise from a dynamic process
of exchange and enter into competition for the power to represent social
reality at any given time. Since the literary work is one of the points of
interaction between different discourses, historicist analysis of literary
discourse seeks to demonstrate how collective systems of representation
function in the production and contestation of social power.

In *Monnè, outrages et défis*, the discursive practices and the knowledge of regimes of power that construct and reproduce different forms of dominance, as well as the discourses that challenge this dominance, intersect and overlap in order to bring out the ill will and naïveté, oppression and resignation, civility and dishonorableness that characterize the human relations described. There is a constant exchange in the underlying relationships between a dominant discourse that claims to represent reality—if not the truth—about the Other and different forms of contestation: colonizer/colonized, sovereign/vassal, king/subject, men/women. Discursive modes—irony, humor, sarcasm, and parody—reflect power while subverting it, often as caricature, allowing all those who are deprived of power to speak. The only ones still deprived of that power of speech are women. Here the commitment of the author stops at the exposure of their condition as dominated: prostitutes, witches, gifts given to patriarchs.

One can speak of multiple voices and perspectives, especially when the narrator comments on various fictional events. The narrator sometimes uses off-color humor in order to represent the culture of citizens, colonizers, the fallen king, and the "Fama"—princes who become servants. Although it is impossible to identify the speaker in many narrative sequences, the indeterminate character of the perspectives represented is yet more complex, leading to both caustic and humorous utterance-based irony. The technique is close to the dialogic forms that are both liberating and subversive (see the discussion of Bakhtin in Selden et al. 42). According to Bakhtin, the words of a discourse are dynamic and active social signs, with different significations and connotations for different social classes and in different historical situations. An attentive reading will reveal the sources and implications of the different perspectives. The narrative voice, adopting all the narrative voices and all the possible forms of point of view (auto-, homo-, and heterodiegetic, sometimes omniscient) one after another, often uses free indirect speech in order to insert his own ironic commentary into this web of perspectives.

The following passage from *Monnè, outrages et défis* offers an example of this functioning of language:

> On the day he took the throne, the griots had chanted, "Djigui! Djigui Keita, king of Soba, the land that you inherit is a finished work. There is no more monnè."
>
> Djigui believed them. During the first seasons of his reign he didn't really devote himself to anything more important than marrying many

virgins—he was the strongest and the most handsome. Being praised
by sycophants and griots—he was the greatest. Turning his slaves into
sbirros and sicarios—he was the most intelligent person in all of Mandingo. Like all young Malinke princes he often went hunting in the
bush. He could retrieve the game faster than the hunting dogs. And
those were the only works that he bothered about. He who was our
king had reigned without blessing the sacred offerings and the alms
distributed in his name to the beggars. Without revoking any of the
verdicts of the lying judges. He lived without convening the wise men
or the sacrificers. Without praying five times a day. Without honoring
the shades of the ancestors. (5)[15]

The new king has just been "reassured" of the permanence of his dynasty by demanding the most desperate prayers of the people of Soba.
Guaranteeing this permanence implies the official sanction of his subsequent exercise of power. The context itself is a demonstration of the
abuse of power and of the lack of statesmanship on the part of a leader.
The voice of a homodiegetic narrator could be best described in this
case as a speaker who is manipulating the utterances of others. The use
of three parallel parenthetical clauses—"he was the strongest," he was
the greatest," "he was the most intelligent"—is the first signal that we
are dealing with an ironical utterance. In these clauses, the speaker
underscores at the same time his own complicity, as a person close to
the king, and his denunciation of the king's self-centered behavior. The
irony is reinforced by the discrepancy between the central sentence describing the king's attitude ("he didn't really devote himself to anything
more important than . . ."—already likely to be a pejorative remark
when applied to kingship) and the attached clauses serving as possible
explanations of his behavior. Interpreted as a narcissistic vision of himself, he could allow himself just about anything, even ignoble acts, since
he is the handsomest and the strongest, hence his right to the best girls.
Moreover, his beauty, virility, and magnificence have been celebrated
by his adulators and his griots—two groups of followers whom one can
hardly trust given their ephemeral and changing words. If he were indeed the greatest, both in physical strength and in social status, why
would he have to make himself the most feared being by surrounding
himself with hired assassins and spies rather than simple slaves? For a
king, a head of state, the father of the nation, who should feel loved and
venerated by the people, the fact that he surrounds himself with hired
assassins and *sbirros*—policemen in a totalitarian state practicing violence in their service to an oppressive authority—and all the measures

taken to solidify his power reveal a pitiless character inhabited by a sense of insecurity. Finally, whether out of naïveté or by intention, he will allow himself to be manipulated by the invaders of his territory. Though fully conscious of the imminent demise of both his kingdom and himself, he will play the game of resistance for all it is worth. At that point, he will sink into collaboration with the colonizers.

As the politician facing failure that he is, he looks for the praise of the most famous panegyrists whom he controls with presents, even if the results are derisory epics: "Assuredly Djeliba was a talented griot, the greatest praise-maker-poet of our century; a king could not let him leave. Djigui must bind him to the Keita dynasty" (30).[16] Then the narrative voice comments again in proverbial form, in the guise of an ironic explanation of the great griot's change of heart when he receives on two occasions presents of beautiful griottes, slaves, horses, and riches: "A benefaction entails obligations. In return for a benefaction, a griot, like any other man, is expected to show appreciation. [. . .] Praises, poems, music. [. . .] A benefaction and honors bind a good man more tightly than force and the rope can ever hold a slave or a shameless man" (31).[17]

In the narrator's commentaries on narrative events, the irony of the proverb depends little on antiphrasis: no one is suggesting that benefaction and honor do *not* bind a man more tightly than ropes. But what is working under the surface is not an argumentative structure as Berrendonner would claim but a view of social reality that implicitly reveals the corruption that underlies the griot's changing positions, discourse, and claim to historical truth. As a man of words, the illustrious hired griot (a symbol of the African writer perhaps?) should be familiar with the history of his culture as oral memory and of the other cultures of his region. Theoretically a writer-griot would want neither to repudiate history completely nor to reconstruct it with nostalgia. Indeed, the griot seems to be engaged in a dialogue with the Négritude writers who tended to idealize the past. The griot's role in the reconstruction of identity and culture, according to the implicit ironic speaker, would be to know how to construct speech, underscoring the specific and the universal in past errors, condemning the colonization of Africa as well as the vainglorious ambition, corruption, and dictatorship that were conducive to the consolidation of that colonization.

The term *monnè* can signify different stages of outrage, defiance, humiliation (submission, slavery, cowardice) among Africans and among their detractors as well as the incommunicable nature of certain types of experience in the context of relations between Africa and Europe.

One could also interpret the term as the expression of the homodiegetic narrator who is speculating on the king's thinking, which he seems to understand intimately and somewhat critically. The discrepancy between the different levels of the narrative voice's utterances becomes manifest in what follows ("He who was our king"), when that voice insinuates that Djigui has not always deserved the honor of being king, whether according to the demands of Islam or according to respect for the spirits of the ancestors.

Throughout the text, the discourse of the characters, with the cultural signifier of the implicit utterances of the Mandingo people embedded in ironical commentaries, assumes different forms in order to interrupt the voice of authority and thus open the way for other voices. The hierarchies are reversed in the sly smile provoked by proverbs that in turn imply an oral culture and traditional wisdom by the living metaphors associated with their images.

The black interpreter, Soumaré, for example, despite his betrayal of the king and his people at the time of the arrival of the French in Soba, does not hesitate to use irony in his discourse as a means of resistance against any effort to suppress his identity: "I'm translating the words of a White Man, a Toubab. When a Toubab talks, all us Niggers shut up, take off our hats and our shoes and open our ears" (42).[18] Superficially, this utterance expresses the tragic fate of blacks under the yoke of colonialism following the slave trade, racially motivated commerce that robbed them of their human, individual, and cultural identities and reduced them to a mass merchandise. This would explain the "Nous, Nègres, on . . . " in the interpreter's utterance. In the same way, the semiotic gestures of humiliation and submission referred to in the rest of the sentence evoke the discourse of the colonial captain: "Glory and joy to the victorious! Misery for the vanquished!" (41) ["Gloire et joie aux vainqueurs! Malheur aux vaincus!" (53)].

The interpreter is not trying to deny the reality of colonization, but the hyperbolic series of gestures of obsequious submission makes the situation all the more ridiculous. Paradoxically, the theatrical gestures transfer the trait of bestiality to the oppressor. The silence of the griot concerning the white man and his words as well as his subsequent excuse ("The griot apologized, he didn't know that the language of white might and power needed the voices of griots in order to prevail" [42][19]) reinforce the interpreter's irony. By insinuation, the latter has just compared the white man's power to that of an awe-inspiring god—"Quand un Toubab s'exprime"; whether verbally or not, he expects the "Nègres" to humble themselves before him. The griot affirms himself by refusing to confirm the oppressor's point of view. The terms of his excuse show more of the wry laughter or raillery of resistance to the subjection of his people. The term *griot* used here acts as a metonymy for Mandingo tradition and culture, epic poetry, and a notion of authentic history. The voice of the griot, symbol of his own affirmation, is not made to sing the panegyric of a colonialist.

Monnè, outrages et défis is a work that out of necessity evokes the history of the "initial" contacts of Africa and Europe as well as the social and geopolitical consequences of this "encounter." In an oral discourse in dialogue with other texts and traditions, both oral and written, an utterance-agent will attempt to blur the distinctions between history and fiction in order to ask a number of pressing questions. What is the meaning of the *mission civilisatrice et évangélisatrice* that the colonizers used as a pretext for "pacifying" Africa? How did they interpret the phenomena that had incited them to undertake such an enterprise? How did they define the concept of a straightforward defeat in combat that they forced the African king to acknowledge? What was the basis of the alterity and the inferiority complex that they were inculcating in Africans through language? Kourouma is aware of the discursive practices of regimes in power that construct various forms of domination. Refusal of domination and resistance to being reduced to nothing will be brought about through language in various contexts by its users— a search for the discursive construction of the past. Utterance-based irony becomes an effective tool with which to correct, denounce, and demystify all claims to infallibility and derisory greatness and, especially, to affirm oneself.

Regarding the question of colonial, neocolonial, or postcolonial power, the novel's narrative voice reveals several levels of social and political hierarchy and their self-proclaimed preoccupation with the economic and political well-being of the continent. The anecdotes of the narrator, often imbued with irony and parody, offer access to the systematic functioning of power structures, such as the invasion of France by the "Allamas," by applying didactic proverbs to characters who are subject to his ridicule. For example, as the French commandant seems to blame Djigui for not recruiting enough *tirailleurs* to prevent France's defeat by the Germans at the beginning of World War II, Djigui thinks to himself: "When each one has to turn against someone weaker, the north wind blows against the empty calabash: the French were horned beasts who only attacked the hornless" (96).[20]

We can retain two principles from Lapp's pragmatic approach in analyzing the sociohistorical background of the narrator's discourse in
Monnè, outrages et défis. First, the ironist is not being ironical only to
show off his or her rhetorical prowess but rather to show something
that cannot be reached through non-ironic expression (Lapp 15). Second, irony not only can function through an abstract opposition between properties such as greatness and smallness but can be based on
the ostensible belief of the speaker in the truth-value of the utterance
put forward and on the corresponding conclusion drawn by the hearer
of a contradictory opposite (25). As Berrendonner's pragmatics of irony
would suggest, this "corresponding conclusion" expected from the
reader can function as a defensive way out for the ironist who can sub-
sequently deny the intention of leading the audience to that conclusion
while still allowing for its possible confirmation in case of a consensus
between speaker and audience. But limiting ourselves to this defensive
view of irony will not account for the possibility of the hearer's conclusion being a trap laid by the ironist in order to confirm the hearer's own
naïveté or inability to understand fully the sociocultural or political
context involved. There is a further possibility that the ironic speaker
intends to set a trap for the hearer but actually traps himself or herself if
the hearer intentionally refuses to draw the conclusion implied.

Irony is inscribed in the process of the *donsomana* of *En attendant
le vote des bêtes sauvages*, in its ritual and traditional properties, its
purpose, and the historical circumstances to which it refers. Although
the close connection between ironic and proverbial expression is even
more central to Achebe's earlier and less obviously postcolonial *Arrow
of God*, the ritual and traditional aspect of irony may be found in Kou-
roma's extensive use of proverbs throughout *En attendant le vote des
bêtes sauvages*. What Lapp claims about the purpose of verbal irony,
to express what would otherwise be inexpressible, is also often true of
the use of proverbs. In the case of Kourouma's *donsomana*, both irony
and proverbial discourse are related to otherwise unattainable expression of cynicism, condemnation, despair, and resistance in a climate of
imposed subservience. At the same time, the prowess that their lavish
and overwhelming power suggests also plays a role in the affirmation
of the moral and traditionally rooted authority exerted by both the *sèrè*
and the *koroduwa* and, ultimately, the implied authorial voice. They become voices of the initiate, agents of purification, and guardians of—or
at least claimants to—truth.

The notion of a claim to truth is crucial to the difference between a structural analysis of irony and any attempt to undertake the pragmatic interpretation suggested by Lapp when he refers to the "ostensible belief" of the speaker and the "corresponding contradictory conclusion" of the hearer. The proverb itself, whether used ironically or not, stands in a highly complex relationship to such contradictory perceptions of the truth. The user of the proverb may be presenting claims to truth at several different levels: the literal truth of the statement as a natural law or a recurring natural phenomenon, for example; the suitability of the truth in relation to life as really lived according to the speaker who has selected the proverb; the same suitability according to the social consensus of a traditional belief system that the user implicitly refers to by placing his or her claim in a proverbial form; and the specific suitability to the context in which the proverb is cited (here traditional or collective claims to truth will play a limited role since the situational appropriateness of the proverb's interpretation can be fully determined only by those directly involved or at least in a position to observe the situation firsthand). There is, however, a further possibility that the claim to truth may function as a litotes, since the proverb's truth-value may be perceived by listeners as more applicable to the context than certain other hearers or targets—such as dictators or corrupt politicians—would themselves wish to recognize.

Three proverbs presented in the opening scene of *En attendant le vote des bêtes sauvages* (4, trans. alt.) will enable us to examine some aspects of this problem:

1. If the partridge flies away, its child doesn't remain on the ground.
2. Regardless of a bird's long sojourn in the baobab, he never forgets that the nest where he was hatched is in a shrub.
3. And when one does not know where he is going, let him recall the place from whence he comes.[21]

As is often the case in *En attendant le vote des bêtes sauvages*, the three proverbs are italicized and clustered, in this case at the end of the prologue of the first *sumu* (the term used in the authorized English translation), or wake. The *sèrè* invokes the theme of tradition as a justification for the use of proverbs as interludes between wakes and then uses the proverbs themselves to underscore the importance of tradition. There already seems to be a paradox embedded in this ritual circularity, as if the proverbs play an ex officio or even token role in the "trial" of Koyaga on more practical and immediate grounds, unless a second and more

subversive voice could be heard in them. But the impression of circularity itself undermines the epistemic and deontic authority of the *sèrè*.
   On closer examination, the three proverbs also present several significant ambiguities. The first proverb suggests the following of tradition more as a necessity of fate than as wise counsel, more as fatalistic
resignation than edifying truth. The second adds the notion of pride
and humility and thus requires for its complete interpretation a critical application to Koyaga. The latter's initiation can be seen as a reminder that his present authority should not isolate him from the people whom he is oppressing because he too witnessed the oppression of
his father at the hands of the French. The third proverb seems at first
glance to resemble Achebe's "If we don't know where the rain began to
fall on us we will not know how to dry ourselves" but in fact represents
a very different view of tradition in that it treats the causal relationship
between past and future more ambiguously. There is no guarantee in
this proverb that knowledge of tradition will help anyone or any society find its way in the future. If we are groping for truth as a people,
it would at least be comforting to know that we did start somewhere.
Although there is nothing in the combined effect of the three proverbs
to dissuade the reader from supporting the *sèrè*'s belief in the importance of tradition, there is also reason for one to reserve judgment on
the applicability of these proverbs to Koyaga's life and regime as well as
on their efficaciousness in responding to the crisis in Koyaga's country.
Does Koyaga remember what it means to suffer oppression? Is knowing
where one began truly useful, and if so, what purpose does it serve? It
should be noted here that it is not really a contrary view of truth on the
part of the hearer that inserts irony into this cluster of utterances, as
Lapp's explanation would lead us to expect, but rather a doubting and
questioning perspective. Although the gradually unfolding atrocities
of Koyaga's regime and the reader's knowledge of contemporary dictatorships are certainly involved, the discrepancy does not come entirely
from knowledge of the context but is already suggested by the way the
utterances themselves are arranged and presented.
   As the *donsomana* progresses, a pattern emerges in which Bingo offers a cluster of proverbs during breaks in the proceedings. For example: "The hunter lying in wait must occasionally pause to take a chew of
tobacco. We too may follow his example. Let us pause in our narrative.
So announces the *sèrè*, and takes up his *kora*. The *koroduwa* dances and
blasphemes. Bingo recites as follows" (57).[22] This passage is situated between Koyaga's initial exclusion from the first independent government

of the Gulf Republic and the bloody coup that will bring him to power. The hunter pauses calmly in the confidence that he will inevitably destroy his prey. This could involve an allusion to Koyaga himself or to the *sèrè* and *koroduwa*, who are determined to press their case against the tyrant. But while the *koroduwa* mockingly expresses his defiance of all authority, the *sèrè* upholds his official function as a public voice of moral authority, as suggested by the verb *proclamer* (translated as "recites as follows"). In this case again, the proverbs come in a cluster of three:

1. Death swallows man; it does not swallow his name and his reputation.
2. Death is an article of clothing that everyone will wear.
3. Sometimes death is falsely accused when it takes the life of old people who had, as a result of their age, already finished their life before it actually ended. (57)[23]

In the third proverb, the surprising and apparently paradoxical innocence of death suggests the superior lucidity of a speaker-analyst. Despite the common theme of death, these three statements are highly divergent in their conceptual content and their relations to the context. As a result, the ways in which they generate or signal irony are also divergent.

The first proverb of this series represents the "double-edged sword" of classical rhetorical theory. The name and the reputation that survive death can be a source of pride, but they also contain the warning that crimes against humanity are neither forgotten nor forgiven at the death of their perpetrator. Cultural memory is not only a form of identity but also a form of justice and even vengeance. The second proverb taken alone would constitute a banal truism but assumes a pragmatic function when its insistence on the inevitability and universality of death is associated with the first proverb, reinforcing its warning of consequences that lie beyond immediate structures of political power.

Technically speaking, the irony in the last of these proverbs is based on an antanaclasis, a play on words through polysemy, from three senses of the word *death*: as an allegorical subject falsely accused, as the cessation of life in a medical sense, and as the moral end of the momentum of human existence. It is this last sense that creates a certain incongruity in the proverb cluster. If the first two are taken as a warning addressed to the dictator that he too will die eventually, just like the victims of his violence who preceded him, and will be remembered for his evil actions, how does this reference to tired old men who have lost their passion for life even before the arrival of death apply to this ruthless and relentless "hunter" of human flesh? One possible explanation would be that the society that Koyaga has hijacked has lost the political and moral strength to challenge him. But a stronger explanation, more heavily dependent on ironic interpretation, would be that Koyaga himself at some point lost the élan vital that had brought him to power and is therefore already metaphorically dead. His continuing violence and even his amazing ability to survive attempts on his life have become more a matter of routine than a manifestation of the magical aura that he had once brought to the national scene as a representative of the passion and dynamism associated with his cultural origins and the accompanying challenge to colonial authority. The *donsomana* is initiatory in the sense that it brings the "father of the nation" back to his beginnings and judges him on the basis of the passionate beliefs he once held. Underlying the open condemnation of the *koroduwa* and the official propriety of the *sèrè*, one finds a discreet vein of scornful (self-)reflection.

Koyaga's Minister of Information, Maclédio, is a figure who mediates between this (self-)reflection and the notion of an official claim to truth. He also mediates between the apparently traditional discourse of the *donsomana* and the technically manipulated and media-based dissemination of politically determined truth. While Maclédio's title is comparable to that of Chris, who is also a Minister of Information, in Achebe's *Anthills of the Savannah*, he functions more as a picaresque complement to the Head of State than as the source of subversive reflection that Achebe's character represents. Yet an interpretation based on verbal and pragmatic irony will allow us to understand a number of underlying subversive questions raised by the way Maclédio is described and addressed by the narrative voice of the novel.

Maclédio's story is told in the third *sumu*, between the second *sumu*, which recounts Koyaga's bloody coup d'état, and the fourth *sumu*, which covers the "consolidation" of the dictator's power as well as his visits to various other African heads of state in whose countries he further learns the art of "modern" despotism. At the end of the second *sumu*, Maclédio is forcibly drafted as Koyaga's media spokesperson, suggesting that he may be Koyaga's "homme de destin" (man of destiny), an idea further developed in the third *sumu*.

The reader has to relate Maclédio's ironic function to the principle of *nōrô* that recurs throughout the chapter and motivates Maclédio's picaresque migration through an imaginary spectrum of West African cultural and traditional spaces. According to the *nōrô* principle, certain individuals are bound from birth to bring misfortune to themselves and their surrounding community by their very presence until they meet their *nörö*, their opposite who will cancel out their evil destiny (118). As Maclédio spends the earlier part of his life wondering who his *nörö* might be, we are led to believe that Koyaga may be his *nörö*, and that would make him Koyaga's *nörö* as well, since the relationship is intrinsically reciprocal.

Maclédio's story itself is introduced as a discursive necessity strikingly similar to the pragmatic function of irony. Words such as the "mountain we have to get around" (117), "the river we have to ford," so that the *donsomana* can "free itself" to express what it otherwise could not express, echo the notion of irony as that which enables us to communicate what otherwise could not be communicated. This offers another way of interpreting the Igbo proverb as "the palm oil with which words are eaten." The unnameable is, according to Gbanou (2002: 59), a significant element of the aesthetic strategy of Kourouma's texts, as put in place by the *incipits* of most of his works: "The aim of such an aesthetic effect is to focus the reader's attention and interest on the self-hood, alterity and deformation of an Ego seen from the outside and from the inside by a voice that is initiated and authorized to say the unspeakable and to name the unnameable."[24] Because it is so difficult to determine which narrative voice fully wields such authority, it is necessary to pay the greatest attention to the rhetorical and linguistic means by which the various narrating agents seek to say what cannot be said, explicitly producing a discursive space charged with implicit irony. At the same time, the *nörö* is presented as a "forgotten principle," which, precisely because it has been forgotten, has brought woe to modern African societies. Given that a key function of the *donsomana* is an ironical "celebration" of Koyaga's story that would simultaneously seek to reveal the horrors underlying that story, the narrative of discovery arising from Koyaga's own (possible) man of destiny opens two important pathways of interpretation. Maclédio's story is a quest for knowledge and understanding, and as such it holds out some hope for renewal and healing through self-discovery. But if Maclédio was indeed Koyaga's man of destiny, that destiny is now known by the reader to have been absorbed in the discursive function of propaganda and deception in a dysfunctional postcolonial state.

This ambiguity is built into the *nörö* from its inception because the narrator insists on the fact that the *nörö* can never be absolutely sure of having met his counterpart, even when all the signs seem to point in that direction. Maclédio clearly misinterprets many situations in the course of his travels on account of quite convincing signs of affinity. The quest for the meeting that would bring African societies back into balance is thus a perpetual solving of an insoluble problem even though the failure to recognize and recreate that quest could be seen as a major if not primary source of the problem, hence the need to understand how Maclédio's story helps us identify the problems that underlie Koyaga's political destiny as a scourge to late twentieth-century Africa as Kourouma envisions it.

Because Maclédio has been detached from his family and community from birth, and his story is one of many attempts at reintegration, he becomes an external focalizer for social and cultural anomalies. He has both the apparent innocence of the earnest youth—echoing the satirical irony of Voltaire's Candide, whose story is similar to Maclédio's in many respects—and the desiring gaze of one who wishes to belong to the satirized community. His implied voice parodies the discourse of colonial anthropology, the outsider's gaze that purports to reduce the Other but that primarily reduces its own claim to understanding, like Ouologuem's Schrobenius. At the same time, this voice scornfully mocks as if from within, as the outcast wishing he were an insider and always succeeding, though temporarily and incompletely.

It thus becomes difficult to know if the problem is the cultures themselves or Maclédio's inability to make sense of them and to restrain his own sexual desire in relation to their sexual structures and rules. His adventure with the Anyi, for example, begins with a misunderstanding stemming from his external ethnographic knowledge: "All of a sudden, he understood everything. He was going to have his throat slit, to be sacrificed and buried with a dead person. Among the Anyi, who belong to the Akan group, a king never enters his tomb alone. He is always inhumed with those who will serve him in the hereafter" (94).[25] The source of this misinformation is difficult to pinpoint, since Maclédio, with his Eurocentric education, Tiécoura, and the overarching ironic voice of the narrator all contribute to the telling of Maclédio's story. What all these contributors have in common is a claim to understanding that presupposes barbaric violence on the part of the (re)encountered Other. Yet when Maclédio, who has been chosen to sire the princess's children, is faced with banishment or death so that the matriarchal tradition can be maintained, he also discovers that the colonial "divide" between barbarity and civilization is strangely contradictory: "Before colonization, the sire had his throat slit and was sacrificed, adds Tiekura. Macledio unhesitatingly begged to have his throat slit, to be killed, to be sacrificed. He preferred death to departure, banishment. [...] The great fetishist answers that, since the arrival of the English in the Gold Coast, the sire has no longer had his throat slit. He is castrated, has his tongue cut out, loses his two eyes, has his eardrums pierced" (96).[26] Preferring escape to the comforting benefits of Pax Britannica, Maclédio realizes later that if no one stood in the way of his flight, the princess herself must have set everything up that way. At that moment of realization, he repents of his cowardice and tries unsuccessfully to return to the village of Kouassikro. "Tearful, demoralized, and discouraged, I continue on my route toward the north" (97).[27] Tiécoura intervenes here: "Those who, like Macledio, have never had any fate other than bad luck and who still look forward to happiness walk relentlessly northward" (97).[28] A certain complicity on Tiécoura's part seems to dull the sting of his irony. Instead of contradicting the propaganda minister who attributes to himself emotions little short of sublime, Tiécoura recognizes his humanity and desire for happiness. But this constant movement toward the north that for Maclédio was a sign of exile, namely, always moving away from his point of departure due the effect of the *nôrô*, becomes in Tiécoura's mouth a sign of Maclédio's separation from the culture he is called to (mis)interpret under Koyaga's regime. This is confirmed by the unlikely transformation of Maclédio from the comic antihero who has the common sense to flee from a mutilation ironically inscribed with colonial hypocrisy into a reluctant hero nostalgic for a sacrificial existence as a being-nonbeing. The mutilated colonized hero remains loyal to a falsified image of traditional culture by becoming visionless, voiceless, oblivious, and unproductive. The symbolic mutilations of the organs of reproduction, sight, hearing, and speech can be ironically linked with Maclédio's subsequent career as the voice without a voice in Koyaga's propaganda machine.

Maclédio is neither the reluctant colonized hero he imagines himself to be nor a true representative of colonial resistance: he is placed by the narrator's ironic stance between the two. His white teacher claims he is the only Nègre capable of pronouncing the French mute [ə] (124). An initial linguistic mark of irony lies in the inherent contradiction since the [ə] itself is nonexistent whenever it is actually mute. Maclédio, at first flattered by this distinction, later rejects his master's praise, opening the way to his northbound adventures, but we also know that the "elegance" of his French is what will attach him to Koyaga and make him an indispensable voice of the dictator's regime. When Maclédio is forced on pain of death to read Koyaga's pronunciamiento over the air waves (114), he begins by disdainfully correcting Koyaga's inelegant French, thereby symbolically placing his ambiguous colonial assimilation at the service of (post)colonial brutality.

If Koyaga is Maclédio's man of destiny, the *nõrô* principle is either contradictory and misleading or eroded by the postcolonial condition that the *donsomana* is addressing. As complementary polar opposites of African leadership, Maclédio and Koyaga have troubling implications: power versus language, unspoken craft versus verbal deceit, colonial militarization of society versus assimilation of colonial values. At the same time, Maclédio's picaresque journey as helper and victim in the third *sumu* compares ironically to Koyaga's journey of apprenticeship as budding oppressor in the fourth *sumu*.

What are the discursive consequences of this irony built into and even determining the narrative structures of Kourouma's fiction? What kind of worldview arises from the voices heard and overheard through this discourse? According to Bisanswa: "His pact in writing will commit him to saying the disillusionment of the African world from an individual perspective, reconciling the functional (the social) and the symbolic through a certain finality, that is by the intensity of his desire to be socially anchored, while the strategies used create a divorce between the two spheres and anchor his novel in idealism" (14).[29] But this anchoring in idealism does not always prevail. Bisanswa himself refers to the notion of destiny that is "the caricature of destiny, because the causes arising from social reality explain it" (20). While this remark was made in the context of *Les soleils des indépendances*, we could also apply it to the *nõrô* principle that plays such a central role in *En attendant le vote des bêtes sauvages*. If the narrator of Maclédio's story claims that the forgetting of that principle has brought woe to Africa, it is not because a discursive practice based on traditional belief systems is being caricatured in the wake of a more "realistic" sociological analysis of "modern" Africa. Rather, it is because "modern Africa" itself is seen as a self-defeating and self-hating caricature, so that the remembrance of a traditional belief in destiny is necessarily double-edged: caricaturing itself because its point of view is inevitably "modern" and caricaturing those who would dismiss its relevance as *passéiste* but who also have no ground to stand on, having lost any claim to identity that could be taken seriously. Irony in African discourse is not likely to be idealist since it is so often necessary. Even when formally based struggles for a literary identity, as Bisanswa has shown in the case of Kourouma, involve resistance to representational functions, the resulting ironic voice is itself involved in a broad social, cultural, and political dilemma.

The Igbo worldview expressed in the proverb that opens this chapter metaphorically pinpoints the unexpected reversal of fortunes embedded in the pragmatics of Kourouma's irony. Both Djigui, the dry tree that has outlived itself and the expectations of others, and Koyaga, the robust tree that, having magically escaped repeated attempts to cut it down, takes itself for granted, are subject to caricature. That caricature is itself subject to a shifting perspective that can surprisingly turn to a warning or to a wry laugh overheard behind one's back.

CHAPTER FOUR

Chinua Achebe's *Arrow of God* and the Pragmatics of Proverbial Irony

Surprise is beyond the great, yet the great is proven in surprise.

—Igbo proverb

Chinua Achebe published his first and now universally canonized novel *Things Fall Apart* in 1958, a sequel, *No Longer at Ease*, in 1960, and *Arrow of God* in 1964. Dan Izevbaye sees as what is perhaps Achebe's most important influence "his contribution to the advancement of a new postcolonial consciousness" (33). Achebe has had enormous influence on African fiction. As Simon Gikandi points out, Achebe's "seminal status in the history of African literature," lies in "his fundamental belief that narrative can [. . .] propose an alternative world beyond the realities imprisoned in colonial and postcolonial relations of power" (3). *Things Fall Apart* and *Arrow of God* are strikingly similar in that both novels build this "new consciousness" on Achebe's "appropriation of Igbo proverbs for domesticating the English language" (Izevbaye 33). In so doing, according to Izevbaye, Achebe connects "the roots of wisdom that are reflected in the speech genres of African oral cultures with the age of literacy and the printing press" (33). Gikandi interprets *Arrow of God* as "a novel predicated on the loss of narrative authority, set in a situation where meanings cannot be taken for granted" (52). One of the most widely recognized thematic problems of *Arrow of God* is precisely that of the need for cultural and social change. Although the protagonist Ezeulu "assumes that the truth is fixed in both time and value" (70) and that his utterances as the priest of Ulu carry that timeless value, he himself paradoxically believes "that doctrines must change to account for temporal shifts" (75). It is important to understand therefore how the traditional proverbs that Achebe incorporates into his fiction can carry meaning while at the same time questioning all authority, old and new, and generating a consciousness of change and the need for change. The double meaning and subterfuge of irony are factors that need to be considered in the analysis of proverbs' role in Achebe's representation of traditional Igbo discourse.

But can proverbs be ironical? Can they be brought together in a novel to facilitate and even generate a writer's ironic vision of shaken wisdom?

Norrick (1985) makes a methodological distinction between the study of proverbs in texts and as texts (2). We have discussed the importance of proverbs in Kourouma's *En attendant le vote des bêtes sauvages* and their role in the production of ironic meaning, but that should not prevent us from recognizing and investigating proverbial expressions as a significant aspect of African literary discourse. Such discourse is not only a modern offshoot of literatures written in European languages but also a traditional mode of expression. To the extent that proverbs are a part of oral and traditional culture, we do well to consider Liz Gunner's assessment: "What the African records and the ongoing production of culture in Africa make clear is that orality is not an amorphous, vaguely communal preliterate state awaiting redemption by various manifestations of modernity. It is rather a protean presence, changing, interacting, and producing a different kind of cultural equilibrium on the African continent, defining its own modernities through language" (8). Proverbs are a source of irony and a witness to the way irony has functioned in African cultures over many generations and continues to function today. By studying both linguistic and cultural aspects of proverbs in Achebe's *Arrow of God*, it will be possible for us to better discern the way irony serves as a conceptual bridge between traditional oral literature and literary texts written in a European language.

Norrick takes the greatest pains to justify the study of proverbs as texts since this is his primary focus. Although he recognizes the frequent if not characteristic conversational use of proverbs, he also notes that they can be and often are anthologized as collections of discrete texts. He adds that "[e]ven when it occurs as an integral part of a larger spoken or written text, the independent meaning of a proverb plays a major role in determining its semantic contribution to the text as a whole" (5). Furthermore, the inclusion of such proverbs in an anthology supports the recognition of their traditional status by showing their value as something to be collected and conserved.

Besides the problem of recognizing true proverbs (namely, proverbs that could be anthologized) in larger texts, Norrick believes—based on his study of a Shakespearean corpus—that the literary text involves a "tendency away from the proverb as a complete, independent utterance and towards the proverb as (a template for) part of a longer speech" (22).[1] He posits that this distance is even greater in the case of the novel because of its typically reduced dialogue quotient. But this hypothesis poses a number of problems in relation to African fiction. First, it does not account for the dialogic character of novels, which, according to Bakhtin, are the most prone to challenge and subvert official, authoritative, and therefore monologic viewpoints. The ironic function of proverbs, as they are found in texts of both Kourouma and Achebe, puts into question the authority of their target—whether the oppressive outsider or insider within the community or even the speaker himself or herself. Norrick's hypothesis is also limited for the most part to proverbs in European cultures, in which the sociocultural status of the proverb may be more readily relegated to "low culture" language uses such as everyday conversation and is brought into high-cultural texts like those of Shakespeare only in a more sophisticated parodic form. Whether or not the binary of high/low culture is easily applicable to traditional African cultures (without certain caveats and nuances), African traditions usually attach greater value not only to proverbs as a textual corpus but also to the *use* of proverbs in many spheres of artistic, political, social, and even religious significance. According to Maureen Warner-Lewis, "[i]n African speech culture appropriate use of proverbs and riddling idioms is a hallmark of high rhetoric" (124). Norrick himself recognizes that as "inventorized units" (25), proverbs can serve as a signal of membership in a local, ethnic, or national community. The speaker who uses such proverbs, instead of quoting an individual author, "quotes the linguistic community itself" (26). Defined by Norrick as persistence in a relatively fixed form over an extended period—that is, at least more than one generation (66)—the traditional is closely related to the didactic function and meaning of proverbs. This generalized meaning for a whole community, a knowledge that is useful to its members, gives proverbs special status as potential indirect speech acts: "My proverbial utterance tips my hearer off to look for further contextual meaning, to the degree that it fails to contribute relevantly to the text/interaction on its literal level" (27). Referring to Grice's conversational maxims and their violation, Norrick suggests that proverbs are prone to carry *implicatures*, which he defines as "what is conveyed by an indirect speech act" (27). In African proverbial discourse—as witnessed, for example, by the perhaps rather sexist Igbo meta-proverb "On anyone who has to have a proverb explained to him, the mother's bride price was wasted"—the onus for recognizing and processing implicatures is often placed more on the hearer than on the speaker, who was, at least in the hearer's view, the original violator of the maxim of relevance. This transfer of responsibility to the hearer gives an advantage to the proverb speaker. According to Norrick, proverbs lend themselves to "double-bind situations, for example when they are called upon for a judgment that might hurt another's feelings or reveal their own private preferences." Proverbs help their speakers "avoid personal commitment and refutation." We can thus see that the proverb's function as a speech act closely resembles the irony described by Berrendonner as a defensive mode of argumentation.

Why then does Norrick exclude irony from the list of figures involved in proverbs' meaning: "Besides synecdoche, metaphor and metonymy, proverbs exhibit hyperbole and paradox, but apparently never irony, litotes, oxymoron, hypallage, etc." (142)? In a pragmatic context in which irony and the proverb have quasi-identical functions, it would seem almost inevitable that at least some proverbs—especially ones bearing typical irony markers such as hyperbole—would carry irony consistently enough for that figure to be related in some way to their linguistic form. The use of the word "apparently" in the previous quotation allows for the possibility that examples of irony were accidentally absent from Norrick's corpus,[2] but that corpus is large enough for this absence to be significant. Since proverbs and irony are parallel forms of indirect discourse, there may be a tendency to attribute a proverb's "suggestiveness" to its own character as a conveyor of double meaning. In that case, irony would seem redundant or even irrelevant to the proverb. The fact that Norrick's proverbs are decontexualized entries in an anthology would certainly help conceal the ironic function, given that a large part of irony lies outside of the realm of textually punctual antiphrasis. That explanation seems inadequate because one could expect the appearance of at least some co-textual signs or irony markers.

The didactic function of proverbs can be seen as a major impediment to irony, if one does not take into account the fact that situational irony can often undermine the authority of the speaker, which is to say that the circumstances in which the proverb is (didactically) used can contradict the general truth-value it seems to affirm. In such cases, although the irony is context-dependent, the ironic meaning itself is contained in the text of the proverb in the form of a potentially questionable, duplicitous, or double-voiced didactic claim to truth. Our analyses of the texts of Achebe, Kourouma, and Beyala also make it clear that in the case of African literary discourse, irony is often subversive or didactic, or both at the same time. The person considered socially inferior or insignificant may use the didacticism of the powerful or prestigious as a means of subverting the very relationship that such didacticism would "officially" imply. Similarly, irony itself has a didactic function when it is used indirectly, whether to teach general truths or to force the hearer to reconsider generally accepted assumptions. Norrick suggests this possibility when he connects the didactic and traditional status of proverbs to the exercise of authority: "speakers generally tend to cite proverbs when speaking (authoritatively) to and for the benefit of hearers younger than themselves. [. . .] Of course, younger speakers may make humorous use of proverbs for just this reason" (28). When a younger in-law uses proverbs to answer the priest Ezeulu in Achebe's *Arrow of God*, or when Édène quotes her own mother, Andela, in *Les arbres en parlent encore* for the purpose of ironically underscoring that character's dependency on banal and unimaginative conventional wisdom, we begin to see the complexity of the relationship between power, tradition, didactic intention, and ironic meaning.

In the case of Kourouma's *En attendant le vote des bêtes sauvages*, when Bingo intervenes in the middle of the narrative of the atrocities Koyaga has committed in coming to power, he quotes three proverbs: "A pirogue is never too big to capsize. Those who have few tears are quick to mourn the dead. The dead nanny goat is a misfortune for her master; but the head of the goat that is placed in the cauldron is a misfortune only for the goat herself" (67).[3] The didactic value of this series of proverbs lies in their lucidity in relation to the hypocrisy of human behavior and the meaninglessness of shows of solidarity in the merciless and treacherous world of Koyaga's new order. Yet the avowed awareness of this underlying hypocrisy on the part of the "official" *sèrè* as well as the suggested warning contained in the first proverb that no dictator is invincible temper the didactic value with implicit subversion and mockery. Even the dead goat that will now feed others at her own expense could be understood as a macabre mockery of Koyaga's bloodbath and his own indifference to his victims.

Norrick recognizes the need to distinguish a supercultural definition of proverbs that would identify characteristic traits of proverbs as a universal linguistic practice and an ethnographic genre definition that would permit us to show the differences between proverbs and other speech practices in a given linguistic or cultural community (28). An examination of the areas in which Norrick's analysis illustrates what might or might not validly apply to an African cultural text will enable us to show how irony can play a key role in African proverbial discourse according to culture-specific features. Not that there is any reason to divorce African proverbs from those of any other culture on the basis of any preconceived ontological difference. Rather, the historical and political circumstances under which African fiction has constituted itself as literary discourse could be expected to influence the value attached to proverbs both as an autonomous sociocultural means of expression and as a strategic component (and not a folkloric local-color additive) of literary texts. When Borgomano (2000) refers to the *sèrè*'s intervention in the *donsomana* as a speaker of proverbs as "intrusions by the discourse of an other" and compares this voice to Barthes's proverbial voice—"collective, anonymous, having as its origin human wisdom" (172–73)—she further insists that the collective voice of the proverb in African society is not really anonymous but instead represents the voice of a people and the social and juridical codes of a particular society.

Norrick claims that among traditional genres, the proverb is the only typically conversational, didactic, or conversational genre (77). Two other features, "potential free conversational turn"[4] and "optional figurative meaning," may be included in an ethnographic definition, though they are viewed as secondary and "not strictly distinctive" features. "The proverb is a traditional, conversational, didactic genre with general meaning, a potential free conversational turn, preferably with figurative meaning" (78). Norrick makes this claim specifically for Anglo-American culture. He rules out entertainment as a part of the proverb's function largely because of its didactic value. When the Igbo meta-proverb states that the proverb is "the palm oil with which words are eaten," this value would be best described not as entertainment, with its implications of passivity and sometimes even escapism, but as enrichment and pleasure. This pleasure is not offered to a passive audience but produced by a speaker and intelligently processed by the hearer. It is therefore both active and interactive, but both speaker and hearer can and should derive pleasure from the communicative exchange itself, even when the didactic purpose of the message conveyed is serious or potentially critical to one's well-being and survival.

A crucial element of this quality, which is absent from Norrick's analysis of the features of the proverb but coincides with his sense of a proverb's cultural and linguistic value, is the "preferable" figurative content of proverbial discourse. Norrick defines the figurative proverb as "one whose literal meaning, even when due to p-grammar or the proverb inventory, differs from its SPI [Standard Proverbial Interpretation]" (108). He also believes that since proverbs are a traditional rather than a literary speech form, their figurative potential reflects a "natural figurative meaning" as opposed to the "irregular and idiosyncratic types in poetic theory" (101). This is an important theoretical consideration, given that Roman Jakobson's well-known linguistic definition of poetic function posits a conscious effort on the speaker's or writer's part to emphasize the quality of the message itself through the "projection of the axis of selection onto the axis of combination."[5] Even if one could demonstrate that a metaphorical or metonymical proverb could be analyzed as just such a projection, it would not be considered poetic except perhaps in a secondary or accidental sense.

If proverbs are seen as a source of enrichment and pleasure within a culture, the gap between the literary and the "natural" figurative will be considerably narrowed. On the one hand, the user will have a heightened awareness of the quality of his or her utterance as message (thereby approaching Jakobson's poetic function). On the other hand, the literary subject, such as a modern African novelist, will have a heightened awareness of the preestablished literary value of proverbs that are already a part of his or her culture *before* integrating them into the overall structure of the literary text.

In Achebe's *Arrow of God*, the frequent proverbs generally depend on some kind of metaphorical meaning that is in turn woven into the literary structure of the text. For example, the long series of proverbs that flows from the mouth of Ezeulu's favorite son, Obika, in the moments leading up to his sudden and tragic death repeat themes that appear earlier in the narrative. They gradually accumulate a number of references to the inevitability of the death and destruction that the character, in the sacred mask of the spirit Ogbazulobodo, is about to encounter. One of the proverbs he pronounces is "An ill-fated man drinks water and it catches in his teeth" (226). Obika is playing a sacrificial role in order to protect the honor of his father and family (see 224), but the slight fever he felt on the night he was asked to wear the mask does not initially seem proportional to the dimensions of his tragic death. He will also say: "The fly that has no one to advise him follows the corpse into the ground." This echoes previous warnings Obika had received from his father. And another: "The very Thing which kills Mother Rat is always there to make sure that its young ones never open their eyes." Death lies in wait for anyone, whether innocent or not.

At the same time, the novel's proverbs serve to underscore recurrent patterns of sociocultural interaction and collectively known sacred practice. What appears clearly as automatic in the production and reception of proverbs in the society Achebe represents is the social appropriateness of the proverbial metaphor. Speaker and hearer recognize the truthfulness and meaningfulness of the proverb according to a shared perception of social reality, even when their discussions imply serious disagreements as to the course of action the speaker's reasoning recommends. These observations suggest that in the context of African literary discourse, proverbs are immediately perceived as figurative from the very moment they are pronounced because their application to life and experience is itself a signifier of shared cultural meaning. This figurative understanding presents itself as a holistic signifier: it is not only that the hearer associates a certain animal with a "typical" human being, for example, but that he or she places the experience of that animal in a situational network involving complex social relationships. For example, an oppressed member of an Igbo community could say: "Constant falling down belongs to the pursuer of the chicken, while the chicken itself continues to enjoy its escape." The speaker of this proverb sees himself or herself as an innocent victim of oppression but rejoices in the irony of his or her vindication in the eyes of all because the oppressor will suffer the greatest derision. Proverbs may include the speaker's wisdom in relation to life, the speaker having wisdom superior to that of the hearer. They may include the verbal encounter of the speaker with the situational irony of fate. Different entailments may arise from different interpretations but are subject to the need for shared understanding in the context of verbal interaction. Thus a paraphrase of the proverb (Norrick's SPI) depends on negotiated activation of collective memory along familiar yet variable and pliable lines of figurative interpretation.

In his investigation of figurative meaning in proverbs, Norrick finds that the most frequent form (constituting 62 percent of the figurative proverbs in his corpus) is what he calls the "scenic species-genus synecdoche" (110). An example is "the early bird catches the worm." The bird is abstracted to any agent, whereas the worm becomes the needed or desired object.

Hyperbole, also present in Norrick's corpus, is described as "a figure which implies the speaker's emotional involvement" (132). There are also paradoxical proverbs involving "apparent contradiction with a deeper sense overcoming the contradiction" (134). One of Obika's proverbs is "The man who likes the meat of the funeral ram, why does he recover when sickness visits him?" (226). If someone thinks death is an occasion for such feasting and celebration, is it not contradictory that the same person, when ill, would try to get better out of fear of death? The contradiction can be overcome only by recognizing that the death of the other is never really experienced as equivalent to our own.

More profoundly suggestive of a major presence of irony in proverbs, however, is the fact that the species-genus synecdoche, which Norrick concludes must be the most fundamental semiotic principle of prover-bial speech, "far from being limited to proverbs and proverbial phrases, provides the basis for our understanding of all kinds of texts which describe a concrete scene to be generalized, e.g. parables and fables in particular, but ultimately, any epic or dramatic text with global par-allels beyond the concrete story told" (143). This seems to be an im-plicit reversal of Norrick's original procedure. Instead of the proverb in the text, the proverb as text becomes a semiotic paradigm for the literary text as a globally signifying unit. In that case, proverbial irony should resemble the dramatic, situational, and verbal (including nar-rative) irony that functions regularly in these broader literary genres. It is clear from our application of Norrick's analysis of proverbs to *Arrow of God* that the analytical model he proposes is conducive to the explanation of irony within the specific context of Achebe's proverbial communication.

Pexman's review of theories of social factors in the interpretation of verbal irony (2005) offers some insights into the way a figurative en-coding of irony could infiltrate proverbial discourse and exchange. The speaker who makes use of verbal irony will tend to have certain attri-butes assigned to him or her: "Compared to speakers who make non-ironic remarks, speakers who make ironic remarks are perceived to be more angry, disgusted, and scornful (Leggitt and Gibbs, 2000), as well as verbally aggressive and offensive (Toplak and Katz, 2000)" (210).

This general impression, quite inconsistent with Berrendonner's de-fensive pragmatics of irony, becomes more specific in the light of differ-ent theories of verbal irony that Pexman summarizes. Pexman explains the echoic mention theory of Sperber and Wilson (1981) by stating that "irony is made possible by an utterance that implicitly or explicitly echoes a previous event, expectation, or social norm" (225). A slightly modified version, echoic reminder theory (Kreuz and Glucksberg, 1989), purports that "the echoic nature of an ironic utterance reminds the listener of a failed expectation or violated social norm. As such, the ironic utterance expresses the speaker's negative attitude about the situation." Another viewpoint described as "pretense models" (e.g., Clark and Gerrig, 1984) observes that "an ironic speaker pretends to be a very optimistic person, addressing an imaginary listener and assuming that the listener would interpret the utterance literally. Consequently, the ironic speaker expresses a negative attitude toward the situation, the imaginary listener, and the pretended optimist" (226). The allusional pretense theory of Kumon-Nakamura et al. (1995) adds that "ironic utterances allude to a failed expectation either by implicit or by explicit echo" and that "ironic utterances involve pragmatic insincerity (e.g. overpoliteness)" (226). Finally, Utsumi (2000) proposed the implicit display theory based on the premises that an ironic utterance assumes an "ironic environment" defined as "a situational setting which motivates verbal irony" (1778) and then displays the ironic environment. Implicit display theory is geared toward explaining how verbal irony functions, distinguishing between irony and non-irony in utterances and assessing the degree of "ironicalness" that can be attributed to a given utterance.

Implicit display theory is based on three claims:

1. Irony depends on an "ironic environment" defined as "a situational setting which motivates verbal irony" (1778), which can be further broken down into three conditions existing prior to an ironic utterance:

    – The speaker has a certain expectation E at one time (t0);

    – the speaker's expectation E fails (i.e., is incongruous with reality) at a later time (t1);

    – the speaker has a negative emotional attitude (e.g., disappointment, anger, reproach, envy) toward that incongruity (1783).

2. Verbal irony is an "utterance/statement that *implicitly displays* ironic environment" (1778). To implicitly display an ironic environment, an utterance/statement:

    – alludes to the speaker's expectation E;

    – "includes pragmatic insincerity by intentionally violating one of the pragmatic principles" (for example, by being more polite than required);

    – expresses indirectly the speaker's negative attitude toward the failure of E (1785).

3. A statement will be understood as ironic in varying degrees according to how close it comes to an "irony prototype": a statement that would be perceived as fully ironic in a given situation. (See 1779.)

Two other points stressed by Utsumi have a direct bearing on this study. He warns of the trap of confusing an ironical environment based on the speaker's failed expectations with situational irony or the observation of ironic situations. In addition, he allows for an utterance to be considered ironic only on the basis of the speaker's intentions: "all expectations which motivate irony must be attributed to or possessed by the speaker" (1784).

Commenting on the applicability of Utsumi's theory, Pexman states: "Lower education levels (strongly correlated with lower social status) may signal a need to express criticism indirectly to lessen the risk of offending higher status others. Because the implicit display theory emphasizes indirect expression of negative attitude, it seems capable of explaining this result. As such, implicit display theory seems able to explain effects of social cues on interpretation of verbal irony" (227). My reading of *Arrow of God* will show that Pexman's suggested association between the motivation to use irony aggressively and the user's socially subaltern status is not adequate to explain irony in African traditional or literary discourses. It is, however, in the context of this assessment of the connection between social status and the use of verbal irony that Pexman reflects on the possibility of the social motivation of irony reaching proverbial discourse: "Other forms of figurative language likely have distinct social functions, although those functions have received little research attention thus far. [. . .] For instance, proverb (e.g., 'Strike while the iron is hot') and metaphor (e.g., 'Children are precious gems') can be used to convey wisdom, although they can certainly be used ironically, perhaps to mock those who would use them to convey wisdom" (228). Further reflection on this possibility leads Pexman to remark that "it has been claimed that proverbs are particularly appropriate for conversation with older adults" (Jackson, 1994), with the further implication "that there may be generational (cohort) effects in use and comprehension of proverbial statements" (229).

How then do metaphorical processing, ironical intention, and proverbial discourse combine in the context of African literary discourse? The didactic function of proverbs, as seen in *Arrow of God*, involves practical wisdom in assessing the stakes in situations of conflict, disagreement, danger, and power relations in general. The answers that proverbs provide to such situations depend on metaphor-based analogies with natural occurrences or logical outcomes to commonly known events. In many cases, thought is anthropomorphically attributed to either an animal or a generic human being ("a man") in order to demonstrate wisdom (or lack of wisdom) exercised in comparable predicaments. Though proverbs are pronounced by characters of different ages, genders, and social status, the source of the wisdom is frequently associated with earlier generations and also frequently accompanies the elder-framed, ritual discourse of older men of respected station such as Ezeulu and Akuebue. Pexman's analysis of the implicit display theory of irony implies that the production of ironic utterances is more likely to be associated with disguised aggressiveness and a socially disadvantaged position requiring the mask of indirect reference. At the same time, both proverb and metaphor can be used, Pexman suggests, to convey an ironic treatment of the wisdom of others, especially if the others belong to an earlier, dominant generation. While the situation encountered in *Arrow of God* lends itself well to implicit display theory through the interpretative demand of the proverb's application to immediate decisions and positions, irony does not rely a priori on the ironist's subaltern status. The proverb-ironist's mission is to display to the other the gap between that person's claimed wisdom and the practical reality imposed by the proverb's implications. By responding intelligently to the interpretative demand of the proverb, the hearer may succeed in bridging the gap of the original ironic imbalance involving speaker and hearer. A subversive/aggressive level of verbal irony is reached in *Arrow of God* at a more discreet narrative level when the death of Obika following a delirium of proverbs and the subsequent dementia of Ezeulu symbolically fuse and obliterate the proverbial "treasury" entrusted to them by the people of Umuaro.

According to Chinwe Okechukwu, the use of language in *Arrow of God* is tied to the social imperatives of rhetoric: "rhetoric has always had the social responsibility of guiding the audience in making the right decisions" (45). Okechukwu's analysis of the novel is based on the failure of Ezeulu to combine his superior wisdom (his "dialectics") with appropriate oratorical means of persuasion: "[Ezeulu] is a good man, but he lacks the ability to speak well, a serious deficiency in an oral society in which oratorical skill is valorized. He goes mad because he cannot fathom why truth, which is supposed to prevail all the time, never does" (47). But the fact that proverbs are interpreted spontaneously, even by those who represent strongly opposing positions on Umuaro's destiny, suggests that the rhetorical issues underlying Ezeulu's confrontation with his changing community involve more than the ability to persuade others. The discursive foundations of the community are being called into action for the purpose of maintaining the semantic and pragmatic operability of a traditional culture under the threat of lapsing into irrelevancy. Germain Kouassi, while recognizing the importance of proverbs and aphorisms as a distinguishing aesthetic feature of African literature, also insists on their contribution "to the equilibrium of traditional society, an oral society whose verbal expression they structured and for which they regularized individual behaviour" (364).[6] Ironic meanings that may have already been a part of a proverb's function within that traditional culture, positioning the speaker in relation to the supposed wisdom of the other, may be expanded to include ways of questioning established authority. The proverb ironically "quotes back" and rails at that authority's arsenal of rhetorical formulas and devices.

It is possible to analyze many proverbs found in *Arrow of God* on the basis of various speakers' claims to wisdom, which may include an ironic echoing of the presumed wisdom of a hierarchically advantaged opponent. But that claim may also include an implicitly shared sense of understanding and an ability (through tradition) to put into words the paradoxes and contradictions of common experience. The proverb may emphasize the natural justice behind unfortunate events, the hidden truths and dangers that force members of the community to reconsider their assumptions, or the "superior" wisdom applied by the speaker to the common situation or problem he or she is trying to share with the audience.

TIT-FOR-TAT NATURAL JUSTICE: AGENT GETS WHAT HE OR SHE DESERVES OR SHOULD EXPECT

The irony in this category stems from the implication that someone's fate corresponds to a predictable relationship of cause and effect and thus reflects a sense of natural justice. The sense of divine retribution accompanied by a tongue-in-cheek notation of the victim's responsibility for his or her own fate can be transformed into an ironic exploitation of the circumstances intended to communicate implicitly the speaker's awareness of and interest in this ironic retributive twist.

The following proverb is pronounced by Akukalia, a member of the delegation sent by Umuaro to the neighboring village of Okperi to threaten war. Since Akukalia's mother was from Okperi, he is speaking to his co-delegates as one who best knows the ways of the "enemy." Using the proverb, he instructs the other delegates not to interfere in the projected discussions: "So leave them to me because when a man of cunning dies a man of cunning buries him" (20). At one level, he is staking his own claim to an insider's knowledge of his mother's people. The narrator is imposing on Akukalia a degree of self-inflicted irony since the use of this proverb implies that he is as slippery as his maternal relatives. But there is another level of interpretation according to which the people of Okperi, who are known for their cunning, are surely going to succumb to the superior cunning of their offspring. The immediate situation makes this interpretation predominant because the village of Umuaro clearly has the confidence and determination to threaten its neighbor with war. The weight of the discursive irony is shifted, though not without leaving a trace, from unintended self-mockery to an appeal to cosmic time (the power of death) as an affirmation according to which the social opponent's supposed strength will become the basis of his demise at the hands of his supposed victim. The burial image fits Norrick's stress on the figurative in proverbs in that its trait of "surviving the other" in time is transferred to the notion of victory in a struggle. A further situational irony that can be attributed only to the narrator is anticipated, given that the very mission to Okperi will lead to the death of one of Akukalia's maternal relatives by his own hand.

But the intention of the character represented as the speaker to demonstrate that an opponent's apparent superiority is destined for ultimate ruin is a recurring ironical pattern of this group of proverbs. Even when the speaker is of high social standing, the central idea is that irony involves the display of an ironic environment associated with an imagined or anticipated reversal of fortune that will demonstrate a principle of natural and/or divine justice.

When Ezeulu uses the proverb "The man who brings ant-infested faggots into his hut should not grumble when lizards pay him a visit" (132), he is answering the accusation relayed to him by his friend Akuebue of having betrayed Umuaro to the white man. He points out that the white men could never have achieved the dominance they now exercise if many people in "Olu and Igbo" had not "shown the way" (132). The proverb's agent—"the man"—is a generic human being who represents the Igbo people collectively. The man's action of bringing ant-infested faggots into his house is a metaphor for the complicity of many people in allowing a foreign power to take over. The agent is treated with irony because he himself is the one responsible for the problem that he is trying to blame on someone else, in this case, Ezeulu. The intended scapegoat of the collective ruin invites those who, like him, are ready to be honest with themselves to move from the camp of the accuser to that of the lucid self-accused. While refusing the role of the lone scapegoat, Ezeulu does not remove himself from the implications of his irony but refuses to be its sole member.

The following passage adds another dimension to the natural justice proverb: "A man might pick his way with the utmost care through a crowded market but find that the hem of his cloth had upset and broken another's wares; in such a case the man, not his cloth, was held to repair the damage" (176). The implied speaker in this case is again Ezeulu, but the object (represented again by "a man") is the English District Officer Winterbottom. Already the modification of the name to "Wintabota" carries an ironic charge since it reflects a parodic transcultural name change. Ezeulu blames Winterbottom for the improper treatment he has suffered at the hands of subordinates. The proverb focuses on the issue of responsibility, displaying the principle of metonymy as a sign of that responsibility. The natural justice implied by the proverb depends on the assumption that Ezeulu is "now even with the white man" because he has defied him through his subordinates and is justified in so doing. In addition, Ezeulu is aware of the ironic fact that the white man, in this failed attempt at oppression, has unknowingly acted as an ally.

HIDDEN TRUTH OR DANGER

Although the ways in which irony can function in the proverbs in this category vary greatly, the common thread is the idea that things are not what they seem because there are hidden dangers that one can never completely foresee or control. Speakers can use the influence of future events in various ways: to threaten an adversary, to warn a loved one, to express a personal or collectively shared anxiety or wariness, or simply to reveal an awareness of the harshness of life. They attempt to exhibit their ironic voice by establishing their ability to perceive and convey the gap between generally expected outcomes and one more probable and more destructive.

Whereas the irony of "natural justice proverbs" may be didactic or aggressive, deriving pleasure from the satisfaction of knowing that the apparent or self-styled superior other may be subject to ill fortune and therefore to verbal irony, the "hidden danger proverb" allows its user to communicate a more anxious fear, but one that nevertheless reflects a hidden layer of truth that either the hearer or the object or both may not have perceived.

One striking example appears early in the text (13) when Ezeulu uses an apparently common proverb—"When a handshake goes beyond the elbow we know it has turned to another thing" (used again later in a different context)—to preface his refusal to allow his son Oduche to help carry the new schoolmaster's personal effects instead of doing his family chores. The proverb warns of the imminent danger of allowing contact with the occupying culture to erode traditional values, authority, and relationships. Ezeulu was the initiator of Oduche's being sent to school, an act that proves highly controversial even within his own family. His warning to Oduche thus further expresses his concern about the possible consequences of his own decision, even though he never backs down. In this case, irony is subtly inherent in the semantic structure of the proverb, since the handshake is portrayed as an insidious prelude to concealed treachery revealed only when it is too late (having already turned into "another thing"). The strongest verbal irony derives from the polyphonic effect of Ezeulu speaking simultaneously with two voices: first, with the voice of the father defending the law and, second, with the voice of the priest-subordinate of Ulu (as the sacred authority of the *communitas*[7]). The priest of Ulu must account for his tentative handshake that involved the sociocultural "sacrifice" of Oduche. The latter is not only a biological offspring but also a potential successor to the priesthood of Ulu. The choice of successor belonged not to the priest but to the god Ulu and was thus a sacred prerogative that Ezeulu's "handshake" has to some extent usurped. Neither the first voice nor the second expresses irony in itself, but irony results from the superimposition of the two because the immediate voice of authority (that of the Father) is subverted by the anxiety of violation and by the consciousness of an uncomfortable relationship to authority itself on a more sacred level.

A much more ominous and troubling version of the hidden truth proverb is provoked by an exchange between Ezeulu and his in-laws, who have come to negotiate the return of one of Ezeulu's daughters to her estranged husband's compound. Ezeulu has said that his death must be near because the appearance of his in-laws is such a rare occurrence, implying inadequate attention to social protocol on their part. This is the irony of collective authority that borders on sarcasm because of its intentionally aggressive tone. In this situation, one would expect an apologetic or argumentatively defensive reply, in keeping with Berrendonner's insistence on the defensive role of irony. The in-laws' spokesman says: "You are right, in-law, it is indeed a long time since I came to see you. But we have a saying that the very thing which kills mother rat prevents its little ones from opening their eyes. If all goes well we hope to come and go again as in-laws should" (61). Onwuzuligbo suggests through this proverb that the very points of contention dividing the two families—the abuse of Ezeulu's daughter, Obika's impetuous attack on the abuser, and the wife's refusal to return to her husband—could have further consequences for the overall good relations between the two families. To the extent that the proverb's figurative (metaphorical) function provides for allegorical interpretation, one could claim that the blind, innocent, and quasi-gestational state of the baby rats reflects the danger posed to the combined families by the divisive effect of one dysfunctional marriage within them. The hidden truth is imminent for all; even elders could be seen as "blind children" unless they recognize the danger. Ezeulu's ritual response of calling for a kola nut and offering *nzu* chalk shows that he is not offended and does not admit, at least openly, to being a target of the ironic implication that he is unaware, as the patriarch of the family and a leader in the community, of the real problems surrounding him.[8] Yet Onwuzuligbo has successfully used the carefully chosen proverb both to neutralize Ezeulo's initial reproach and to assert his ability to appropriate the didactic function of the proverb for his own self-affirmation.

The mother rat proverb seems ominous in its referential content but only indirectly alludes to possible catastrophe, whereas the successful negotiations surrounding the disrupted marriage tend to further attenuate any such allusion. Other proverbs of this category function quite differently in that they reinforce didactic positions on both personal and collective fate and even foreshadow—thereby generating dramatic irony—impending demise or death. The first time the Court Messenger and his escort, an Umuaro man, visit Ezeulu with Winterbottom's summons to Okperi, Ezeulo, in a dramatic aside to his friend Akuebue, notes how significant it is that an Umuaro man would show the foreign messenger—an Igbo from another clan representing the colonial authority—the way to the priest's house. This reiterates a point he had already emphasized in previous debates about responsibility for the collective surrender of Igbos to colonial domination. He then adds: "Our sages were right when they said that no matter how many spirits plotted a man's death it would come to nothing unless his personal god took a hand in the deliberation" (136). This proverb refers to the role played by Igbos in general and by a son of Umuaro in particular in the handover of power to the European occupier, in that the "personal god" is to some degree a synecdoche for the self. The fact that such a grave scenario is evoked suggests a very serious underlying problem—one that involves both personal destruction and tragic betrayal with spiritual implications. We must remember that Ezeulu has been summoned by some-one considered almost legendary in his power (The Breaker of Guns) to leave his house and travel to another town, all in complete violation of his sacred role and place. In a sense, therefore, this summons is a form of impending death: the end of the sanctity of Ezeulu's person, an un-certain future as an individual, and the desecration of Ulu, whose sa-credness is the foundation of Umuaro. It is ironic that a body would be destroyed by one of its own members, but Ezeulu's choice of this prov-erb to express that irony as a secret destiny inscribed in each person's relationship with the *numen* or divine authority displays an environ-ment subject to mourning and an implied sense of loss.

SUPERIOR WISDOM

The advice proverb, or superior-wisdom proverb, is not automatically ironic. If the proverb's purpose is simply to propose a wise course of ac-tion in the interests of the recipient, it does not have to imply an ironic intent. In many cases, however, the proverb establishes a comparative scale of wisdom in which the speaker or narrator claims greater under-standing than another. The proverb represents either a metaphorical agent who occupies a position analogous to that of the recipient and who makes an unwise decision or an agent who has the same cunning and intelligence as the speaker. The speaker in turn invites the recipient to join him or her in this position of practical, moral, and intellectual superiority. Once the proverb or proverb frame, such as "You have for-gotten that . . . " contains an indication of this imbalance, the speaker's ironic intent is implied by a consciousness of his or her own greater awareness.

A very early example of the superior wisdom proverb occurs in the initial description of Ezeulu's family. The narrator reports one of Ezeu-lu's typical warnings to his son Obika, a favored but quick-tempered person prone to the abuse of alcohol and impetuous bravery: "His fa-ther who preferred him to Edogo, his quiet and brooding half-brother, nevertheless said to him often: 'It is praiseworthy to be brave and fearless, my son, but sometimes it is better to be a coward. We often stand in the compound of a coward to point at the ruins where a brave man used to live. The man who has never submitted to anything will soon submit to the burial mat'" (11). The narrator makes it very clear to us that Ezeulu's claim to superior wisdom is motivated by affection and not by arrogance or self-importance, a fact that excludes ironic intent at the illocutionary level. This does not, however, exclude the possibility of an argumentative function of irony at a didactic level. Given the axiological relation between courage and cowardice, and the two men's shared admiration for strong, assertive behavior, the proverbial claim that cowardice may in some circumstances be a better stance must strike Obika as an anomaly, especially coming from his father. The second, supporting, proverb (or adage), "The man who has never submitted to anything will soon submit to the burial mat," provides a necessary gloss to this anomaly. The issue is not dependent on the axiological opposition, as it may seem, but is rather one of submission in the context of a society in which authority is complex and multifarious, involving the "order" of the community as well as the fatalism combined with personal responsibility associated with the spiritual world and one's own destiny personified as one's *chi*. The verb "submit" in "submit to the burial mat" is an antanaclasis (a figure of speech in which the same word is used in two different senses) based on the special sense of *submit* as "succumb willy nilly to a greater force than one's own life." The notions of both cowardice and submission are part of an ironic expression not aimed at the hearer but arranged for his benefit, in order to transmit to him the superior wisdom he needs for survival. The failure of this process of transmission over time may or may not be causally linked to Obika's unexplained death, but such a possibility heightens the rhetorical effect of these proverbs in the text.

A more aggressive application of the superior wisdom proverb arises directly from Ezeulu's quarrel with the priest of Idemili. When Akuebue reminds him of the opposition stirring against him in the other villages, Ezeulu indirectly challenges the rival priest: "But if it is jealousy, let him go on. The fly that perches on a mound of dung may strut around as it likes, it cannot move the mound" (130). This proverb affirms the solidity of the speaker's own foundations in relation to the challenges of an ultimately ineffectual opposition. But the fly's major problem is not its powerlessness, which would simply be a function of its natural condition, but its self-delusion and ignorance of its real place in the world: Ezeulu's use of this proverb in speaking to Akuebue as the ear of the community, as the passive equivalent of a vox populi, can be seen as a perlocutional act to the extent that the priest of Ulu wishes Akuebue to carry his response to others, eventually reaching the ear of his intended target or of those who may be supporting that target.

The display of superior wisdom is clearly associated with irony since it points to the gap between the target's or hearer's self-assessment and what the ironist presents as a truer perception of reality. This is not always patriarchal or antagonistic, as in the two previous examples, since it is also possible for the speaker to reveal superior wisdom through a shared sense of the situational "irony of life" when fate plays a trick on all the members of a community. Thus the proverb used by Moses Unachukwu in order to discourage revolts against British exactions for building roads acts as a call to acceptance of a modus vivendi based on a collective understanding of changing circumstances: "When Suffering knocks at your door and you say there is no seat left for him, he tells you not to worry because he has brought his own stool. The white man is like that" (84). Moses's proverb is a didactic allegory, with Suffering personified as the protagonist of an ironic narrative in which the abstract notion expresses its own inevitability in response to the human character whose resistance is made to look not only vain but rather laughable. Moses provides an interpretative gloss for this allegory by telling us that Suffering in this case is the white man. In this way, the more general didactic concept of the inevitability of suffering becomes the reality of colonization and the unwanted presence becomes the imposition of alien culture as authority. Moses thus positions himself, like the interpreter of Kourouma's *Monnè, outrages et défis*, as an ironist-interpreter. He reveals to his Igbo audience the situational paradox of foreign domination, an unwelcome presence that simply welcomes itself, as a form of didactic warning and control. At the same time, for the sake of that same Igbo audience, he is playing the role of the lower-placed trickster who makes fun of the white man by discreetly equating him with a disease or natural misfortune. He also seeks to overcome, at least in discursive terms, his alienation as a double-voiced figure by establishing his own belonging to the oppressed community. Yet the irony that sustains this allegorical attack on the Other and the reintegrating positioning by the speaker is already embedded in the ironic-aggressive voice attributed to Suffering. The latter mocks the ineffectual "politeness" of the host who thought he could diplomatically exclude the inconvenient Other from his existence through a claim to fullness of life.

Although I will endeavor to explain the relevance of implicit display theory to proverbial irony in African literary texts such as *Arrow of God*, several caveats are needed. I will show the importance of recognizing the limits of this theory, as of any one theory of irony, in the overall work of understanding required by such texts. I will also point out that despite Utsumi's critique of mention theory and its later versions, mention remains a valid and useful tool of analysis in the context of African literary discourse. These considerations lead to an approach to proverbial irony that will contextualize the three notional-didactic categories that we have seen in *Arrow of God*: natural justice, hidden truth, and superior wisdom.

The notion of an ironic environment is suitable for explaining the cultural and historical anomalies of the colonial state—not because they generate situational irony, which they certainly do, but because they require a speaker as colonized subject to find the means to express dissatisfaction with the boundaries to freedom of expression while still maintaining a certain degree of discursive autonomy and even personal authority. This can be seen, for example, in all the traditional formulas and rituals brought into play in arranging a formal declaration of war with the village of Okperi when everyone involved knows that the days of intervillage wars have passed. Each time a proverb is used, the speaker affirms the continued existence of cultural frames of reference while implying a bitter awareness of the passing away of once established norms and values. In addition, the centering of irony on the speaker's intention of expressing it helps us account for the didactic and sometimes subversive intention behind the proverb's use and thus allows us to bridge the conceptual gap between the apparent "seriousness" of proverb use and the often caustically playful use of irony. By the same token, the individual act of expressing the irony found by the speaker in verbal exchange can be reconciled with the more community-based purpose of the proverb. The proverb user has appropriated a traditional quasi-fixed expression by which to articulate dissatisfaction with the situation at hand, the attitude of the direct or indirect addressee, or the latter's likely future course of action. Finally, the central importance that Utsumi accords to the implicit character of the speaker's allusion to the ironic environment corresponds to the indirect operation of figurative proverbs. Since the meaning of proverbs is normally the result of an indirect comparison, any ironic intention they display has to be incorporated into the implicit verbal communication involved.

Utsumi himself recognizes (1804) that implicit display theory does not yet have any means of accounting for the functions of irony, that is to say, alternative goals that speakers may have in deciding to allude to their failed expectations. Implicit display theory is designed to determine whether or not an utterance is ironic but not to explain how or why a didactic or subversive intention related to proverbial expression can combine with the perceived choice of speaking ironically.

If we are to reflect on the reasons a speaker might have for resorting to irony and what he or she might hope to accomplish by subverting the expectations of a proverb's audience, we need to look at the larger picture, namely, one that takes into account both the rhetorical function of ironic argument and the sociohistorical contexts of the cultures involved. Berrendonner's defensive bias in his explanation of ironic function as well as Perrin's emphasis on raillery as a subversive imitation of the other need to be seen in the light of the larger problem of self-representation in times of fragmented but persistent cultural identities. In his book *Domination and the Arts of Resistance*, James Scott discusses the notions of a "public transcript," the record of "the public performance required of those subject to elaborate and systematic forms of social subordination" (2), and a "hidden transcript," which he defines as "discourse that takes place 'offstage,' beyond direct observation by powerholders" (4). As long as these two transcripts represent separate, competing discourses, there is little room for irony in either. Although Scott makes few references to the problem of irony, he does recognize that "the frontier between the public and the hidden transcripts is a zone of constant struggle between dominant and subordinate—not a solid wall" (14). As subaltern speakers seek and find "a thousand artful ways to imply that they are grudging conscripts to the performance [of the public transcript]" (15), they are necessarily building the double-voiced discourse of irony. As these practices become embedded in traditional cultures over time, the dynamics of authority, subversion, and subordination will continue to change. As long as subordination continues to exist in one form or another, the relationship between speakers and their audiences will continue to reflect "the smuggling of portions of a hidden transcript, suitably veiled, onto the public stage" (157). Irony in this sense may shift from an official display of wisdom that implies the contradictory logic of life, or of the too predictable fate of human beings who defy the advice of more experienced relatives, to an ironic question that challenges the authority of the old and wise. The problems of irony in African culture are based on the fact not only that there have been and continue to be relations of subordination, oppression, and exploitation but that the same discourses that carry the arms of rebellion and subversion also carry the signs of culture, memory, and community.

That is why the association of irony with a single speaker is very appropriate both to a linguistic theory that needs to provide a clear-cut and relatively simple set of rules by which to test the likelihood of ironic intent or to psychological experimentation that can equate one speaker to one subject; however, it is not always adequate to the type of analysis needed for African literary texts. A single speaker may represent several points of view: those of a "character," an implicit *vox publica*, an implied voice that the speaker is consciously or unconsciously representing, a heterodiegetic narrator, and an implied author. Any combination of these voices may carry the intention of ironic expression, and in this sense the role of mention or echo-based approaches to irony cannot be discounted as easily as Utsumi has argued. This is doubly true of proverbial irony in *Arrow of God* because this practice presupposes both the discursive complexity that I have just alluded to and the polyphony inherent in the social use of proverbs. One speaks both for oneself and on behalf of the cultural community that has nurtured the verbal patterns of particular types of proverbs in order to address multigenerational sociopolitical issues such as the disruption of family marriage ties by the behavior of young people, as with Obika and his in-laws.

The diagram in figure 1 illustrates the conditions for the transmission of verbal irony in the context of proverbs represented through literary discourse. It indicates that the proverb speaker may represent more than one utterance-agent. Within the text of the proverb, the agent can be an ironic speaker (in that case, Speaker 2), the agent of a verbal action that indirectly alludes to the failed expectations of Speaker 1, or the agent of an action that has caused the existence of an ironic environment to be assumed by Speaker 1. The proverb can have its own ironic target—P-target (or "victim," following Utsumi's terminology). The P-target stands in for the actual target of the utterance (U-target), that is, of the speaker's ironic intention.

To illustrate how this schema works, let us take a second look at an example discussed earlier in the context of the superior wisdom proverb. In Moses's warning speech to his age-group, he assures his fellow citizens that "there is no escape from the white man." He then states his proverb: "When Suffering knocks at your door and you say there is no seat left for him, he tells you not to worry because he has brought his own stool" (84). Who are the actors involved in this proverb? First of all, from the inside of the proverb, if we were to detach it momentarily from

Speaker 1 → Proverb → Agent (Speaker 2) → P-target
Voice 1   → U-target → Addressee
Voice 2 . . .

Figure 1. Conditions for verbal irony of proverbs in literary discourse.

Moses's communicational context, there is a speaker who makes the statement, the "you" to whom the statement is addressed and who seeks to send Suffering away before he can get his foot in the door, and Suffering, who completed the exchange with his "reassuring" answer. Within this limited initial framework, Moses may be seen as Speaker 1. The agent, or Speaker 2, is the actor whose words determine the meaning of the exchange, that is, Suffering. It is also Suffering who pronounces the irony of the situation by offering a reassurance to the person at the door that is in fact ominous, threatening, and inevitable. Suffering has put in place the ironic environment that Moses is now apparently accepting and peddling as the new reality. The P-target is the "you": to the extent that the proverb is understood to be part of traditional discourse, "you" is anyone, past or present, who could be confronted with the hard realities of life, tries to resist those realities, and finally realizes the futility of that resistance.

As we move outside the proverb and consider it as an utterance embedded in a novel, some important adjustments become necessary. The U-target is not a manifold, transhistorical "you" but the people of Umuaro in relation to Mr. Wright (the supervisor of the road project that caused the conflict with Obika and his age-mates), blacks in relation to whites, the colonized in relation to the colonizer.

Speaker 1 embodies no less than four voices as the responsibility for his utterance-act is fully deployed. Voice 1 is the tradition that spoke the proverb into being through "our people." Moses needs this voice in order to draw his U-target into its place as P-target, to see itself as a transhistorical victim of Suffering's irony but at the same time as possessed of the integrity of being part of a community that could freely think out its fate in an internal, private dialogue with its own hardships and challenges. Voice 2 is the voice of the "new" superior wisdom that Moses now brings as one who has learned the secrets of modern reality. Suffering now speaks its irony directly into the situation of the U-target because he is no longer just Suffering in general but the white man—who is in turn allegorized as a symbol of the inevitable. At this point, the agent of irony (Speaker 2) is made to coincide with the second voice of Speaker 1, but Moses also needs to assume the ironic power of

Suffering in order to affirm his superiority by transferring that power to the new situation. As mentioned earlier in my first discussion of this passage, Moses is also sounding a third voice, that of the trickster who purposely puts the white man in a profoundly negative light by equating him with a traditional allegorical representation of everything harmful and undesirable in life. Voice 4 is that of the narrator who may very well subsume the other three voices but who faces his own dilemma in regard to his audience. If his own U-target is the colonizing world that he might legitimately hold responsible for this new figure of Suffering that Moses evokes, the P-target of his proverb could seem somewhat detached and neutralized, seen from the outside as a folkloric victim. If instead he means to keep as his U-target "his own people," a people of shared values and tradition among whom the U-target is still very close to the P-target, a collective and meaningful "you" that has never ceased to know itself as it engages in dialogue with Suffering, then he also runs the risk of the ambivalence of being, like Moses, Voices 1 and 2 at the same time, telling people to remember themselves but also to remember the reality of change. Voice 3, the trickster voice, is an important but dangerous threshold.

On the basis of this schema, I would like to propose the following pragmatic conditions for ironical proverbs in African literary discourse:

1. The environment necessary for establishing that the proverb is spoken with ironic intent derives from several potential factors, and not necessarily from the speaker's negative emotional attitude alone. There will be a perception on the speaker's part that negative consequences have resulted from certain actions on various occasions over several generations, in keeping with Norrick's definition of tradition. Thus the speaker expresses a recurrent experience of failed expectations over time in relation to a putative family or community living at some point in relative harmony. Though the speaker will be responsible for alluding to this tradition, neither the intention of displaying irony nor the negative emotional attitude is necessarily his or hers alone. He or she has adapted a preexisting verbal template to the present situation, suggesting that similar reactions have been known by others. Due to the didactic function of proverbs, the proverb speaker may be speaking for an entire family group, community, or even race in the case of racially motivated colonial oppression. Either the target's implied deed or

misdeed affects the fate of that collectivity or the moral judgment involved brings a whole community's voice to bear on the target's actions. This factor explains the ironic environment of both the natural justice proverb and the hidden truth proverb. In both cases, moral judgment is suggested through the figurative representation of an imaginary scenario in which incongruities between behavior and justice are exposed, redressed (natural justice), or drawn to their inevitable conclusion (hidden truth).

2.   When a Speaker 2 is an agent of proverbial action or speech, he or she is using mention or echo in order to display the incongruity between his or her own behavior and/or thinking and a superior perception of truth that Speaker 1 implicitly attributes to himself or herself or to the community that provided the pattern of speech involved. Speaker 1 attributes to Speaker 2 (in the case of self-inflicted irony, the two speakers coincide) a stereotypical mistake that implicitly lowers that speaker's prestige (hence failed expectation) in the eyes of Speaker 1. Thus explaining the functioning of superior wisdom proverbs in general requires mention-based analysis. Mention theory also offers the only possibility of explaining how both didactic and subversive proverb use can be ironical. In the former case, superior wisdom is used to mock, influence, or control a target or addressee of lower station, whereas in the latter, the lower-placed speaker mocks the other's superior wisdom by implicitly displaying the other's words. After all, the didactic tendency of irony places it in the armory of the social leader. For example, bitter sarcasm or an attempt at raillery can be suggested by negative connotations attached, according to specific cultural contexts, to the signifying terms of the proverb. In *Arrow of God*, Matefi's use of the vulture in proverbs referring to the behavior of one of her co-wives's children could suggest an underlying insult indirectly aimed at the mother of the metaphorical agent (Nwafo), since the comparison of a woman to a vulture is extremely offensive in Igbo society. When she hears that Nwafo, a co-wife's son, has eaten the soup prepared for her husband, Ezeulu, Matefi remarks: "'Do you blame a vulture for perching over a carcass?' [. . .] 'What do you expect a boy to do when his mother cooks soup with locust beans for fish?'"

(9–10). Although Matefi occupies a position superior to that
of a younger wife and even more so the position of that wife's
child, she is still limited in her ability to attack another member of the household by the authority of the patriarch, who
would be sure to intervene in the case of direct conflict threatening the social order within the compound.

The need to maintain a semblance of balance between respect for traditional authority and the use of mention-based irony to question relevant aspects of that authority results in what seems to resemble Socratic irony. In complaining to Ezeulu about the humiliating treatment
inflicted on their kinsman by Obika, the delegation's leader says: "We
have not come with wisdom but with foolishness because a man does
not go to his in-law with wisdom. We want you to say to us: You are
wrong, this is how it is or that is how it is" (12). Based on a very direct
and nonmetaphorical proverbial premise ("a man does not go to his
in-law with wisdom"), this speaker constructs a mention-based challenge by implying the superior wisdom that Ezeulu would need to use
in refuting their complaint against Obika and by implying at the same
time that such a challenge cannot be met because Ezeulu would have
to speak unreasonably or even foolishly to do so. Given that Ezeulu's
demise as symbolic leader is intimately connected with Obika's tragic
destiny, we can see this apparently polite challenge as an initiation into
the ironic narrative discourse of desacralization that makes up the underlying story of *Arrow of God*.

Finally, it should be noted that the relationship of verbal irony
to culture and literary discourse plays an important role in the
way in which proverbs become both the vehicle and the focus of
irony in a text such as *Arrow of God*, which attempts to represent
a particular African culture at a moment of profound disruption
and change.

The use of irony as a trope for historical crisis and the internal contradictions of African societies is not unknown to African literary critics. Kenneth Harrow sees an overarching situational irony in the historical universe of Ngugi's *A Grain of Wheat* in which all the characters
betray themselves and their own people in the face of colonial oppression: "Like the flat, sterile, burning desert or the dreary expanses of
mist and darkness, irony is life-denying when it embraces all actors,
all hopes. Finally, irony denies freedom, and with it responsibility,
by incorporating guilt into the fabric of the universe" (258). Modupe

Olaogun's view of irony, as she presents her insightful hypothesis on Bessie Head's *Maru*, would seem to be similar to Harrow's. She sets out to demonstrate that "*Maru* portrays specific ambiguities engendered by the Botswana and South African historical conditions fictionally represented by Head. These ambiguities are akin to schizophrenia and are best captured by the figure of irony. Contrary to the interpretations of *Maru* as a simple dramatization of good versus evil, or male power [...] versus female submissiveness [...] I shall argue that the dominant images of these characters, and of the society they represent, are above all those of ambiguity" (70). But whereas the ambiguous middle ground of Harrow's interpretation of Ngugi is life-denying even at its most promising moments, as it absorbs all human effort into its ambiguity, Olaogun sees Head's ironic tropism as a turning away from "things as they are" to "things as they can be" (84). Irony in African literature can be a trope of creative thought as much as a historical witness to endless ambiguity and contradiction. By analyzing verbal irony through oral tradition, we can better understand the latter's creative, playful, and self-affirming speech. Such analysis does nothing to counter an open-ended critique of all agents and voices involved in the narratives of African historical experience.

This chapter opened with an Igbo proverb: Surprise is beyond the great, yet the great is proven in surprise. Communities can withstand betrayal, challenge, imminent ruin, and internal contradiction even when they are least prepared for them, but only to the extent that an ironic voice can be found to remobilize shaken wisdom and put it back into circulation.

Proverbs in *Arrow of God* are ironical. They reflect relations of power that call for expressions of incongruity between expectations and actions. They have been marshaled in a particular historical conjuncture to respond to underlying situational ironies such as the fact that a fellow Igbo could show the way to the house of the sacred priest to the greatest desecrator of culture in African history: the leper whose handshake has become another thing.

CHAPTER FIVE

Calixthe Beyala

New Conceptions of the Ironic Voice

It's because respect is mutual that a woman gives birth to
another woman.

—Igbo proverb

Given the fact, well documented in Irène d'Almeida's *Francophone African Women Writers: Destroying the Emptiness of Silence*, that women
writers arrived relatively late on the scene of African literature and that
many representations of what constituted African literary discourse as
well as African tradition itself were already in place when the early novels of Ama Ata Aidoo, Flora Nwapa, Aminata Sow Fall, and Mariama
Bâ began to appear in print, the question of how women authors perceive and use irony is crucial in several respects. Although mention-
based irony and subversive raillery are major elements in the discourses
of authors such as Achebe and Kourouma, the questioning of authority, whether colonial or traditional, does not necessarily imply a fundamental questioning of patriarchy or of male-dominated colonial and
postcolonial societies. Whether discursive irony in a text written by an
African woman is formally distinguishable or not, the objects of irony
and the reasons behind its necessity are in themselves different. Yet research on African women's writing has tended to emphasize thematic
and sociocultural issues much more than formal ones, with the notable
exception of Nfah-Abbenyi, who emphasizes theorization through fiction. The study of irony offers the opportunity to gain insight into the
narrative strategies involved in the production of an ironic voice in the
face of both sexual and racial oppression. Finally, without some degree
of awareness of the potential ironic intention behind the discourse of

women struggling to be heard above the din of traditional barriers to their speech, the reader of fiction produced by African women could mistake genuine subversive and contesting thought with reflection for diatribe or, worse still, cultural portraiture.

Ironic discourse appears frequently in the recent fiction of African women. Three notable examples are the Gabonese author Sandrine Bessora, the Senegalese Fatou Diome, and the Nigerian Chimamanda Adichie. The remarkable diversity of these authors and their approaches is a witness to irony's scope and strategic importance as African women writing in the early twenty-first century extend the reach of their thinking to many aspects of social and political life, both within Africa and throughout the constantly self-renewing African diaspora of postcolonial migrations.

Adichie's short story "The Headstrong Historian" (2009) incorporates cultural traditions and translinguistic onomastics—playing on the presence of an African language embedded in an English-language text through character names—into the construction of situational ironies of postcolonial experience. Widowed at a relatively young age and harassed by acquisitive in-laws, the story's heroine, Nwamgba, sends her only son to a Catholic mission school in the hope that he will someday be able to defend her rights in the colonial court system (207). Ashamed and discouraged by her son's subsequent cultural alienation, "she prayed and sacrificed for Mgbeke [her daughter-in-law] to have a boy, because it would be Obierika [her late husband] come back and would bring a semblance of sense back into her world" (213–14). When the first child is born, however, though a male child, Nwamgba "did not feel the spirit of her magnificent husband" (214). It will be the second child, a girl, who will fulfil Nwamgba's desire: "From the moment Nwamgba held her, the baby's bright eyes delightfully focused on her, she knew that was the spirit of Obierika that had returned; odd, to have come in a girl, but who could predict the ways of the ancestors? Father O'Donnell baptized her Grace, but Nwamgba called her Afamefuna, 'My Name Will Not Be Lost'" (214). Though Afamefuna will become a "Western"-trained academic and historian, her attachment to her grandmother will lead her to seek to rewrite colonial history from what she sees as an African perspective. Nwamgba was following her traditional beliefs in looking for a male grandchild to embody her husband's spirit, whereas it was actually her own spirit as a strong, self-affirming, and capable woman that she needed to embody. The crossing of gender roles fulfils Nwamgba's dream by playfully switching it around. At the same time, Father O'Donnell's imposition of the name Grace ironically confirms the grandmother's intention by inscribing the notion of redemption in what he considered to be an acculturating act.

Sandrine Bessora's *53 cm* (1999) generates irony within a framework of social and political satire that attacks the inability of the French immigration bureaucracy to understand the intricate and anti-normative features of postcolonial migrations, particularly those of women. As Ben K'Anene Jukpor explains: "As an indirect attack, irony is an arm particularly belonging to satire. Just as the satirist, so as to not put his or her life on the line, avoids going directly to the target, the ironist, for the same reason, avoids a direct attack on the object. Irony is specific to satire because in every irony there subsists implicitly a censure that the subject addresses to an object, or expresses about that object" (35).[1] When Zara, the protagonist, born in Belgium of a Swiss mother and a Gabonese father, always in and out of illegality in France, calls "definitive" (14) a "carte de séjour" that will last one year minus the six months already used up under the temporary residence permit, her irony questions a system predicated on the precariousness of the outsider's existence, a life that is always controlled but never affirmed. As Odile Cazenave points out, in *53 cm*, Bessora "subverts the norms and justly questions the authority of the discourse that determines what constitutes central and peripheral discourse" (2005: 35). This subversion translates into a recurring play on the language of identity, as every person, fruit, and vegetable has to justify its racial and cultural authenticity or face expulsion.

While Bessora's satire emphasizes the ridiculous in postcolonial migration control, Fatou Diome, in *Inassouvies, nos vies* (Our lives remain unsatisfied) (2008), integrates philosophical reflection on the social condition of women and social satire on issues such as dysfunctional and missed marriages, marginalization of the elderly, and postmodern isolationism. When Félicité, the elderly friend of the protagonist, Betty, is forcibly consigned to a nursing home, the narrator comments that "those who had placed her there *for her own good* had forgotten her, to her misfortune" (48).[2] Later, in discussing an unexpected visit by a previously unknown niece, the narrator uses free indirect discourse: "they were expecting the pompous contribution [to the niece's upcoming wedding] from *an old aunt who had nothing more to do with her savings*" (149).[3] The device of mention—using the typical words of someone else in order to show one's scorn—is both satirical, in that it criticizes the current state of family and social relationships, and ironical, in that it simultaneously showcases exploitative social practices and the victim's conscious resistance to that exploitation. An even greater and subtler irony of Diome's novel is that behind the mask of the observer-protagonist Betty (also referred to as the "Loupe," or Magnifying Glass), her understated Senegalese origins are spread throughout the novel. As in all of Diome's novels, there are references to places and names, an abundance of proverbs woven into the texture of the narrator's discourse, and recourse to the music of the kora, a Senegalese musical instrument, as an overarching symbol of sustained identity in ironic contrast to a world with "so many signs for so little meaning" (72).[4]

Among this new generation of African writers, Calixthe Beyala, who comes from Cameroon but has been living in and writing from Paris for more than two decades now, has distinguished herself as a prolific, personal, and diverse author in terms of themes as well as linguistic and stylistic devices. Though Beyala is not universally recognized as the best representative of African culture and tradition,[5] her fiction incorporates many of the diverse tendencies we have seen in the irony of writers such as Adichie, Bessora, and Diome, for all of whom questions of migration, identity, and authenticity are both thematic and subject to irony.

Beyala seems to be motivated by the urgency of dismantling, or at least shaking up, the world of both men and women in their apathy and conservatism, forcing the sacred and the profane to coexist in order to reveal social realities and the contradictions that underpin them. This may be why her protagonists have constant recourse to irony and humor as strategic rhetorical devices that make their voice(s) heard in their polyphonic resonance. To this end, the women characters, who tend to be central in her novels, function in relational contexts with other women as well as with men in marginalized communities; hence the abundance of problems related to sexuality, race, and marriage presented through varied modes of narration in a way that generally reveals the plight and suffering of women and other marginalized members of society.

Amours sauvages (1999) and *Les arbres en parlent encore* (2002) illustrate the importance of irony in relation to the self-construction of the ironist as writer, and especially as an African woman writer, and to the representation of colonial history. Beyala's work offers many examples of ironic narrative and discursive strategies. *Le petit prince de Belleville* (1992; *Loukoum: The Little Prince of Belleville* [1995]) produced

an implied ironic voice through the juxtaposition of two interlocking
and mutually contradictory male voices (see Onyeoziri 2001). *Assèze
l'Africaine* (1994) more fully develops a woman narrator's voice that
uses irony as a means of revealing the contradictions and internal crisis of identity of her "Westernized" and ultimately suicidal half sister.
Comment cuisiner son mari à l'africaine (How African women cook
their husbands) (2000) uses irony to explore the relationship between
identity and sexuality without capitulating to the stereotypes of submission to patriarchy or exoticism. *La plantation* (2005) rehearses and
revitalizes the ironic tone of colonial times by reviewing racialized and
racist perceptions. A third-person narrative voice ironically represents
white Zimbabwean landowners faced with expropriation by a postcolonial African regime. The principal source of both verbal and situational
irony in *L'homme qui m'offrait le ciel* (The man who offered me heaven)
(2007) is the narrator's adolescent daughter. Her mother presents her
as the irresponsible representative of a new, culturally alienated generation, and yet she sees through the racially determined barriers to
her mother's relationship with a white man. Though the narrator is a
well-established and experienced African woman writer, her analysis
of race and gender is shown to be incomplete by the very generation she
has judged to be less conscious of the imperatives of emancipation and
self-affirmation.

In *Amours sauvages* (1999), pungent irony and caustic humor
through hyperbole, preterition, onomastics, and scatological imagery
enable the writer to reveal and denounce various levels of tragic human
conditions and the fallacious myths and manipulations that perpetuate oppression, exploitation, and privation, as well as self-depreciation,
self-deception, and/or utter lack of consciousness. As an attentive social
critic, Beyala is aware of current literary and political issues of the postcolonial, postmodern world, such as transculturalism, *métissage*, and
miscegenation, misogyny, racial conflict, and racism, not to mention
the eternal problem of marriage. The auto-reflexive principal character, Ève-Marie, moves and acts through clichés and stereotypes, leaving
theory and practice to coexist. As the homodiegetic narrator, she puts
in place herself, the stereotypical strong-willed black woman prostitute
who reinvents herself and becomes the center of life in a marginalized
community; Flora-Flore, the archetypal oppressed white woman/wife
who mortgages her life in the name of savage love for her archetypically
violent white husband, Jean-Pierre Pierre, and yet secretly seeks solace
elsewhere in the most incongruous ways; the marginalized black men

and women nostalgically looking for communal acceptance in a mul-
tiracial racist society; and Pléthore, the marginalized white man who
chooses a black prostitute in an attempt to alleviate his suffering and
alienation. Following the various dislocations and fragmentations involved in the different strands of social relationships, the novelist seems
to be saying that interracial and intercultural relationships are conceiv-
able only to the extent that they intersect and form part of a new, growing postcolonial immigrant community. Pléthore's betrayal or infidel-
ity through an affair with Flora-Flore, though initially condemned by
Ève-Marie, is treated as an antithesis to Jean-Pierre Pierre's white male
violence, while Flora-Flore's son, whose biological father is a black ho-
mosexual, is very well integrated into the community as a positive symbol of *métissage*, in opposition to the racial hatred and impossible interracial relationship to which the innocent and helpless offspring is
sacrificed in Mariama Bâ's *Un chant écarlate*, for example.

Beyala, like other African writers, many of whom are at least as well
rooted in Africa as she is—Kourouma, Diabaté, Labou Tansi—draws
her narrative and discursive inspiration largely from African oral traditions but also from French literary traditions. She integrates tradition
and modernity in a way that produces the burlesque in the language
and behavior of the characters (see Matateyou and Diallo, respectively,
in Godin, *Nouvelles écritures francophones*).

An analysis of several passages will help bring out some of the
sources of humor and irony and show how they function, often creat-
ing laughter and sadness at the same time. The first passage describes
the arrival of Ève-Marie's mother in Belleville. Here the author con-
fronts or integrates tradition with modernity and postmodernism. In
the first place, Ève-Marie's mother has just arrived from Africa and,
however educated she may be, still carries with her a certain number
of stereotypical ideas of what life in the metropolis should look like.
She expects her son-in-law to have a high-paying white-collar job in
big business or as an engineer in charge of construction companies.
The daughter, to be accepted as a "been-to," should have been able to
secure a well-paying job too, as a secretary or a nurse. Since there are
no signs of such socioeconomic success, in spite of the couple's effort
to make their home clean and comfortable for her, Ève-Marie's mother
still finds reasons to look down on them from the castle that she has
built in the air and placed herself in. Her attitude evokes in the reader
images of unfounded claims and unrealistic expectations that lead people in modern societies to dress in borrowed robes, a subject similar to

what Aminata Sow Fall has figuratively dealt with in *Le Revenant* (The ghost) as *xeessal*. Perspicaciously picking up the borrowed-robes figure from African oral tradition, Ève-Marie responds accordingly in an interior monologue, but not without falling into the trap or the temptation of wishing her husband had dressed himself in borrowed robes in order to impress her mother.

Distracted from Flora-Flore's interest in Pléthore, Ève-Marie reflects bitterly on her own mother's refusal to recognize her newfound dignity in marriage: "I had my own grievances to air: against Mama who had had the nerve to not notice that my relations with the universe were what they should have been, against Pléthore who didn't know how to wear the borrowed robes of the so-called elect and how to tell Mama he was a store-owner, or an engineer or a construction project manager" (34).[6] Ève-Marie herself prolongs the unrealistic expectation in the ironic tone of her interior monologue. She dreams of the orphan girl in folk tales who stumbles on wheelbarrows of gold and buckets of diamonds, who is able to silence her mockers and even to arouse some envy in them.

One might say that her mother is playing the role of the conscious African woman who refuses to be mystified by the Western world, showing her self-affirmation by condemning everything, from her daughter's husband's socioeconomic status to their white culture and values, which consider a poet's socioeconomic condition a valid one. Unfortunately, her ideology, which involved a certain degree of self-affirmation in order to counter the contempt in which the colonialists and their *mission civilisatrice* held Africans and everything African, invariably hurts her daughter and strips her at least at the time of any form of dignity and self-worth she might otherwise possess. The strongest irony in this passage lies in Ève-Marie's feigned anger against Pléthore for not lying to her mother and claiming that he has one of the officially accepted social positions. This mocking of the self is addressed to herself because of the attitude she is ready to adopt in order to impress the world, the self-denial and lack of integrity to which she is tempted to succumb. But she also seems to be poking fun at the world and what impresses people in general.

In a later passage, Ève-Marie adopts more heightened irony and self-mockery in her social criticism as she claims to play the role of a saintly person who cares for the poor and the oppressed in a selfless way. Meeting a "destitute" Senegalese immigrant girl carrying a baby, she claims: "Suddenly an illumination rose to my head, standing my nerves on end, and I began to sense the fatality represented by Maya lost and alone in the city [. . .] I felt I had wings because I was not abandoning this unknown woman to an early grave. I couldn't allow the suffering of this poor soul to be increased by my own indifference" (37–38).[7] Ève-Marie not only sees herself as a Good Samaritan but goes as far as to evoke the Christic image implied in her name by metonymy, not only as the image but even as Christ himself, who is there for the rejected of the world.[8]

The description of the situation that follows heightens the irony. First of all, this woman who bears the combined names of two key biblical women, in metonymic relation with Adam and Jesus Christ, introduces her African protégée to a brothel, where she had made herself an associate manager with the white male owner, Mr. Thirty Percent, who has already been revealed to be a corrupt individual. Of course Ève-Marie immediately asks for her share of the profits for her collaboration in this "fruitful" business, in which the female body is exploited and treated with indecency, and for her self-serving act of charity "while sensual pleasures bought and sold spread out their tentacles and crushed humanity" (40).[9] Whereas Ève-Marie reveals her consciousness of the contradictions and hypocrisy of her so-called act of charity, the supposedly innocent and abandoned Maya whom Ève-Marie is "helping" immediately reveals herself to be an accomplished prostitute. This revelation creates a double irony and ambiguity. Whom does the reader believe? Ève-Marie's intervention in Maya's life begins as a satire of sainthood combined with hyperbole and then points to several ambivalent situations. Hyperbole arises from a number of cultural allusions such as "le boat people des temps modernes," cultural icons of heroism and survival. Here the imagery that conveys the irony is highly polymorphous. Who is finally responsible for the moral degradation of the growing community? Or is this moral degradation in the first place?

Ève-Marie mentions, among a number of young immigrant African women, one who came to study in France and now claims to find herself in an impossible situation because her home government has cut off her scholarship. Ève-Marie combines a kind of mocking description of such young women with a representation of their utterances in the form of mention. Rather than offering a real quotation of the student's words, she subtly repeats the typical statements such a person would make in a way that insinuates her skepticism, thus adding to the ambiguity of the situation. In imposing this mention-based irony on the different young immigrant women who approach her for help, she shifts a good part of the responsibility onto them and with a wink enlists the reader's complicity in seeing that these women are playing a game too. Here the mention, a general overarching discourse presented as a quotation and attributed to the type, makes the situation all the more difficult to assess in terms of both truth-value and point of view.

Self-mocking irony is seen in the fact that the young women whom Ève-Marie, in her implicit role as *maquerelle* (female pimp) takes to Mr. Thirty Percent, the first victims of her bid to make money at any cost and raise her socioeconomic status, are all African. This is a conscious act that, on the one hand, underscores the degree of their *déchéance*, or disastrous circumstances, and, on the other, puts into question their self-awareness as well as racial solidarity. Or is it an ironic way of affirming the loss of and need for racial solidarity, since Ève-Marie, at this moment in her life and narrative, is functioning within a racialized community as a treacherous symbol of (African) motherhood, luring and betraying women of "her own race" if not women in general?

At the same time, her discourse reveals that she is conscious of what is wrong with her behavior, and the hypocrisy it involves, but she is not entirely, if ever, apologetic about it. This further complicates the situation. The refusal to be apologetic about her betrayal of her race and sex is very complex. It reveals her lucidity and strength as well as her weakness; she succumbs to this behavior perhaps in order to survive. Irony and ambiguity are seen in the hypocrisy of her attitude of sainthood as well as in the fact that she reveals her own self-awareness of this hypocrisy. Both her discourse and her acts continually give a double message, at once accepting responsibility and dissociating herself from it. The ironic self-depreciation continues throughout the narrative of help and betrayal, as it were, given that prostitution is a form of oppression. At the same time, she seems to be saying that if French society, because of its racist structure, is not ready to give immigrant African women a place in which to realize their aspirations, then prostitution is a legitimate means of getting a foothold in a country that has rejected them. She thus presents prostitutes as victims of oppression and not as the source of social evil and moral degradation. One wonders if the author is justifying and exonerating Tanga's mother, whom she seems to have condemned in an earlier work, *Tu t'appelleras Tanga* (1988; *Your Name Shall Be Tanga* [1996]).

Ève-Marie leaves us with a sense that there are many unresolved issues currently under debate in diaspora society: social criticism in relation to self-affirmation and self-expression, lucidity in relation to

cynicism, solidarity in relation to exploitation, true oppression in relation to self-immolation, or denial of one's identity in order to satisfy the
Other's imagination. What is our position in this debate? Beyala's literary career, which has not been without its own peculiar vicissitudes and
ambiguities, may be on a collision course with contemporary identity
politics.

Irony in the fictional discourse of Calixthe Beyala is an irony of positioning, of creation of place. It is closely tied to the problem and challenge of being an African woman writer. This type of positioning or
identity-claim irony can be seen in *Amours sauvages*, in which Ève-Marie conceives the idea of writing a novel and at the same time has to
come to terms with multiple forms of rejection, ridicule, and ultimately
her own self-doubt.

For Ève-Marie, writing is a desire, an ambition for which she is not
about to abandon her ardent determination. The reader cannot yet determine the future and scope of her success or failure as a writer: the
novel gives us no closure on that front. We cannot yet know if the polite
rejection of Ève-Marie's manuscript represents a definitive dead end or
a provisional moment of frustration implicitly negated by the concrete
reality of Beyala's published novel.

What the reader can directly and indirectly conclude is that the desire to write comes from an unshakable resolve on Ève-Marie's part to
voice in a more open way than ever before what she has learned both
from her mother and grandmother and from her immediate social mi-
lieu. In the context of this novel, writing takes on such significance that
this woman of limited formal education has decided to teach herself
independently to read and write in order to gain a broader hearing,
whatever the obstacles or cultural limitations. The reader has to try to
understand how the problems of the community and of individuals, as
well as the subversive ironic intention of the heroine, combine to evoke
the notion of an African woman who writes in order to be a writer but
also to denounce individuals and groups who perpetuate marginalization and sexual, emotional, and economic violence against women.

Consciously using her cultural heritage, Ève-Marie assumes the voice
and the freedom needed to speak for all marginalized and oppressed
people while repudiating the inauthenticity of gratuitous erudition.
She is a prototype in every sense of Beyala's "femme-rebelle" (Cazenave
1998): an African woman, often illiterate, who claims her freedom to
be, to have, and to do, her pleasure as well as her place in anticolonial
and antiracist struggles, whether she be a prostitute, a fortune-teller, a

cleaning woman, or a petty trader. Ève-Marie is prepared to push her way forward not only for her own survival and well-being but also to take over her own self-representation within the narrative. To do so, she neither plays down nor exaggerates the obstacles of a world and a society built by men in general and by colonizers in particular. In all her efforts to survive, including learning to read and write, she listens to a litany of misery and exclusion from her sister immigrants. Before beginning to imagine any possible literary enterprise, she passes through a gamut of professions, reflecting both her socioeconomic and sexual oppression and her street smarts and cleverness. As for the African men who excluded her and smothered her voice for years, she not only exposes them to ridicule by treating hyperbolically what was already hyperbolic—their empty erudition, since they consider themselves as "knowing more French than the French Academy" [plus férus en français que l'Académie française]. Monsieur Rasayi says: "It is purely out of courtesy that I dare to call language the gibberish that comes out of your mouths. It's not with the three hundred odd word vocabulary that Ève-Marie commands—and the rest of you as well I might add—, these two dozen catch-all verbs that you keep peddling, the total disregard for prepositions and coordinate conjunctions all of which you abuse to reveal your ignorance, that a work worthy of the name is going to emerge" (173).[10] Whether or not Ève-Marie's novel-writing project corresponds to Beyala's thinking as a writer, it suggests important emotional, intellectual, political, social, and cultural traits that underlie the ways in which African women have taken command of their own representation through writing. By conceiving and assuming the work of writing, Ève-Marie is trying to fight a confusion of values, for according to what she observes, she is not sure of what is good and useful for the community around her or what is valid as personal choice. All the more so because, while reflecting on writing—the subject and how to weave it—she is also asking herself questions on several aspects of her experience: the chances of success of interracial marriages, a certain disillusionment concerning white couples, sexual relations in general related to Océan's bisexuality, and a certain siege mentality provoked by Mlle Personne's initially unexplained murder.

When she feels the need to write and conceives of possibly doing so, she is aware that she is not necessarily equipped or trained for writing, even if the need to write has become almost an obligation. Her surprising if not troubling question to her entourage—"How does one commit a perfect murder?"—is a rhetorical pretext for hurling herself into writing, to start weaving her story, constructing a plot and characters. In answering this call to writing through which she will speak for a hybrid community, Ève-Marie reflects on her relationship with that community. Though she seeks encouragement ("good grades") from her entourage, her awareness of her lack of formal education does not prevent her from making efforts. Her tenacious struggle to gain admittance into the circle of the "elect" of literature seems to transform the initial skepticism of her friends into admiration mixed with curiosity. While some of them try to dissociate themselves from her for fear that her book may cause them trouble by revealing day-to-day social problems, such as murder and violence, others, including her husband, Pléthore, rally around her, expressing their optimism and support for the future of her artistic enterprise.

Ève-Marie wishes to have a voice, through the writing of her novel, to show that she too has something to say about the sexual, physical, economic, and emotional violence inflicted on women and the social injustice and indignities suffered by the marginalized people of Belleville, a situation of which she herself has been a victim and to which, by her own admission, she has sometimes contributed. She wants to write not only to make known her experience as an African woman immigrant among immigrants but also to show herself fruitful, prolific, and smart in a "hostile world," where one could easily succumb to sterility in the face of enormous material, financial, and cultural obstacles: "I ran after them, showed myself prolific, ingenious, reassuring, upholding my claim to be the most likely to survive in a hostile universe" (169).[11] In order to calm her entourage, she adds: "It's not for real that I want to know how one commits a perfect murder; I'm writing a book."[12] Ève-Marie constructs the idea of her manuscript with subtlety and complexity, despite her language, which sometimes seems to border on slang, often including possible transliteration of an unnamed mother tongue. What Ève-Marie presents as a pretext reveals itself in her utterances and actions to be the sign of the malaise she feels in a society dominated by violence.

The surprise, skepticism, and incredulity with which her neighbors receive this affirmation of selfhood, of the freedom to think, to say, and to act, coming from the oppressed of the oppressed (a former sex-trade worker) illustrate their low level of consciousness: they have accepted the limitations that white society has placed on them. They find it normal that Ève-Marie would make ends meet in any other field—hooker, cleaning woman, cook—but not in the field of literature. "They were pushing each other, stepping on each other's feet to have a look at the miracle of this literary birth" (170).[13]

The first attempts at writing by African women were certainly not encouraged, even by those who most needed to support them. One cannot but recall how the harshest criticisms of Mariama Bâ's *Une si longue lettre* (1979; *So Long a Letter* [2008]) came from male critics of African origin. In this case, those close to Ève-Marie almost shake her confidence: "I was trembling, my hands were trembling [. . .] I feared the worst" [Je tremblais; mes mains tressautaient (. . .) je craignais le pire (171)]. The modalization is noteworthy here. The imperfect tense underlines the indefinite character of these fears. An African woman wishing to write has to go beyond this stage of having to seek the world's approval, even the approval of one's own "friends." For them, it is a transgression to which Ève-Marie has added the sin of translocation. She informs us that one of her African friends, the *tirailleur sénégalais*, no doubt accustomed to seeing women exercising agency in the kitchen, is shocked to see an African woman, and especially one much younger than himself, dare to conceive of the ambition of writing a novel. "What's the world coming to, if women are writing stories?" [Où va le monde, hein, si les femmes écrivent des histoires? (171)]. He already called Ève-Marie to order by denying women any right to take part in public affairs: "Your sisters, your fellow-women, had better understand that their place is at home, [. . .] Not in the streets!" [Faut que tes consoeurs comprennent que leur place est au foyer, (. . .) Pas dans les rues!] (165). This prohibition of freedom of expression and action, an almost absolute authority, which men like Jean-Pierre Pierre arrogate to themselves in order to silence temporarily or permanently (by death) the women they oppress, is the reason for Ève-Marie's writing. It is what gives birth to her words of survival, resistance, and revolt.

The fact that the others applaud the *tirailleur*'s words emphasizes their own lack of consciousness and self-esteem. But Ève-Marie herself, in her caustic irony, does not fail to respond to this gesture with her own diatribe: "The tirailleur sénégalais charged at me, growling like a mad dog, his eyes popping out of his head" (171).[14] It is as if the struggle between the sexes were operating on two levels—animalistic physical gestures and the subtle ferocity of writing. These are the "sanctions" Berrendonner discusses in relation to the pragmatics of irony, "sanctions à cercle vicieux." The fellow black man, believing Ève-Marie guilty of transgression, reacts in an aggressive way that the narrator allays in advance with her own aggressively hyperbolic but ironic terms.

Ève-Marie's husband, rather than separating himself from his wife,
gives up his vocation as a poet. "I'm going to stop writing. [. . .] We
can't have two writers in the house!" [J'arrête d'écrire. (. . .) Il ne peut
pas y avoir deux écrivains dans la maison! (187)]. The presentation of
this act may be ironical since we do not know if it is motivated by lack
of inspiration, by respect for Ève-Marie's passion, or by bitterness at
seeing his wife take up writing in his place. Pléthore, perhaps to protect his self-esteem and dignity, refuses to place himself in a position of
competition with her—especially knowing that her life has greater significance for their community.

Although Ève-Marie does not claim to have at her disposal the greatest facility of language, and though she is not confronted with the same
ruptures with her own "family" because of writing, she gives us the impression—through her actions, her observations on the dictatorships
that reign in certain African countries, her views on the suffering of
marginalized individuals, especially women, of the expropriated of the
world—that writing is a means of bombarding both injustice and racism in the diasporic world in which she lives.

Of her friends, Ève-Marie says: "they were convinced that by abandoning me they were avoiding problems that would otherwise have led
to their lives as outcasts being further displaced" (169).[15] The expression
"dislocation de leur vie d'exclus" doubly negates the notion of life fully
lived. The irony resides in the fact that they are seeking, at this point in
their relations with the narrator who sneers back at them, to defend a
state that is hardly worth living in, much less defending.

After she sends her manuscript to a publisher, there are at this stage
of Ève-Marie's narrative two radically opposed reactions to her vocation. On the one hand, Pléthore's enthusiasm is presented hyperbolically in line with a romanticized notion of his wife's genius: "'You'll see,
they're all going to beg you to publish with them.' He ran around the
cafés singing about my extraordinary talent in Latin, Greek and even
Chinese. 'Wait and see!' he proclaimed, 'my wife is the greatest writer of
her generation'" (195).[16] This is a reaction to which Ève-Marie responds
in her own hyperbolic terms in the way she presents his excitement. She
establishes her ironic distance in relation to the superfluous information Pléthore offers in order to elevate, somewhat gratuitously, the status of his wife's writing. On the other hand, we find the skepticism of
those around her in the community who have accepted the place society has assigned to them. "They ranked their own intellects according
to the realities of social determinism" [(Ils) plaçaient leurs esprits à la

clarté des réalités du déterminisme social (195)]. This is the social determinism already inculcated in them. They cannot imagine that one of
their own, much less a woman, could become a serious writer. Yet this
social/intellectual determinism, so well described by Simone de Beauvoir in "La femme et la création," does not in this context come from a
social elite that imposes inferior status on these "damnées de la terre,"
"la putasserie réunie," the poor, the black immigrants of Belleville, all
those who occupy the lower rungs of the social ladder. It comes from
themselves. The implication is that if Ève-Marie, as the "daughter of
nobody," is incapable of becoming a writer for this reason, they themselves will always be limited in the execution of their life goals, since
they have all joined, in their judgment of her, in this determinism.

Faced with these two opposing positions, Ève-Marie herself reacts
ironically to her husband's enthusiasm, and this is a sign of her lucidity.
At the same time, she does not subscribe to the social determinism of
her entourage. She describes the sources of authority that are supposed
to determine who is qualified to be a writer and who is not. According to her, the skepticism of these authorities derives from the fact that
they "knew that I did not belong to that world where the authoriza-
tion was given to be or not to be considered a woman" ["savaient que je
n'appartenais pas à ces mondes où se délivraient les autorisations pour
être ou pas une femme" (195)]. The allusion to the identity papers of the
postcolonial metropolitan state represents metaphorically the "autho-
rization" to have a voice, in that some women are recognized as having
the authority to express themselves. It is not all women who have the
right to be women in that sense, since there are women whose voices
are denied on the basis of the values of established literary institutions.
The others knew she did not belong to "those galaxies that gave directives on how things should or should not be invented" ["ces univers qui
donnaient des directives de comment devraient ou pas s'inventer des
choses" (195)]. This hyperbolic and ironical reflection on cultural elitism alludes to the whole concept of writing and publishing. According
to Ève-Marie, this principle of literary production is apparently determined by a certain authority that cannot recognize her as a woman
writer who should or could speak in the name of other women. Finally,
her friends know that she does not belong to "those circles that determined what is or is not necessary and that attacked whatever they
judged inappropriate to the well-being of society" ["ces milieux qui
déterminaient ce qui était nécessaire ou pas et qui s'attaquaient à ce
qu'ils jugeaient impropre au bien-être social" (195)]. This is a reference

to literary institutions that assume the right to determine what kinds
of writing are pertinent or useful in the context in which the writing is
produced. This could also apply to the language of writing, since "the
well-being of society" includes the maintenance of the quality of literary language as a cultural, national, and racially determined French
cultural heritage.

In reflecting on the perspectives and modes of thought of her community, as she interprets them, Ève-Marie responds by saying that she
could not care less about such authorities because, in the first place—
and this is what I consider to be a key affirmation of *Amours sauvages*
regarding African women's writing and the African woman, a kind of
manifesto of the African writer and woman that Ève-Marie wants to
be—she is "convinced that [she] does not need the little earthly powers to survive, think and do what [she judges] good for [her] existence"
(196).[17] The "little earthly powers" are the powers that be of literary institutions whom she considers essentially insignificant because they are
based on narrow-mindedness and consider themselves more important
than they really are. She is convinced that she does not need their approval to attain three goals as a woman and writer in her social context: survival, thinking, and doing what one considers good for one's
own existence. Survival is a part of her practical efforts to earn a living by various means. Surrounded by confusion in her community, she
needs to put her ideas down in writing in order to make sense out of
her life and identity-constructing origins. In order to think, the African
woman writer has the ability, the right, and even the obligation to intervene intellectually in her society. What she judges to be good for her
own existence is what is valid in the light of that evaluation.

Ève-Marie supports this affirmation with a reference to two proverbs
that she learned from her mother, a fact that contradicts the initial idea
of those around her who thought of her as a "daughter of nobody." Implicitly, she affirms her cultural and familial identity. "'The greatest chief
loses his powers if you decide that he possesses none,' my mother used to
say. And also: 'the only hold the other has over us is the power we give
him'" (196).[18] She is the daughter of another woman who has a voice and
who could affirm her existence and the authority to transmit to her descendants, orally in this case, a cultural experience and knowledge on
which Ève-Marie can base her stand vis-à-vis the authorities that exclude
her. The proverbs represent the voice of her mother as well as an oral African literary tradition. Not only is Ève-Marie constantly thinking about
her country or continent of origin, desiring "those returns to the palm

trees because they were reassuring" ["ces retours aux palmiers parce qu'ils étaient rassurants" (166)], but she progressively puts herself in the center of the life of Belleville's exiled people. She hosts griots during the evenings in her apartment, where African exiles come to listen and to relive an oral culture that transports them briefly back to Africa:

> because the griots explained to them how much African lands were warmer, they took root in the tropics and their hearts became as vigorous as the trunks of the baobabs and their bodies bloomed with the strength of flowering bougainvilleas. They were capable of spending another thousand years in exile without worrying about the suffering. You will certainly have understood, my dear readers: I wasn't such an imbecile as to enjoy life without a cloud, but I wasn't intelligent enough either to gather apples with Newton or to flirt with Einstein! In those moments, my hard heart, my heart of a savage, would soften. The griots' words gently intoxicated my spirit; Paris faded into the background; Africa came to hover over my head with her suns and her nights filled with the sounds of reptiles. (141)[19]

This passage shows the connection that Ève-Marie makes between her literary work and value and the memory of her identity and oral culture. While allowing the griots to evoke the beauty and warmth of African lands, the narrator insists on the fact that she is conscious of the ambiguous ground she occupies. She tells the reader that she is not naive enough to believe in a purely euphoric experience emerging from the relationship between the exiled subject and her geographically and temporally distant origins. At the same time, implicitly arming herself with an irony reminiscent of Césaire ("Those who invented neither powder nor compass / those who never tamed steam or electricity" [*Return to My Native Land* 110]),[20] she recognizes that she is not accepted in the place of exile as an equal partner and that the laws of physics, the discoveries of Einstein, lie beyond her reach. But these cultural evenings bring hope in the sense of a world to be built through writing, the promise of a better future for the exiled individuals who are discovering their potential solidarity. The magic of the spoken word that one finds completely natural and ordinary, and about which one has no need to reflect when still living in one's own culture—as Ève-Marie's mother had pointed out in questioning the need for "professional" poets like Pléthore—is now a kind of "magic" for Ève-Marie and her fellow exiles. This is precisely because they miss their culture and become more conscious of its value as they are further removed from it in time and space. Ève-Marie does not want this remembering to be a vague euphoria, even as a source of inspiration, while she does recognize the value of the experience in relation to her native land and cultural past. The baobab that she refers to is not an empty cultural signifier but an appropriation, again with inspiration from Césaire, of the power and solidity of the association of the baobab with Africa, whether such an association represents a stereotype for others or not. The tree is used to signify Africa and to be African. It is Barthes's "maison basque" in Paris and in the "pays Basque" at the same time (*Mythologies* 210).

Ève-Marie is constructing the aesthetics of her writing before seeking publication in order to show that writing is not simply an intellectual or scholarly exercise but the fruit of an aesthetic forged in the experiences of the writer and the frustrations, dreams, and self-delusions of herself and her community. By making herself the center of that community, she orchestrates the experience, observes it, and senses it for her own fulfilment and validation in a way similar to her application of the two proverbs mentioned earlier that she has learned from her mother. One could compare her attitude, albeit an implicit one, toward oral tradition to what is said by the narrator of Malika Mokeddem's *La transe des insoumis* (The trance of the rebellious) (2003): "As for me, tradition is always something I've been against. I'm with tradition when it vibrates with emotion, nourishes the mind, enriches memory. But I stand up to it, in fact I repudiate it, when it freezes over as prohibition and sets itself up as a prison" (25).[21] The two proverbs told by her mother symbolize an oral tradition that nurtures Ève-Marie's spirit, reassures her, and enriches her memory, reminding her of the strong women among her ancestors who did not allow anyone to crush them. Her confidence reinforced, her existence validated, she becomes unshakable. According to the experience and collective memory contained in the two proverbs, the power of the Other is reduced to the level of an imaginary existence: we grant it validity only if we acknowledge it as a force that can control us.

The last sentence in the passage adds a rather surprising twist to this manifesto of the African woman writer. Ève-Marie says that, according no importance to the "little earthly powers," she lies down on her sofa to contemplate the cracks in the ceiling. This suggests a state of reflecting and waiting, neither overly confident nor prematurely discouraged. It is like the state of lucidity referred to by the narrator of *La transe des insoumis*: "it is in insomnia that I unearth lucidity" ["c'est dans l'insomnie que se creuse la lucidité" (25)]. Ève-Marie is waiting for the time when her voice will be affirmed while knowing that there is no guarantee of this happening. It is not an empty state of resignation. The foregoing explanation and analysis of Ève-Marie's artistic enterprise allow us to bring out several important points related to this development in the work of writing, the motivation and the measures to be taken: the desire and even the obligation on the part of an African woman in exile to break out of the private and personal domain that has been assigned to her as her place, to raise her voice, or to speak out in order to participate in the domain of public discourse through the production of a novel. To prohibit her from doing so, the dominant voice, as represented by the publishing house that rejects her manuscript, reminds such a woman of her place outside of the public domain. What logically follows is Ève-Marie's tenacity in not recognizing the voice of the dominant power or allowing it to control her thinking.

Schiappa, in *Defining Reality*, examines the way that those who hold power or have authority use different definitions of the terms *personal*, *public*, and *technical* in different situations in order to include or exclude people from participation in particular discourses or in public conversation. Referring to Jay (1981), Schiappa notes that the distinction between the personal and public domains creates one of the binary oppositions that have long been used to repress women in the world: "The distinction between the personal and the public sphere has been one of the most persistent dichotomies used throughout the history of western civilization to repress women. [. . .] [T]he more entrenched the public-personal dichotomy becomes the more the distinctions drawn typically perpetuate gendered differences" (158). Ève-Marie would add, through the mouth of the "heir to the French Academy," with his gratuitous elitism: . . . the more the African woman's linguistic competence is belittled and denied.

It is precisely to preclude prejudice and any hasty stereotyped conclusion that would designate the black world or Africa as inherently guilty in this regard that Beyala chooses a white couple (Jean-Pierre Pierre and Flora-Flore) as a "typical" and extreme example of dehumanizing domestic violence against women. Jean-Pierre Pierre's acts of violence are central to Ève-Marie's decision to write a novel. By both her actions and her words Ève-Marie abstains from defining her own space in the world as either personal or public so as to avoid subscribing to relations of power that would limit her options, given that the participation of women in public discourse, in the form of writing, is discouraged by means of violence, derision, and sociocultural clichés.

This is what, according to Jamieson (1988), makes women who speak in the public arena, by writing books, for example, suspicious.

Another critic (Elshtain 1982, quoted in Schiappa 158) maintains that current dominant political language, holding in place the public/personal dichotomy, functions as a means of silencing certain individuals: "to silence particular persons or groups and proscribe particular topics and spheres of life from discourse." Ève-Marie refuses to be silenced or crushed. She confirms her personal power by infiltrating several different professions, not allowing, in her discourse, for any topic to be blacked out among the areas of life she has known. In her writing, the dichotomy between the personal and the public remains ambiguous. Ève-Marie subverts the dichotomy through her practice of discourse, which continues to present itself as politically liberating.

The radical positioning of Beyala's discourse, as seen in the example of Ève-Marie's ironic self-initiation into the practice of writing, should not, however, diminish the importance of the relationship between traditional culture, proverbial discourse, and irony that, as a reading of *Les arbres en parlent encore* (2002) shows, plays a key role in the structure and function of Beyala's narrative practice and also suggests a much closer connection than has hitherto been recognized with earlier texts of African literature such as *Arrow of God* and with Ahmadou Kourouma's writing.

Like Kourouma's *En attendant le vote des bêtes sauvages, Les arbres en parlent encore* is organized through the orality-evoking device of the *veillée* and implicitly connects a traditional narrator to a listening audience. *Les arbres en parlent encore* is also initiatory in that it traces the woman protagonist's development within an African traditional community through colonialism into the implied postcolonial world of the narrative present. Beyala's *veillée* differs, however, from Kourouma's in several ways. Instead of exposing a dictator to trial by his peers, Beyala presents the testimony of one elderly woman who had modestly claimed that her father's story *was* the story of Africa (7). After a lifetime of observer status in her father's Africa, she is suddenly put on trial by the colonial authorities. She relates this incident toward the end of the book. Having refused to be beaten up by the old man who was forced on her as a husband, she is now being prosecuted for refusing to hand over her twin boys from another father to the traditionally official husband. Her trial is like a lightning-fast glint of a reflection of Koyaga's *donsomana* in *En attendant le vote de bêtes sauvages*. It in fact mirrors the trial of authority and

abusive patriarchal power. The layered web of ironies that results from
Édène's trial offers a glimpse of Beyala's subversive treatment of the
traditions that she has constructed and deconstructed from within as
an African woman.

The irony that will culminate in the trial scene is already planted in
the way Édène presents her life. Unable to fully possess Chrétien No.
1 because she is not as beautiful and womanly as her weak half sister Opportune des Saintes Guinées, Édène is forced to accept being an
abused second wife to Chrétien No. 1's father, Gazolo. Her defiance and
independent spirit lead her to abort Chrétien No. 1's child, conceived
even before the "marriage" with the child's grandfather, to strike her
husband, to nearly kill Chrétien No. 1, and then to flee the village to
live with her equally rebellious stepmother, Fondamento de Plaisir, in
a brothel-bar. Édène eventually conceives twins of undetermined pa-
ternity. Whether for the sake of patrilineal avidity—eyeing the twins
as potential male descendants—or simply out of a need to reaffirm
male power, Gazolo appeals to the French colonial authority to shore
up his own power, thereby implicitly affirming his lack of it. When the
judgment against her is pronounced by the French commandant Michel Ange de Montparnasse, Édène's only recourse is to remind him
that he himself is responsible for offspring living in her village who
were conceived while he lived with them as a refugee and adopted son.
While no one in the community is ignorant of Michel Ange's numerous métis progeny, it is Édène's verbal irony alone that forces him to
recognize publicly the inconvenience of assuming legal responsibility
for offspring produced outside of the registries of colonial officialdom.
But instead of simply triumphing from the effectiveness of her logic and
discursive brilliance, Édène turns her ironic gaze inward: "Only later I
realized that I owed that happiness to the same colonial system that had
stripped us, including us women and children, of all our wealth and
lands, and that added spice to the farce" (462).[22] Édène's reflection is
neither a sign of second thoughts nor an apology since the "piment" she
alludes to suggests a kind of sensual pleasure, as Achebe suggested in
the meta-proverb according to which proverbial discourse is the palm
oil that enables us to digest words. Yet the consumption of ironic words
and thoughts is at the same time an awareness of self-contradiction, of
empowerment through disempowerment, and of freedom ironically attained both through and in opposition to oppression.

The association that Édène creates in this case between the colonial
judge and the irony of the "native" voice suggests a reading of this novel

in which the theme of trial and judgment frames the story. When Michel Ange de Montparnasse first enters the Issogo community as a stray French soldier from Gabon, Édène is the first person to see him. She mistakes him for a wild pig and then for a "whiteghost," thereby implying her own ironic evaluation of the "new god" who will soon attempt to mystify the village with stereotypical gadgetry and prowess. But it is her father, Assanga Djuli, the patriarch whose story she says is the story of Africa, who first "judges" the future judge. Because Michel Ange sees fit to make fun of his hosts by saying he expects to be cooked and eaten, Assanga Djuli summarily and nonchalantly, and with obvious ironic intent, sends him off to be hanged. At this point, Michel Ange seems to be seriously frightened, though we immediately learn that the condemnation was nothing more than an elaborate "farce," to use the French term for practical joke that Édène applies to her situation in the closing trial. Édène reports that later, after Michel Ange settled in as an adopted member of the community, she asked her father why he had played this practical joke. Assanga replied that Michel Ange "was already carrying death in his head" before stumbling on their village and that in order to run away "he would have to have been aware of his own freedom" (18).[23]

The problem of self-awareness is a major element of the ironical judgment that Beyala has built into this narrative framework. At the beginning of the novel, Michel Ange, with his assumptions of superiority, is discountenanced by the commanding wit of Édène's father. She casts herself at this point in the role of an apprentice, asking her father to explain to her the hidden meaning behind his verbal act. What she appears to learn from her father is that the power of the colonial intruder, the uninvited guest who brings his own stool—like the allegorical Suffering of Achebe's proverb quoted in *Arrow of God*—is founded on a mistaken belief in his own superiority. Assanga Djuli's almost superhuman prophetic foresight enabled him to see that the white man who seemed bound to his Africa and his civilizing mission is in fact a very ordinary human being who on many occasions needs the help of stronger men and women in order to exercise the freedom of action and the control that he automatically assumes to be his. Assanga Djuli's logic is consistent with the fact that when Michel Ange's Issogo wife, Espoir de Vie, tries to send spirits to curse him after his departure from the village, they are unable to locate him and consequently turn their wrath back on the Issogo. Michel Ange's "adoption" by Édène's people was not the romantic "going native" of an extraordinary savior, the irony of which illusion the reader must also accommodate, but rather the right/ rite of association between two equal and equally responsible cultures in which each party had to live with its own commitments. The same Assanga Djuli who was ready to condemn Espoir de Vie for misunderstanding her "hold" over Michel Ange, thereby exposing the community to internal spiritual disruption, is the first to insist on taking her to her husband when the news comes that he has returned as the new French commandant. Michel Ange does not belong to "his" colonized people, there is no mystical union between him and them, but he had freely chosen to live with a woman as his wife and was no less bound by his decision in Assanga's eyes than anyone else.

We can now see that the final judgment scene is a completion of the initial one. Michel Ange has no truly superior place even in the context of his fullest colonial authority. His imposition of French civil law as the legal basis of marriage, while designed to cancel the authority of African tradition, is in reality a tacit admission of that tradition's hold over him as the underlying reality of the people whom he seeks to dominate and control.

Édène uses a graphically symbolic incident at the end of the novel to emphasize the ironic fact that the Other discovers himself through the failure of a selfhood constructed from a supposed and imposed notion of superiority and gratuitous, self-serving "solidarity." In the aftermath of World War II, Michel Ange has scheduled a ceremony "honoring" the Cameroonians who died on the field of battle while helping to save the Republic. Men and women dream of sacks of money sent from France as a well-deserved reward. When Michel Ange concludes the ceremony with a hollow speech and no suggestion of reward, the crowd riots, leaving the commandant with a severed arm he cannot take with him as he departs. The severed arm is an ironic symbol that represents Édène's view of his relationship with the colonized. Neither a true sacrifice—it becomes more ridiculous than sacred—nor an investment in the future, having outlived any usefulness either to France or to Édène's people, the arm is closer to a phallic aftermath, an imaginary and unfruitful emblem of a relationship that never really was, or at least that never was what Michel Ange imagined it to be. Assanga Djuli had already undermined Michel Ange's paternal dignity by producing as a daughter Akouma Labondance, the ape-woman rebel who would publicly expose the governor's nakedness. Although Michel Ange secretly spares Akouma for the sake of his old friendship with her father, even this gesture of solidarity is rendered meaningless by Édène's ironical postscript that places the former rebel half sister in a reestablished position of subalternity: "The moral of the story: some years later I ran into Akouma on a visit to Douala. She looked withered. Her breasts were sagging. Her companion was beating her so much that his hands were white. I said to myself that we'd rather see those we love dead than living a life in the garbage heap" (468).[24] The sparing of Akouma's life becomes in Édène's account a useless exchange between two old men.

The problem of Assanga Djuli's relationship with Michel Ange leads us to suspect that if the colonizer is the primary target of a postcolonial ironic voice, Assanga Djuli, the emblematic subject of the narrative, may also be a more than incidental target of his daughter's irony. He does in fact have an ambiguous connection with both of the framing acts of judgment: the mock death sentence at the beginning of the novel and the judgment against Édène, which is pronounced only to be rescinded, at the end. Immediately the narrative slips into a mythopoetic mode ("In the beginning was the world" [Au commencement, était le monde]), in a text that attempts to explain the origins of racial difference in relation to human conflict. The poem concludes:

> [The spirits] still got bored.
> They painted humans without consulting each other.
> […]
> Boredom begat races;
> Selfishness begat war. (20)[25]

In order to explain the positioning of an ironic voice in this passage, one has to understand the relationship between the meaning of this myth, Édène's exchange with her father, and the colonialist context of that exchange. The concluding lines of the myth suggest that while the "creation" of races was a largely arbitrary and stereotyped act to which only the value of variety should be attached, the root of human conflict is not in this arbitrary difference but in the pride and selfishness of individuals who are bound to build on the arbitrary differences in order to lord it over others. As C. L. R. James noted in his discussion of the Haitian revolution, "The race question is subsidiary to the class question in politics, and to think of imperialism in terms of race is disastrous. But to neglect the racial factor as merely incidental is an error only less grave than to make it fundamental" (283). Arbitrary difference will always be arbitrary, but its concrete political consequences will always be real.

Is this birth of wars the death that Michel Ange, according to Assanga

Djuli, was carrying in his head? It is difficult to know if this sequence is placed here by Édène as an interpretative gloss on her father's cryptic pronouncements or if she is reporting a speech that she recalls her father adding to his more prosaic answer to her question. There is, however, an implicit polyphonic effect resulting from Édène's reproduction of Assanga's cryptic statements about Michel Ange. Polyphony also underlies the abrupt insertion of a mythic tale, a different form of language that normally represents a collective voice and thus cannot easily be assigned to an individual fictional character.

Through this polyphonic intervention, Édène positions herself as a witness both to her father's wisdom and to the possibility of a complementary wisdom and knowledge that either belongs to the whole community and reaches the reader and listener through her or has actually accrued to her through her bildungsroman conveying her experience of colonial history. Although at this point in the novel there is little to suggest a competitive stance on the part of this woman's voice, later developments, including Assanga Djuli's rather conventional and disloyal reaction to his daughter's self-affirming struggle with an abusive husband and his own occasional recourse to physical violence, will bring about a subtle change in the way Édène modalizes her language about her father.

With the second judgment sequence at the end of the novel (454–62), Édène, on seeing the people of her village arrive, hides "to observe them better" [pour mieux les observer (455)]. The person summoned to judgment assumes the place of a judge in relation to the people she has been working to represent from the beginning of her narrative. Among the others, she sees her parents: "Papa and Mama were no exception to the rule, and after a long life together, had ended up looking alike. They were bald. Their faces were craggy and on their dried out hands the veins protruded like the roots of a wild mango tree. They were standing up a few feet away from me, so near to each other that their heads almost touched each other. I had the impression I was experiencing an illusion and I remained perfectly still" (455).[26] There is nothing very surprising in this description of an ordinary old couple, unless the reader did not realize the seriousness of the rupture caused by Édène's departure. The distance that now separates her from her parents evokes a strong sense of both personal and social alienation. She watches them from her hidden vantage point, like strangers transformed into the spectacle of physical and social decay. In her prologue, Édène had described Assanga as a towering tree: "He was as tall as a baobab and in his black eyes was concentrated the serene force of a Roman pope" (7).[27] We know that at the time of Édène's trial, he has even been replaced by Gazolo as chief of the Issogos.

After a life of spectacular and at times socially disruptive polygamy, Édène's father appears in her eyes reduced to a conventional partnership with a conventional partner (Édène's mother) whom he now resembles. In the same way that their heads are now almost joined, the near-epic proportions of the earlier Assanga are assimilated with the wife whom he once ignored or scorned for the sake of prestige or egocentric infatuation. Édène has in fact succeeded in turning her father's patriarchal wisdom—judging the dominant Other to be carrying death in his mind—and her mother's submissive-conventional proverbial wisdom back on themselves, back on the earlier colonial generation. Her parents' generation had mediated the "death" that was in the colonizer's mind into a hybrid form of oppression passed on to a second colonized generation, an example being Édène's suffering at the hands of Gazolo. Yet the illusion that Édène feels she is living through in secretly observing this aged couple is not only Assanga's reduction to human proportions but the notion that he and his wife are now somehow equal, quasi-identical partners in life. Édène's experience of family life is founded largely on the marginalization of her mother through Assanga's successive infatuations with other women. Following Perrin's analysis of raillery, one could say that Édène is discrediting any reading of this scene that would interpret it as a sign of social harmony and closure.

From her hidden vantage point, Édène hears a private dialogue between her parents that allows her to go even further in this ironic turning back on her original subject, namely, Assanga's story as the story of Africa. As if for the first time, Assanga notices that Édène's mother, Andela, has grown thin. Since they have shared the same compound for decades, we have to assume that this remark is meant to imply that Assanga has never particularly thought about Andela's health, state of being, or efforts in life, all of which would be reflected in her present physical state. At the risk of generalizing a little, we might say that in an African context, a woman's thinness often suggests suffering and hardship. His second reflection is that Andela has been his wife since the age of twelve, or thirteen, as Andela rectifies. He seems to suddenly realize that she had no life at all outside of her connection with him, such that the entire responsibility for her

existence has been thoughtlessly given to him. When Andela wonders why he is only now thinking about the passage of time (presum-
ably interpreting his question as a sign of his impending death), he
answers by suggesting that their shared life was intentional and coherent at least from his point of view and by hoping that she has no
regrets. Suspicious, as are Édène and perhaps we, her readers, that
Assanga is conveying a hidden message through this "small talk,"
Andela answers: "What exactly would you like me to tell you? You
want me to reassure you that I'll take good care of your memory after
your death?" (455).[28] Édène has always presented her father as a practitioner of hidden meaning and double entendre. In a sense, that is
the guiding theme of Édène's narrative as a memorial to traditional
discourse: "He was an old man in the Eton sense of the term, that is
to say that a magnetizing light gave him the power to mask his true
thoughts" (7).[29] In this last example of masked thought at the colonial
courthouse, Édène unmasks her father as a *vieillard* in a somewhat
less Eton sense. His hidden thoughts are still hidden and displayed at
the same time, but they are full not only of the anticipation of death
but also of worry about who will care for his memory. Moreover,
both his wife and his daughter are able to read his "hidden" message
so easily that the power of irony has effectively passed from his hands
to theirs. When the intended receiver of an ironic message shows
herself already ahead of the game, shows that she has read the hidden
meaning and finds it no more significant than the explicit meaning
of the utterance, she has switched the ironic effect to her own subjec-
tivity as a receiver who has already processed and laid claim to the
implied sense.

The ironic effect of Édène's representation of her father is not simply
that she has found her own ironic voice—the whole novel and its tone
are proof enough of that—but that she has significantly modified the
social and cultural ownership of ironic discourse in relation to men, in
relation to the father, and in relation to the colonial master. But with
the change in ownership comes also a change in style and method and
ultimately a change in content. The new ironist has not only a new target and audience but also a new purpose, notably the emancipation and
fulfilment of women, even though that new purpose does not preclude
a memorial function in relation to the ironist-father she claims to have
originally intended to reveal.

A complex shift in ironic discourse is further elaborated in subsequent encounters as Édène concludes her story. When Assanga Djuli

dies a few days after the trial, Édène begins by suggesting a logical connection with that event. "From the very next day, Papa decided to die, as
if he wanted to avoid taking this path of madness into which the black
continent was plummeting" (462).[30] This path of madness would logically refer to his daughter's colonially supported triumph over patriarchy, which Assanga cannot accept. Édène still sees her father's passing
as the instauration of a profound disorder, a "cacophonie des existences"
left in the wake of this social and political father figure: "My God did
I suffer afterwards from watching humanity squirming, singing, fuck-
ing, while no trace remains of my father!" (464).[31] Of course her life did
continue, and even his funeral is seen both as a departure from tradition ("His funeral was strange" [Ses obsèques furent étranges]) and as
a mixed, ironic commentary on the value attached to him as a leader of
the Africa of Édène's past ("Some came out of duty, others in the hope
of getting into the good books of Mama . . . Some out of curiosity, others to make sure that there would be lots of people at their own funer-
als" [465]).[32] There is very little in Édène's account to suggest the passing of a leader whose story was the story of Africa. Even Andela sees her
widowhood as the harvest of the fruit of her years of sacrifice, as if her
long unrewarded alliance with Assanga has little to do with any feelings of respect toward him.

While returning from the burial, Édène is met by Michel Ange,
who significantly did not attend the funeral and whose secret purpose
is to reveal to her that he recognizes his debt to Assanga although that
recognition could not be acknowledged publicly. This recognition is
an allusion to the first judgment and to the freedom of being Assanga
taught him. But his second secret purpose is to reveal to Édène that he
has repaid his debt to Assanga by sparing Akouma Labondance from
death by execution after her arrest as the rebel ape-woman. Though
Édène is initially shaken by the news, she presents as the moral of the
story the fact that Akouma's life turned out to be uninspiring and
insignificant. The colonialist's mercy, his gift that is designed to convince Édène of the authenticity of his desire to be buried in the Africa he loves, turns out to be an empty gift. Although this judgment is
directly related to Akouma's fate, it could also be seen as a reflection
of the postcolonial conditions in which the colonialist's gift of civilizing love is worse than worthless. Édène's ironic treatment of Michel
Ange's news and of the peace of mind that he sought to procure for
himself with it evokes the colonialist as the giver, the father as the
dead recipient—a memory of tradition and community—and the lost

half sister as an unsatisfactory vestige of resistance to both male and colonial oppression.

Beyala's African women ironists, as represented by figures such as Ève-Marie and Édène, are like the woman given birth by another woman out of respect. She is able to seize what patriarchy and colonialism threatened her with—the forbidden space in which she did not belong. She has learned tradition as a woman, though that tradition sought to deny her (sometimes even through her mother's own voice), and yet it is from out of that tradition that she is able to speak of re-creation.

When the Handshake Has Become Another Thing

I have emphasized linguistic and pragmatic approaches to irony, not because I expected to invent a new method of analysis, but because I was and still am convinced that in addition to being an artistic medium, African literary discourse is a particular form of pragmatic communication intimately connected with cultural and historical problems of identity, oppression, and voice. It is important to confront some of the major issues of irony, according to recent theoretical models, with issues of representation and narrative voice raised by such authors as Achebe, Kourouma, and Beyala.

The preceding analyses have also shown that the problem of irony in African literature and cultural traditions is too complex, controversial, and multifaceted to be discussed within the limits of one or two models, schools of thought, or even disciplines. Irony is a problem of language, but it is also one of behaviors, intentionality, interpersonal relationships, community, and history. Irony is not only a problem for the (ex-)colonizer and the (ex-)colonized but a problem for the old and the young, and for men and women: a barrier, an arm, a refuge, a lesson, a dry smile of ambivalent complicity.

The limits of various approaches to irony become apparent in the light of both critical literature and the needs arising from their application to African culture. Wayne Booth's discussion of the difference between stable and unstable irony is significant because under the growing influence of reader-response theory in the latter part of the

twentieth century, he was concerned with the dynamic interaction between two poles of communicative process or event: the implied author and the reader. Booth's notion of "stable irony" reflects the need
to establish structural limits to the plausible meanings of a text. Such
boundaries would reveal themselves to be more and more difficult to
maintain in the face of the growing power and complexity of theories
and narratives of difference—not the least of which has been that of Africanity, caught in the double bind of self-affirmation and the admission of its own hybridity.

In general, theories of irony such as that of Kaufer, based on semantic hierarchies, with an initial, apparent interpretation to be rejected
in favor of a second, intended meaning, run into difficulty on several
fronts. Because of their emphasis on lexical interpretation, they rely
heavily on textual and/or co-textual signals and thereby offer little help
in knowing how to account for situational context and oral or gestural
conditions of communication in the relationship between speaker and
audience. Kohvakka's schema of concentric contextual levels of contradiction goes a long way toward clarifying the locus of the contradiction
that signals the presence of irony, but as Berrendonner has argued, contradiction alone is not necessarily a sign of irony, so that a further step
is still needed to reach a convincing means of predicting ironic understanding or intent. Kerbrat-Orecchioni's approach attempts to situate
irony at the level of connotative semes, where the figurative meaning of
an ironic utterance—what the ironist is really getting at—becomes the
denotative meaning and the ironic form becomes the utterance's connotation. Although this allows us to discern micro-semantic contradictions in textual environments more effectively, the flaunt/flout problem
in *Anthills of the Savannah* being a prime example, her decision to view
irony as a trope or "figure of meaning" rather than a "figure of thought"
ensures, according to Perrin, continued dependence on antiphrasis and
consequently failure to recognize the crucial role played by the speaker's attitude toward what he or she is saying.

Both Perrin and Berrendonner argue against the primary role of antiphrasis in the production of irony and propose pragmatics-based explanations in which the role of antiphrasis becomes secondary, functioning as a source of semantic specification at best. For the latter, irony
consists primarily of an argumentative ambiguity. To qualify as ironic,
an utterance must present an argumentative value. Once that value is
established, the ironist uses the effect of mention to discredit the point
of view he or she is apparently advocating. This is made possible by the

"multiple coded nature of communication," which is to say that just as more than one code can be employed in a given act of communication, more than one viewpoint can be represented and more than one audience can be called upon to interpret what is conveyed. The argumentative function of irony, according to Berrendonner, is largely defensive because it allows the ironist to deny the negative implications of his or her reference to the discourse of the real or potential opponent.

While also according a central place to mention, Perrin emphasizes the importance of raillery and thereby gives irony a much more aggressive and discursively destructive edge than did Berrendonner's pragmatics. But the two theorists offer important ideas for the understanding of irony in African literary discourse. African writing began as an alienated discourse, with texts such as *Force-Bonté* and *Batouala*, and then struggled to stake a claim to self-expression through ironic imitation, with feigned naïveté, of the discourse of the colonizer (see Ferdinand Oyono's *Une vie de boy* and Mongo Beti's *Le pauvre Christ de Bomba*), through cultural celebration of African historical agency (*Things Fall Apart* and Bernard Dadié's *Béatrice du Congo*), and through images of collective action (Ousmane Sembène's *Les Bouts de bois de Dieu* and Ayi Kwei Armah's *Two Thousand Seasons*). African writers eventually sought, through satirical criticism, to denounce a marked deterioration of African self-respect related to corrupt and repressive regimes (for example, Ousmane Sembène's *Xala* and Kourouma's play *Le diseur de vérité*). Through this history of searching and speaking, the voice of the Other has never ceased to be either foregrounded or implied as an underlying issue. The narrative forms vary widely from dialogue and direct quotation, to free indirect speech, to stylistic imitation. A striking example in recent years is Henri Lopes's *Le lys et le flamboyant* (The lily and the flame-of-the-forest) (1997), in which the narrator, Victor-Augagneur Houang, struggles with another métis, "Henri Lopes," to tell the story of Kolélé, a popular singer who has become a national icon. The narrative from its inception is presented as a rectified, more intimate portrait of Kolélé than the one presented in an earlier text he attributes to Lopes. Then, at the end of the novel, we discover that Lopes got to the publisher before Victor, leaving us with the impression that the fictional Lopes, like the implied author Lopes, is the traitor-usurper of the narrative voice.

We have seen also how the problem of the ironic voice is closely related to the right to voice, particularly in the case of women authors. Beyala's Ève-Marie of *Amours sauvages*, in defending her right to speak

as an author, cites the voices of both canonical and patriarchal authority in order to display and discredit their power to suppress her as well
as their power to convince the very people she seeks to represent of the
absence of value in their own stories.

In this sense, there is good reason to believe that African literary
discourse incorporates at least three major elements of Berrondonner's
and Perrin's pragmatics of irony: mention as the primary discursive
act signaling irony; an argumentative value, since irony was needed as
an arm in multiple and complex situations of oppression and suppression; and raillery, in that there was a real need to take one's distance
from a voice that one was forced to imitate. At the same time, Norrick's
curious conviction that irony is essentially absent from proverbial discourse leads us to believe that a theory of irony appropriate to African
culture is needed in order to show that the argumentative and didactic
character of traditional wisdom can be used in a way that subverts the
voice of another implied speaker, thus making irony for Africans a significant part of both traditional and modern literary discourse.

This possibility of subversion suggests, however, that Berrendonner's
emphasis on the defensive posture inherent in the use of irony constitutes a major divergence from the practical conditions of ironic language in African culture. While it is true that irony generally offers the
speaker the way out of denying the original ironic intention, this does
not necessarily mean that the original intention was itself defensive.
We have seen, for example, in *En attendant le vote des bêtes sauvages*
that when the *koroduwa*'s railing is apparently suppressed but in fact
complemented by the *sèrè*'s raillery, the purpose of irony can be both
aggressive and destructive. In a text such as *Arrow of God*, which focuses on a crisis of traditional authority, irony can be used to question
that authority, whereas Édène's narrative strategies in *Les arbres en parlent encore* illustrate the vast potential for irony and self-affirmation to
coincide.

Studies such as Pexman's, which suggest a relationship between disadvantaged social status and the frequent recourse to sarcasm and irony,
seem to fit well into the general problematic of subalternity. Utsumi's
implicit display theory, while in itself limiting because of its failure to
recognize multiple voices, audiences, and purposes behind the use of
irony, offers the advantage of indirectly revealing a sense of failed expectations. While the writings of Achebe as well as of Kourouma evoke
weighty failed expectations on both the social and political fronts,
Beyala complicates and internalizes this sense of failed expectations

through awareness of the voice of the Other that scorns and excludes her, even when that voice is as close to self as neighbor, mother, or father. In *Amours sauvages*, Ève-Marie recalls the proverbial discourse of her mother as a means of self-affirmation, yet that same mother discourages her by refusing to validate her fantasy of "arrival" and integration as a successful immigrant in French society. Again, in *Les arbres en parlent encore*, in which a representation of traditional society is emphatic and not entirely negative, Édène's own mother, Andela, is characterized by a conventional and rather uncreative use of proverbial discourse designed largely to express spite and envy. Édène as narrator is ultimately responsible for the ironic deconstruction of her mother's socialization, although she is perfectly aware of her father's contradictions as well as the selfishness and cynicism of her stepmother, Fondamento.

If some insights have been gained into theories and methods of analysis that are appropriate and effective in the context of African literature, there remain several open-ended and difficult questions to which this study can only suggest possible answers as African literatures continue on the road to and of self-understanding. Some of these questions are technical in nature and have more to do with the discussion of linguistic theories in relation to artistic media. The study of irony itself is notoriously problematic in this regard, breeding a rich but awkward cohabitation, as, for example, of literary theory (Wayne Booth, Jonathan Culler, Philippe Hamon), stylistics (Kauffer, Kerbrat-Orecchioni), *Textlinguistik* (Kohvakka, Lapp), pragmatics (Berrendonner, Perrin), and even cultural studies and postmodernism (Hutcheon, Rice). Many of these positions overlap, and no one has attempted to explain systematically exactly why the same object has been subject to so much methodological and epistemological difference, despite Muecke's effort to broaden and fine-tune the definition of irony. Certainly the stylist who examines textual and literary representation of verbal irony is not oblivious to the possibility of similar uses of ironic language in everyday life. The theoretical linguist who is looking for a model of verbal behavior that can be confirmed in experiments with children or adult subjects also knows that any explanatory model with potential general application is likely to be effective in describing the way authors perceive human interaction as aesthetically represented events, whether in the form of drama, dialogue, or narration. Literature is a form of discourse among others but also a discourse on discourse, a linguistic medium concerned with itself, among other things. In this sense, the review of some linguistic theories related to irony in the context of fiction does not claim to advance the precision or rigor of those theories but rather to show that the explanation of irony is itself an endeavor that occupies the intersection of language as a means of human interaction, as a critique of that interaction, and as a mode of creative endeavor.

More pressing questions arise concerning the cultural and historical context of the types of irony examined in this study. If we admit that what we have encountered reflects a tendency in various postcolonial societies to respond in certain ways to a cataclysmic change in codes of linguistic and social behavior, does this give us a broad enough picture of African literary discourse? Besides the geopolitical issues—the size and limits of African culture in relation to the problem of diaspora, overarching representations that would have to include many vastly different cultural traditions—how far does the use of the term *African* go in affirming either racialized or Afrocentric presuppositions? There is also the question of manifestly ancient oral traditions and the many colonial writings from authors such as Amos Tutuola and the first novels of Mongo Beti, which, though mentioned in this study, have not been analyzed as ironic discourse. Is irony, as a centerpiece of the struggle for voice, not only to be heard but also to be heard for oneself at the expense of a borrowed, overthrown, and discredited Other's voice, more characteristic of postcolonial African literature than of African literature in general?

To a certain extent, the texts we have considered do provide some answers to these questions. Although they are postcolonial in perspective as well as in time, they show a remarkable amount of interest in the colonial experience, even reaching back to the earliest encounters between the colonizer and the colonized. The ironic scene of encounter between the colonial chief and the local authority, complete with the double play of the interpreter who (mis)represents the Other in relation to his own people, occurs strikingly in *Arrow of God* (Moses and the white foreman, Ezeulu and the Court Messenger), *Monnè, outrages et défis* (Djigui, the French officer, and the interpreter), and *Les arbres en parlent encore* (Assanga Djuli, the German commander, and the interpreter Monsieur Taxes, in a scene later ironically "replayed" between Édène and Michel Ange).

The texts discussed in this volume also show a deep engagement with oral tradition. Since African oral tradition was a subject of denigration and ridicule, postcolonial African writers can hardly be expected to play the naive role of representing traditional beliefs, ideas, or modes of discourse without taking a critical and questioning perspective alongside the denigrating voice of their detractors. This positioning can range from the need to show the other side of things, as in Achebe's then iconoclastic painting of Igbo culture, to the in-your-face sarcasm of Kourouma's "hommes nus." In each case, however, the problem of tradition as a construction of meaning and belief is inherently related to the cultivation of a strategically ironic tone of voice.

At the same time, Beyala's demonstrable importance as a practitioner of ironic discourse in terms of volume, complexity, and subtlety is significant. This suggests a direct relationship between what I have described as a struggle for voice through the ironic mode and the rise of African women's determination to achieve self-creative freedom as well as social, political, and cultural empowerment. Furthermore, the diasporic situation of Beyala herself is directly reflected in the themes of *Amours sauvages*. It is highly significant as well that Ève-Marie's effort to be a writer can be conceived only in the context of an already displaced cultural community, precisely because the desire to write arises from the need to bring that community into focus for her, for itself, and for the world. Yet that taking up of a cause can be ironic only because that same community, hegemonically still colonized, does not spontaneously recognize its own voice and hope in Ève-Marie's unauthorized use of language.

In a sense, *Les arbres en parlent encore* also combines irony and diaspora. Although Édène never leaves the colonial locus as far as we know, her departure from her village to live with Fondamento de Plaisir, the symbolic "colportrice" of global consumerism and sexuality, is a diasporic movement that challenges and disrupts the "Africanity" of her own narrative world and creates a space of change and rupture. The "return" to her people becomes at that point the ironic gaze, verbalized through the narration of the book, which makes the critical equation of Assanga Djuli's story with that of Africa itself profoundly ambivalent, perhaps the novel's greatest irony.

There is, finally, a difficult question that remains: the political usefulness and significance of ironic discourse in the African societies represented by authors such as Achebe, Kourouma, and Beyala. This question is related to the problem Lapp refers to in defining irony as a verbal behavior. Is there something that can be said through ironic expression that cannot or should not be said otherwise? It would be absurd to argue that irony belongs to one culture more than another or even more so that irony is something to be outgrown. But the struggle for voice and the irrepressible imperative of responding to denigration by others that translates into a shifting multiple perspective in many postcolonial African texts could conceivably give way to other configurations as the memories of old colonies fade and new forms of oppression—including globalization—and resistance emerge in Africa and throughout the world.

NOTES

INTRODUCTION

1. A trend in the field of archaeology started in the 1960s, moving away from emphasis on cultural history and diffusionism toward a claim to more rigorous scientific method. See Trigger 1989.

2. Gates rarely uses the term *irony* in what was no doubt intended to be a work of cultural differentiation. But in that he defines black tradition as "double-voiced," he evokes a terrain closely tied to verbal irony as a discourse of double meaning. He recognizes this relatedness when he describes a sixteenth-century black poet (Latino) "signifying" about King Philip of Spain: "This subtle and witty use of irony is among the most common forms of Signifyin(g)" (90).

3. John Lyons (26) translates énonciation as "utterance-act," which Benveniste defines as "the actualization of language by an individual act of use." The term *utterance agent* will be used in the sense of énonciateur, the person or viewpoint to whom the speaker's beliefs are imputed: this person or viewpoint could represent the speaker himself or herself, whether a character or a narrator, but it could also represent an implied author or someone else whose thinking it is alluding to, with an opinion at variance with that of the person actually pronouncing the words. That is why two (or more) utterance-agents can appear in the words of the same speaker.

4. "Dominée par la clarté d'un journal rédigé au quotidien [par Denis], l'écriture semble […] viser par cette recherche d'une plus grande clarté à situer le personnage du prédicateur lui-même dans une plus grande lumière."

5. See Tobner 17.

6. According to the *New Princeton Encyclopedia of Poetry and Poetics*, "[i]n irony proper, the speaker is conscious of double meaning and the victim unconscious; in *sarcasm* both parties understand the double meaning" (634). This does not preclude the possibility that the victim may only become aware of the double meaning later on, so that the subtlety of irony eventually turns into the humiliating bite of sarcasm.

7. "peignent indifféremment des dictateurs sanguinaires qui, aux lendemains des indépendances des États africains, ont accaparé le pouvoir, transformé leur pays en goulags et leurs concitoyens en bagnards sans recours."

8. "Il n'y a dès lors plus de doute que l'exclusion et la marginalisation dont sont frappés leurs 'héros' au niveau paratextuel et énonciatif, participent d'une stratégie délibérée et consciente des deux écrivains."

9. "'L'indépendance' du chef par rapport aux auxiliaires du pouvoir que sont la police, la 'coopération technique' et les partis politiques (pouvoir et opposition) induit une déliquescence du pouvoir lui-même et des centres éclatés de décision qui se trouvent dès lors divisés en groupuscules indépendants d'un pouvoir central inexistant."

10. In *L'Implicite*, Kerbrat-Orecchioni distinguishes between context as the totality of referential factors rendering a given utterance intelligible and co-text as the words and sentences surrounding the utterance in a text (see 300).

11. It is also interesting to note that Kourouma's first novel, *Les soleils des indépendances*, is punctuated by a proverb at the beginning of each chapter.

12. As V. Y. Mudimbe (76) points out, even when some anthropologists evoked the "possibility of interpretation [of African societies] from a new perspective" based on more immediate experience of those societies, "the methodological rules remained essentially the same. They [. . .] still imply that Africans must evolve from their frozen state to the dynamism of Western civilization."

1. FROM RHETORIC TO SEMANTICS

1. "L'école où je pousse nos enfants tuera en eux ce qu'aujourd'hui nous aimons et conservons avec soin, à juste titre. Peut-être notre souvenir lui-même mourra-t-il en eux" (63–64).

2. "Le projet littéraire de Chinua Achebe s'inscrit dans la littérature en anglais comme un anti-roman sur l'Afrique: il veut démontrer que Joseph Conrad dans *Au coeur des ténèbres* (1902) et Joyce Cary dans *Mister Johnson* (1939) n'épuisent pas la matière romanesque africaine."

3. See Garnier (104–5) for a discussion of the relationship between irony and humor in Kourouma's fiction.

4. "seule à notre avis peut valablement être portée au compte du transport esthétique l'ironie par dramatisation en ce qu'elle est bien le reflet de la vivacité de la parole

africaine et constitue en même temps un témoignage sans équivoques de l'art verbal africain généralement célébré dans les veillées de conte au clair de lune lorsque sont mises en scène pour être raillées les attitudes et les façons d'être ou de faire des êtres et des choses."

5. Other examples of such ruptures are the division of ethnic groups through imposed national borders, the creation of artificial ethnic hatred that in some cases leads to acts of genocide, and reduced knowledge of native languages due to compulsory learning of colonial languages.

6. Koyaga is a ruthless dictator in the Gulf Republic who has taken power and holds on to it by violent means. A ritual council of hunters (Koyaga's brotherhood) has been convoked to review Koyaga's life and politics. This event, called a *donsomana*, resembles both a trial and a purification ritual. Its social, political, and moral function is complex and ambivalent (heaping epic compliments and various accusations on the same subject).

7. "L'image d'une Afrique subsaharienne précoloniale vivant dans le chaos, sans organisations politiques véritables et sans États est restée longtemps prégnante en France, comme dans les autres pays occidentaux."

8. See, for example, Yambo Ouologuem's *Le Devoir de violence* (1968).

9. "[. . .] est un chantre, un aède qui dit les exploits des chasseurs and encense les héros chasseurs" (9).

10. "[. . .] est un initié en phase purificatoire, en phase cathartique. Tiécoura est un cordoua et comme tout cordoua il fait le bouffon, le pitre, le fou. Il se permet tout et il n'y rien qu'on ne lui pardonne pas" (10).

11. Deixis is a use of language in which "the referent is identified on the basis of the environment in which the utterance takes place" (Blakemore 66). For example, "today" can make sense only in reference to the time and place in which the word is uttered. Such terms are also called "shifters."

12. See Gagiano's discussion of Achebe's methods (60).

13. "Ce n'est pas difficile, dit Silmang Kamara, il m'a suffi de penser à une quelconque canaille, c'est tout. Nous connaissons tous des canailles et j'ai eu l'un d'eux constamment à l'esprit en faisant ce travail. Voilà ma méthode artistique."

14. As this example suggests, it is storytellers of oral tradition who use both proverbs and irony most frequently and compellingly. (See Okpewho; Ogunjimi and Na'Allah.)

15. "[L]e roi eut la force de se redresser et de s'achever de sa propre main pour honorer son serment: 'Moi vivant les nazaréens n'enteront pas à Sikasso!'" (21).

16. "Lorsque nous parlons d'ironie 'référentielle', nous entendons bien que le référent est, déjà, un objet sémiologique."

17. The verb *flaunt* is defined by the *New Shorter Oxford English Dictionary* as "1. display oneself ostentatiously or impudently; 2. flutter or wave proudly; 3. flout (often considered to be erroneous)." The verb *flout* is defined as "treat

or behave with disdain; mock, jeer; express contempt (for) by action or speech. Now usually denoting indirect expression: openly disregard (a law, an opinion, etc.)." Chris's first level of meaning, as he "corrects" the Attorney General, is based on the claim that the right word would be *flout*, as defined here, that is, openly disregard the will of the people. At a second, or ironic, level, Chris is suggestively alluding to the "correct" meanings of *flaunt* (senses 1 and 2 in the dictionary): impudently displaying a propaganda-generated "will of the people" in order to circumvent any real respect for people's freedom to choose their own leader.

18. The President had promised to visit Abazon, the rebellious fourth province of Kangan, but later changed his mind, while still declaring to his cabinet that as a soldier he is bound to keep his word. In the meantime, Chris, the Commissioner for Information, has relayed the President's initial promise to Ikem, the editor of the national *Gazette*, who has in turn commented on the promise in an editorial, thereby placing both his friend Chris and the President in an awkward position. This explains the Attorney General's reference to Ikem as a saboteur (see particularly page 45).

2. INTERPRETING IRONY

1. "Une jeune femme était allongée sur le plancher. Personne ne l'avait jamais vue dans le quartier, ni croisée, voilà pourquoi je la surnommai Mlle Personne."

2. "Le soir de l'enterrement, sans qu'aucune menace de pluie l'ait justifié, la nuit opaque s'est épaissie au point que seuls les hiboux au vol puissant pouvaient la fendre. Nous les avons vus venir sans surprise, mais ne les attendions pas si nombreux. C'est par centaines que les grands ducs envahirent le Bolloda, et, tard dans la nuit, ululèrent, huèrent et holèrent. De nos cases, nous étions convaincus qu'ils organisaient à leur manière les funérailles du défunt qui était sûrement le chef de la confrérie des mangeurs d'âmes, ces sorciers qui se travestissent en hiboux pour détruire le principe vital des victimes qui leur sont offertes" (200).

3. "Figure par laquelle on veut faire entendre le contraire de ce qu'on dit."

4. "L'attribution conjointe des deux propriétés au même objet produit donc bien une contradiction."

5. See Amadou Koné's remark that in *Monné, outrages et défis*, Kourouma creates a "double representation de la réalité [...] où le roi Djigui et les siens voient et tentent de vivre une réalité qui objectivement est une réalité fictive" (37).

6. "[La métaphore] remplit alors une fonction argumentative, et [...] la contradiction qui la fonde aboutit à conjoindre deux valeurs d'argument incompatibles. Tel est souvent le cas dans les métaphores animales."

7. "A la sixième lune, dit Édène, les épis de maïs deviennent si jaunes qu'ils

rendent limpide la pensée des hommes. Les eaux se reposent; les serpents oublient de mordre; les oiseaux ne construisent pas leurs nids; les parents ne donnent pas d'ordres et les enfants peuvent briser tout ce qui leur tombe sous la main.

"Et cette sixième lune-là, un éblouissement nous arriva. Il fut si intense que la plupart d'entre nous n'eurent plus envie de lever les yeux. Si je me souviens bien, cela se passa au moment où Michel Ange de Montparnasse décida de nous quitter: 'Je dois servir la République française!' nous avait-il dit."

8. "'Vous savez comme je vous estime', ' Votre bonté me bouleverse'— des compliments en manche de veste—des compliments qui se retournent à volonté en blâme."

9. "Ironiser, ce serait produire un énoncé en l'utilisant non comme *emploi* (pour parler de la réalité), mais comme *mention* (pour parler de lui, et signifier la distance qu'on prend à son égard). L'ironie s'apparenterait ainsi à un fait de discours rapporté."

10. "ces mentions sont interprétées comme l'écho d'un énoncé ou d'une pensée dont le locuteur entend souligner le manque de justesse ou de pertinence."

11. "Une confession écrite dans ne langue étrangère est toujours un mensonge. C'est dans la langue de Baudelaire que nous mentons. On racontera de préférence ce qui est facile à exprimer, ou laissera de côté tel fait par paresse de recourir au dictionnaire. On comprendra aisément que cette historie racontée dans notre dialecte n'aurait plus la même teneur.

"Notre existence n'avait rien de spectaculaire. Mais mon émotion en vous transmettant ces souvenirs est sincère et intense."

12. "Faire de l'ironie [...] c'est s'inscrire en faux contre sa propre énonciation tout en l'accomplissant."

13. "Il importe peu que l'ironie soit morale ou non. L'essentiel [...] est qu'il s'agit d'une manœuvre à fonction fondamentalement *défensive*."

14. Other examples include Ken Bugul's unmasking of the dignified white man's secret violence toward women in *Cendres et braises* (1994) and Calixthe Beyala's depiction in *Amours sauvages* (1999) of an abusive white husband who attempts to attribute the consequences of his own sadistic violence to his black neighbors.

3. PRAGMATICS AND AHMADOU KOUROUMA'S (POST)COLONIAL STATE

1. From his detailed and precise semantic and syntactic study of Kourouma's use of French in *Les soleils des indépendances*, Makhily Gassama concludes that Kourouma "has emptied the words of France of their Gallic content in order to fill them, in the manner of Malinke hawkers, with new merchandise for the francophone to consume" [a vidé les mots de France

de leur contenu gaulois pour les charger, comme des colporteurs malinké, de nouvelles marchandises, proposées à la consommation du francophone] (118).

2. I am grateful to R. Miller for his assistance in the translation of key passages of this book from German.

3. Kourouma's writing does offer examples of antiphrasis, as shown by Annik Doquire Kerszberg (119), who quotes the narrator of *Allah n'est pas obligé* . . . speaking about "les droits de la femme" (34) and notes that the expression is ironic because it means precisely the opposite. Since this is an example of sarcastic irony (explicit and biting antiphrasis), it underscores the need to understand the pragmatic function of Kourouma's ironic stance in relation to the sociocultural contexts he is writing in and about.

4. "avec Ramsès II et Soundiata l'un des trois plus grand chasseurs de l'humanité" (9).

5. "grain de sel" (10). Sélom Komlan Gbanou (55) places the *sora (sèrè* in the English translation) at the center of the purification ritual: "The ceremonial seriousness with which the *sèrè*—narrator/story-teller of the *donsomana*—exposes the official and unofficial biographies of the character gives to his presentation connotations that are at the same time humorous, witty and impartial." [Le sérieux cérémonial avec lequel le Sora—narrateur-conteur du *donsomana*—expose les biographies officielle et non officielle du personnage donne à sa présentation une connotation à la fois humoristique, spirituelle, grave et impartiale.] The reader could easily miss the embedded comic side of the *sèrè*'s discourse without the counterpoint effect of the *koroduwa*.

6. "—Président, général et dictateur Koyaga, nous chanterons et danserons votre *donsomana* en cinq veillées. Nous dirons la vérité. La vérité sur votre dictature. La vérité sur vos parents, vos collaborateurs. Toute la vérité sur vos saloperies, vos conneries; nous dénoncerons vos mensonges, vos nombreux crimes et assassinats . . . " (10).

7. "Arrête d'injurier un grand homme d'honneur et de bien comme notre père de la nation Koyaga. Sinon la malédiction et le malheur te poursuivront et te détruiront. Arrête donc! Arrête!" (10).

8. Sélom Komlan Gbanou (2002: 57–58) points out that contradictory "*sous-entendus*" associated with Koyaga's titles (hunter, president, and dictator) contribute to the distance created between the myth and the reality of Koyaga's symbolic role.

9. "L'ironie ne saurait [. . .] être assimilée à une simple inversion de la signification des mots et des phrases puisqu'elle consiste avant tout à se moquer de quelqu'un en feignant d'adhérer et de chercher à faire croire à ce qui est précisément exprimé littéralement."

10. "L'écriture se situe dans cette épreuve: faire le point entre deux polarités du même sujet, respectivement entretenues par une rhétorique d'État

fossoyeuse de légendes et par une rhétorique de contestation encline à un portrait pathologique de son objet."

11. "l'effet le plus immédiat de ces jeux de miroir est de mettre le lecteur dans une posture instable. On ne sait jamais dans quel récit on est, celui du narrateur ou celui du personnage."

12. This game of deception is explained in structural terms by Bisanswa (16) as a "doubling of the 'I' as narrator and narratee, the second constantly measuring up the first" [dédoublement du je narrateur-narrataire, le second jaugeant constamment le premier]. This doubling can also be explained in pragmatic terms as a game of identity and (shirked) responsibility on the part of the speaking actors, the imagined or intended spectators, and the reader.

13. "asservit la langue française, [. . .] l'interprète en malinké, pour rendre le *langage malinké*, en supprimant toute frontière linguistique, à la grande surprise du lecteur."

14. See Frantz Fanon's essay on the relationship between the national bourgeois class and the problems of the postcolonial nation, "The Trials and Tribulations of National Consciousness," in *The Wretched of the Earth*, 97–144.

15. "Il n'y reste aucun *monnè*, avaient chanté les griots le jour de son intronisation.

"Djigui les avait crus. Les premières saisons de son règne, il ne s'était livré à rien de vrai qu'à épouser de nombreuses vierges—il était le plus fort et le plus beau. Se faire célébrer par les adulateurs et les griots—il était le plus grand. Transformer ses esclaves en sbires et en sicaires— il était le plus intelligent du Mandingue. Comme tout jeune prince malinké, il avait chassé. Dans la brousse, on l'avait vu souvent arriver avant les chiens sur le gibier. C'étaient là les seules œuvres qui l'avaient préoccupé. Lui qui était notre roi, il avait régné sans bénir les offrandes et l'aumône qu'en son nom on distribuait aux mendiants. Sans casser aucune des sentences des juges mensongers. Il avait vécu sans rassembler les savants ni les sacrificateurs. Sans prier cinq fois par jour. Sans honorer les mânes des aïeux"(15).

16. "Assurément, Djeliba était un griot talentueux, le plus grand poète louangeur de notre siècle . . . Djigui devait l'attacher à la dynastie des Keita" (42).

17. "Un bienfait toujours oblige. A un bienfait un griot, comme tout homme, est tenu à la reconnaissance . . . des louanges, des poèmes, de la musique. [. . .] Le bienfait et l'honneur enchaîne plus solidement l'homme de bien que ne parviennent à l'accomplir la force et la corde qui retient l'esclave ou l'éhonté" (43–44).

18. "Je traduis les paroles d'un Blanc, d'un Toubab. Quand un Toubab s'exprime, nous, Nègres, on se tait, se décoiffe, se déchausse et écoute" (54).

19. "Le griot s'excusa: il ignorait que le langage de la force et du pouvoir blancs avait besoin de la voix des griots pour s'imposer" (54).

20. "Quand chacun doit se retourner contre moins fort, la bise souffle

contre la calebasse vide: les Français étaient des cornus qui ne donnaient des coups qu'aux bêtes décornées" (113).

21. "1. Si la perdrix s'envole son enfant ne reste pas à terre. 2. Malgré le séjour prolongé d'un oiseau perché sur un baobab, il n'oublie pas que le nid dans lequel il a été couvé est dans l'arbuste. 3. Et quand on ne sait pas où l'on va, qu'on sache d'où l'on vient" (11).

22. "Le chasseur à l'affût de temps en temps interrompt la poursuite pour chiquer son tabac. Imitons-le nous aussi. Suspendons notre récit. Annonce le sora, et il joue de sa cora. Le cordoua danse et blasphème. Bingo proclame: . . . " (81).

23. "1. La mort engloutit l'homme, elle n'engloutit pas son nom et sa réputation. 2. La mort est un vêtement que tout le monde portera. 3. Parfois la mort est faussement accusée quand elle achève des vieillards qui par l'âge étaient déjà finis, déjà bien morts avant l'avènement de la mort" (82).

24. "L'enjeu d'une telle esthétique est de focaliser l'attention et l'intérêt du lecteur sur l'*ego*, l'altérité et l'altération d'un 'Moi' vu du dehors et du dedans par une voix initiée et autorisée à dire l'indicible et à nommer l'innommable."

25. "Tout de suite, il a tout compris. Il allait être égorgé, sacrifié et enterré avec un défunt. Chez les Agnis, ethnie du groupe des Akans, un chef ne va jamais seul dans sa tombe. On l'inhume toujours avec ceux qui dans l'au-delà le serviront" (132).

26. "Avant la colonisation, le géniteur était égorgé et sacrifié, ajoute Tiécoura. Maclédio, sans hésitation, demanda à être égorgé, tué, sacrifié. Il préférait la mort à l'éloignement, ou bannissement. [. . .] Le grand féticheur lui répond que depuis l'arrivée des Anglais en Côte-de-l'or, on n'égorge plus le géniteur. On le castre, lui tranche la langue, lui crève les yeux, lui perce les tympans"(135).

27. "En pleurs, démoralisé et découragé, je poursuis ma route toujours vers le nord. . ." (136).

28. "Ceux qui, comme Maclédio, toute la vie n'ont eu comme lot que la déveine et qui aspirent au bonheur marchent sans désemparer sur le Nord" (136).

29. "Son pacte d'écriture sera de dire le désenchantement du monde africain à partir d'une position individuelle, réconciliant le fonctionnel (le social) et le symbolique par un certain finalisme, c'est-à-dire par la fulgurance de son désir d'ancrage social, alors que les stratégies utilisées créent un divorce entre les deux sphères et ancrent son roman dans l'idéalisme."

4. CHINUA ACHEBE'S *ARROW OF GOD* AND THE PRAGMATICS OF PROVERBIAL IRONY

1. The template is a form of parody/mention (see Norrick 22).

2. The first two hundred entries under the letter F in the *Oxford Dictionary of English Proverbs*.

3. "Une pirogue n'est jamais trop grande pour chavirer.
Ce sont ceux qui ont peu de larmes qui pleurent vite le
défunt. La chèvre morte est un malheur pour le propriétaire de
la chèvre; mais que la tête de la chèvre soit mise dans la marmite
n'est un malheur que pour la chèvre elle-même." (95)

4. "Free conversational turn" is defined as "a discrete contribution to an ongoing conversation, which the speaker ends voluntarily (i. e., without being interrupted)" (Norrick 68).

5. A simple illustration of such projection is the poetic function of an academic protester's placard saying "More dollars for scholars" instead of a more prosaic "More funding for researchers." The reader is led to focus on the language of the message by the noticeable selection of rhyming terms in forming the syntactic sequence.

6. "C'est précisément dans [leur] rôle à la fois didactique et coercitif que aphorismes et proverbes purs contribuent, au-delà de leur valeur esthétique indéniable, à l'équilibre de la société traditionnelle, société d'oralité dont ils structurent l'expression verbale régularisent [*sic*] les comportements individuels" (364).

7. See Mathuray (52), who defines the *communitas* as an unstructured, liminal, and sacred sense of community that constantly threatens the hierarchical structure of society.

8. Okechuckwu views this exchange with the in-laws as evidence of Ezeulu's strength in dealing with "forensic occasions" (establishing facts to address a case involving litigation): "Ezeulu carefully placates [his in-laws] while not admitting to any serious misdemeanor on his son's part" (51).

5. CALIXTHE BEYALA

1. "En tant qu'attaque indirect, l'ironie est une arme particulièrement propre à la satire. Tout comme le satiriste, pour ne pas compromettre sa vie, évite d'aller tout droit à son but, l'ironiste, lui aussi pour la même raison, évite une attaque directe contre l'objet. L'ironie est particulière à la satire car dans toute ironie subsiste d'une manière implicite une censure que le sujet adresse à l'objet, ou exprime vis-à-vis de cet objet."

2. "Ceux qui l'avaient placée là *pour son bien* l'avaient oubliée, pour son malheur."

3. "on attendait d'elle la pompeuse contribution *d'une vieille tante qui n'avait plus que faire de ses économies.*"

4. "[t]ant de signes pour si peu de sens."

5. Odile Cazenave (2000) suggests that Cameroonian readers do not always find Beyala's work as an African writer as convincing as her French readership does (124).

6. "J'avais des griefs à brandir: contre Maman qui avait eu l'outre-cuidance de ne pas s'apercevoir que mes relations avec l'univers étaient convenables; contre Pléthore qui n'a pas su prendre l'habit des faux élus et raconter à maman qu'il était magasinier, ou ingénieur, ou chef de chantier."

7. "Soudain une illumination me monta au cerveau, exposa mes nerfs et je flairai la fatalité de Maya perdue seule dans la ville. [...] J'avais des ailes parce que je n'abandonnais pas cette inconnue à des tombeaux prématurés. Je ne pouvais laisser les peines de cette pauvre âme s'accroître par mon indifférence" (37–38).

8. Similar ironic figures of women as pseudo-saviors who are in fact violent, manipulative, and dangerous beings are found in the Mother Superior of Kourouma's *Allah n'est pas obligé* and the "Mother Superior" Geneviève of Mongo Beti's *Branle-Bas en noir et blanc*.

9. "Tandis que les sensualités marchandées déployaient leurs tentacules et broyaient l'humanité."

10. "C'est par pure courtoisie si j'ose appeler langage le charabia qui sort de vos bouches! Ce n'est pas avec les quelque trois cents mots de vocabulaire que possède Ève-Marie—et vous autres aussi, soit dit en passant—, ces deux douzaines de verbes à tout faire que vous écoulez sans cesse, l'incurie réelle de prépositions et de conjonctions de coordination dont vous abusez et qui trahissent votre ignorance, qu'une œuvre digne de ce nom verra le jour."

11. "Je courus derrière eux, me montrai prolifique, ingénieuse, rassurante, justifiait ma prétention à être la plus apte à survivre dans un univers hostile."

12. "C'est pas pour de vrai que je veux savoir comment on commet un meurtre parfait; j'écris un livre."

13. "Ils se bousculaient, se marchouillaient sur les pieds pour assister au miracle de l'accouchement littéraire."

14. "Le tirailleur sénégalais bondit vers moi, en grondant comme un chien méchant et ses yeux sortaient de sa tête."

15. "ils étaient convaincus qu'en m'abandonnant ils s'évitaient des problèmes qui auraient eu pour conséquence la dislocation de leur vie d'exclus."

16. "'Tu verras, ils vont tous te supplier de publier chez eux.' Il courait dans les cafés et psalmodiait mes extraordinaires talents en latin, en grec et même en chinois. 'Qui vivra, verra! lançait-il. Ma femme est la plus grande écrivaine de sa génération.'"

17. "convaincue [qu'elle n'a] pas besoin des petites puissances terriennes pour survivre, penser et faire ce [qu'elle juge] être bon pour [son] existence."

18. "'Le plus grand chef perd ses pouvoirs si tu décides qu'il n'en possède pas', avait coutume de dire ma mère. Et aussi: 'L'autre n'a sur nous que le pouvoir que nous lui accordons.'" This wisdom of the mother is comparable to the wisdom of the father evoked by Achebe, according to Okechukwu.

19. "parce que les griots leur expliquaient combien les terres africaines étaient plus chaleureuses, ils s'enracinaient sous les tropiques et leurs cœurs devenaient aussi vigoureux que les troncs des baobabs et leurs corps s'épanouissaient avec autant de puissance que les bougainvilliers en fleur. Ils pouvaient encore passer mille ans en exil sans se soucier des souffrances. Vous l'avez sans doute compris, chers lecteurs: je n'étais pas assez imbécile pour vivre un bonheur sans nuage, mais pas assez intelligente pour cueillir des pommes avec Newton ou courir la bagatelle avec Einstein! Dans ces moments-là, mon cœur endurci, mon cœur de sauvage s'amollissait. Les paroles des griots enivraient doucement mon esprit; Paris se raréfiait; l'Afrique venait planer au-dessus de ma tête avec ses soleils et ses nuits croassantes de reptiles."

20. "ceux qui n'ont inventé ni la poudre ni la boussole / ceux qui n'ont jamais su dompter la vapeur ni l'électricité" (*Cahier* 111).

21. "Moi, la tradition, j'ai toujours été contre. Je fais corps avec elle quand elle vibre d'émotion, nourrit l'esprit, enrichit la mémoire. Je l'affronte, la répudie quand elle se fige en interdits, s'érige en prison."

22. "Plus tard seulement je m'apercevrais que ce bonheur-là, je le devais à ce même système colonial qui nous avait dépouillés de tous nos biens, terres, femmes et enfants compris, ce qui donnait du piment à la farce."

23. "La mort, il la portait dans sa tête avant même de se perdre dans notre village. [. . .] Encore faudrait-il qu'il ait conscience de sa propre liberté."

24. "Morale de l'histoire: des années plus tard, je rencontrai Akouma lors d'un séjour à Douala. Elle s'était flétrie. Ses seins tombaient bas. Son compagnon la battait jusqu'à ce que ses mains blêmissent. Je me dis qu'il existe des situations où nous préférons la mort pour ceux qu'on aime à une vie de suie."

25. "[Les esprits] s'ennuyèrent encore.
Ils peignirent les humains sans se consulter. [. . .]
De l'ennui naquirent des races.
De l'égoïsme naîtront les guerres."

26. "Papa et maman n'échappaient pas à la règle et, à force de vivre ensemble, ils avaient fini par se ressembler. Ils étaient chauves. Leurs visages étaient burinés et sur leurs mains desséchées des veines saillaient comme les racines d'un manguier sauvage. Ils étaient tout debout à quelques pas, si proches l'un de l'autre que leurs têtes se touchaient presque. J'eus l'impression de vivre une illusion et ne bougeai pas."

27. "Il était haut comme un baobab et concentrait dans ses yeux noirs la force tranquille d'un pape romain."

28. "Que veux-tu que je te dise au juste. Que je t'assure que je prendrai soin de ta mémoire après ta mort?"

29. "Il était un vieillard dans le sens éton du terme c'est-à-dire qu'une lumière magnétique lui conférait le pouvoir de masquer ses vraies pensées."

30. "Dès le lendemain, papa décida de mourir comme s'il voulait éviter de prendre ce chemin de la folie dans lequel le continent noir s'engouffrait."

31. "Mon Dieu que j'ai souffert par la suite à regarder l'humanité qui grouille, qui chante, qui baise tandis qu'il n'y a plus trace de mon père!"

32. "Certains venaient par devoir, d'autres dans l'espoir de s'introduire dans les bonnes grâces de maman. [. . .] Les uns par curiosité, les autres pour s'assurer qu'à leur enterrement, il y aurait beaucoup de personnes."

REFERENCES

Achebe, Chinua. *Anthills of the Savannah*. London: Heinemann, 1987.

———. *Arrow of God*. 1964. London: Heinemann, 1974.

———. *Things Fall Apart*. London: Heinemann, 1958.

Adichie, Chimamanda Ngozi. "The Headstrong Historian." In *The Thing around Your Neck*, 198–218. New York: Knopf, 2009.

Allemann, Beda. "De l'ironie en tant que principe littéraire." *Poétique* 11 (1980): 345–97.

Amadi, Elechi. *The Concubine*. London: Heinemann, 1966.

Armah, Ayi Kwei. *Two Thousand Seasons*. London: Heinemann, 1979.

Bâ, Mariama. *Un chant écarlate*. Dakar, Senegal: Les Nouvelles Éditions Africaines, 1981.

———. *Une si longue lettre*. Dakar, Senegal: Les Nouvelles Éditions Africaines, 2000.

Bakhtin, Mikhail. *The Dialogic Imaginaton: Four Essays*. M. Holquist, ed.; C. Emerson and M. Holquist, trans. Austin: University of Texas Press, 1981.

Barbe, Katharina. *Irony in Context*. Amsterdam: Benjamins, 1995.

Barthes, Roland. *Mythologies*. Paris: Éditions du Seuil, 1957.

Beauvoir, Simone de. "La femme et la création." Text from conference in Japan, September 1966. In C. Francis and F. Gontier, eds., *Les Écrits de Simone de Beauvoir*, 458–74. Paris: Gallimard, 1966. Translated by Roisin Mallaghan as «Women and Creativity,» in Toril Moi, ed., *French Feminist Thought*, 17–32. Oxford: Basil Blackwell, 1987.

Behler, Ernst. *Irony and the Discourse of Modernity.* Seattle and London: University of Washington Press, 1990.

Berrendonner, Alain. *Éléments de pragmatique linguistique.* Paris: Éditions de Minuit, 1981.

Bessora, Sandrine. *53 cm.* Paris: Le Serpent à Plumes, 1999.

Beyala, Calixthe. *Amours sauvages.* Paris: Albin Michel, 1999.

———. *Les arbres en parlent encore.* Paris: Albin Michel, 2002.

———. *Assèze l'Africaine.* Paris: Albin Michel, 1994.

———. *Comment cuisiner son mari à l'africaine.* Paris: Albin Michel, 2000.

———. *L'homme qui m'offrait le ciel.* Paris: Albin Michel, 2007.

———. *Le petit prince de Belleville.* Paris: Albin Michel, 1992.

———. *Plantation.* Paris: Albin Michel, 2005.

———. *Tu t'appelleras Tanga.* Paris: Stock, 1988.

Bhabha, Homi K. *The Location of Culture.* London and New York: Routledge, 1994.

Bisanswa, Justin. "Jeux de miroirs: Kourouma l'interprète?" *Présence francophone* 59 (2002): 8–27.

Bjornson, Richard. *The African Quest for Freedom and Identity: Cameroonian Writing and the National Experience.* Bloomington: Indiana University Press, 1994.

Blakemore, Diane. *Understanding Utterances.* Oxford: Blackwell, 1992.

Booth, Wayne. *A Rhetoric of Irony.* Chicago and London: University of Chicago Press, 1974.

Borgomano, Madelaine. *Des hommes ou des bêtes? Lecture de "En attendant le vote des bêtes sauvages" d'Ahmadou Kourouma.* Paris: L'Harmattan, 2000.

Bouaka, Charles-Lucien. *Mongo Beti: Par le Sublime.* Paris: L'Harmattan, 2005.

Bugul, Ken. *Cendres et braises.* Paris: L'Harmattan, 1994.

Cazenave, Odile. *Afrique sur Seine : A New Generation of African Women Writers in Paris.* Lanham, Md.: Lexington Books, 2005.

———. "Calixthe Beyala's 'Parisian Novels': An Example of Globalization in French Society." *Contemporary French and Francophone Studies* 4:1 (2000) : 119–27.

———. *Femmes rebelles: Naissance d'un nouveau roman africain au féminin.* Paris: L'Harmattan, 1996.

Césaire, Aimé. *Cahier d'un retour au pays natal/Return to my Native Land.* Paris: Présence Africaine, 1971.

———. *Discours sur le colonialisme.* Paris: Présence Africaine, 1955.

Clark, Herbert, and Richard Gerrig. "On the Pretense of Irony." *Journal of Experimental Psychology* 113 (1984): 121–26.

Colebrook, Claire. *Irony*. New York: Routledge, 2003.

Cox, Tim. *Post-modern Tales of Slavery: From Alejo Carpentier to Charles Johnson*. New York: Garland, 2001.

Culler, Jonathan. *Structuralist Poetics: Structuralism, Linguistics and the Study of Literature*. Ithaca, N.Y.: Cornell University Press, 1975.

Dadié, Bernard. *Béatrice du Congo*. Paris: Présence Africaine, 1970.

d'Almeida, Irène. *Francophone African Women Writers: Destroying the Emptiness of Silence*. Gainesville, Fla.: University Press of Florida, 1994.

d'Almeida-Topor, Hélène. *L'Afrique*. Paris: Le Cavalier Bleu, 2009.

Diallo, Bakary. *Force-Bonté*. Paris: Nouvelles Éditions Africaines/Agence de Coopération culturelle et technique, 1985.

Diallo, Mamadou Bani. "Les sources traditionnelles du comique dans l'œuvre romanesque de Massa Makan Diabaté." In Jean Cléo Godin, ed., *Nouvelles écritures francophones: Vers un nouveau baroque?* 154–62. Montreal: Presses de l'Université de Montréal, 2001.

Diome, Fatou. *Inassouvies, nos vies*. Paris: Flammarion, 2008.

Diop, Boubacar Boris. *Le cavalier et son ombre*. Abidjan, Ivory Coast: Nouvelles Editions Ivoiriennes, 1999.

Ducrot, Oswald. *Le Dire et le dit*. Paris: Éditions de Minuit, 1984.

Elshtain, Jean. "Feminist Discourse and Its Discontents: Language, Power, and Meaning." *Signs: Journal of Women in Culture and Society* 7 (1982): 603–21.

Erling, Holger, ed. *Critical Approaches to "Anthills of the Savannah."* Amsterdam: Rodopi, 1991.

Ezenwa-Ohaeto. "Patriots and Parasites: The Metaphor of Power in Achebe's *Anthills of the Savannah*." In H. Ehling, ed., *Critical Approaches to "Anthills of the Savannah,"* 23–34. Amsterdam: Rodopi, 1991.

Fandio, Pierre. "*Trop de soleil tue l'amour* et *En attendant le vote des bêtes sauvages*: Deux extrêmes, un bilan des transitions démocratiques en Afrique." In O. Pfouma, ed., *Mongo Beti: Le proscrit admirable*, 113–35. Paris: Menaibuc, 2003.

Fanon, Frantz. *The Wretched of the Earth*. Richard Philcox, trans. New York: Grove Press, 2004.

Gagiano, Annie. *Achebe, Head, Marechera: On Power and Change in Africa*. Boulder, Colo.: Lynne Reinner, 2000.

Gallimore, Rangira Béatrice. *L'oeuvre romanesque de Calixthe Beyala: Le renouveau de l'écriture féminine en Afrique francophone sub-saharienne*. Paris: L'Harmattan, 1997.

Garnier, Xavier. "Le rire cosmique de Kourouma." *Études françaises* 42.3 (2006): 97–108.

Gassama, Makhily. *La langue d'Ahmadou Kourouma ou le français sous le soleil d'Afrique*. Paris: ACCT/Karthala, 1995.

Gates, Henry Louis, Jr. *The Signifying Monkey: A Theory of African-American Literary Criticism*. New York and Oxford: Oxford University Press, 1988.

Gbanou, Sélom Komlan. *"En attendant le vote des bêtes sauvages* ou le roman d'un 'diseur de vérité.'" *Études françaises* 42, no. 3 (2006) : 51–76.

———. "L'incipit dans l'oeuvre d'Ahmadou Kourouma." *Présence francophone* 59 (2002): 52–68.

Gikandi, Simon. *Reading Chinua Achebe*. London: James Currey; Portsmouth, N.H.: Heinemann; Nairobi: Heinemann Kenya, 1991.

Gilroy, Paul. *The Black Atlantic: Modernity and Double Consciousness*. London: Verso, 1993.

Gunner, Liz. "Africa and Orality." In F. A. Irele and S. Gikandi, eds., *The Cambridge History of African and Caribbean Literature*. Vol. 1 : 1–18. Cambridge: Cambridge University Press, 2004.

Hamon, Philippe. *L'ironie littéraire*. Paris: Hachette, 1996.

———. "Stylistique de l'ironie." In G. Molinié and P. Cahué, eds., *Qu'est-ce que le style?* 149–58. Paris: Presses universitaires de France, 1994.

Harrow, Kenneth. "Ngugi wa Thiong'o's *A Grain of Wheat*: Season of Irony." *Research in African Literatures* 16.2 (1985): 243–63.

Head, Bessie. *Maru*. London: Heinemann, 1971.

Honeck, Richard, and Jon Temple. "Proverbs: The Extended Conceptual Base and Great Chain Metaphor Theories." *Metaphor and Symbolic Activitiy* 9 (1994): 85–112.

Howe, Stephen. *Afrocentricity: Mythical Pasts and Imagined Homes*. London and New York: Verso, 1998.

Hutcheon, Linda. *Irony's Edge: The Theory and Politics of Irony*. London and New York: Routledge, 1994.

Izevbaye, Dan. "Chinua Achebe and the African Novel." In F. A. Irele, ed., *The Cambridge Companion to the African Novel*, 31–50. Cambridge: Cambridge University Press, 2009.

Jakobson, Roman. "Linguistics and Poetics." In S. Chatman and S. Levin, eds., *Essays on the Language of Literature*. Boston: Houghton Mifflin, 1967.

James, C. L. R. *The Black Jacobins: Toussaint L'Ouverture and the San Domingo Revolution*. New York: Vintage Books, 1989.

Jamieson, Kathleen. *Eloquence in an Electronic Age: The Transformation of Political Speechmaking*. New York: Oxford University Press, 1988.

Jankélévitch, Vladimir. *L'ironie*. Paris: Flammarion, 1964.

Jay, Nancy. "Gender and Dichotomy." *Feminist Studies* 7 (1981): 38–56.

Jukpor, Ben K'Anene. *Étude sur la satire dans le théâtre ouest-africain francophone*. Paris: L'Harmattan, 1995.

Kane, Cheikh Hamidou. *L'aventure ambiguë*. Paris: Julliard, 1961.

Kaufer, David. "Irony, Interpretative Form, and the Theory of Meaning." *Poetics Today* 4.3 (1983): 451–64.

Kenyatta, Jomo. *Facing Mount Kenya*. New York: Vintage, 1965.

Kerbrat-Orecchioni, Catherine. *L'Implicite*. Paris: A. Colin, 1986.

———. "L'ironie comme trope." *Poétique* 41 (1980): 108–27.

———. "Problèmes de l'ironie." *Linguistique et sémiologie* 2 (1976): 10–46.

Kerszberg, Annik Doquire. "Kourouma 2000: Humour obligé." *Présence francophone* 59 (2002): 110–25.

Kohvakka, Hannele. "Ironie als Textuelle Erscheinung: Eine linguistische Erklärung der Enstehung von Ironie." *Neuphilologishe Mitteilungen* 97.3 (1996) : 239–53.

Koné, Amadou. "Figures d'hier et d'aujourd'hui: Vers une nouvelle perception du roman africain." In Christiane Ndiaye and Josias Semujanga, eds., *De paroles en figures: Essais sur les littératures africaines et antillaises*, 23–38. Montreal: L'Harmattan, 1996.

Kouassi, Germain. *Le Phénomène de l'appropriation linguistique et esthétique en littérature africaine de langue française: Le cas des écrivains ivoiriens: Dadié, Kourouma et Adiaffai*. Paris: Publibook, 2007.

Kourouma, Ahmadou. *Allah n'est pas obligé*. Paris: Éditions du Seuil, 2000.

———. *Le diseur de vérité*. Paris: Acoria, 1998.

———. *En attendant le vote des bêtes sauvages*. Paris: Éditions du Seuil, 1998.

———. *Monnè, outrages et défis*. Paris: Éditions du Seuil, 1990.

———. *Monnew*. Nidra Poller, trans. San Francisco: Mercury House, 1993.

———. *Les soleils des indépendances*. Paris: Éditions du Seuil, 1970.

———. *Waiting for the Vote of the Wild Animals*. Carrol Coates, trans. Charlottesville and London: University of Virginia Press, 2001.

Kreuz, Roger, and Sam Glucksberg. "How to Be Sarcastic: The Echoic Reminder Theory of Verbal Irony." *Journal of Experimental Psychology* 118 (1989): 374–86.

Kumon-Nakamura, Sachi, Sam Glucksberg, and Mary Brown. "How About Another Piece of the Pie: The Allusional Pretense Theory of Discourse Irony." *Journal of Experimental Psychology: General*, 124 (1995) : 3–21.

Labou Tansi, Sony. *La vie et demie*. Paris: Seuil, 1979.

———. *Les yeux du volcan*. Paris: Seuil, 1988.

Lapp, Edgar. *Linguistik der Ironie*. Tübingen, Germany: Gunter Narr, 1992.

Leggitt, J. S., and Raymond Gibbs. "Emotional Reactions to Verbal Irony." *Discourse Processes* 29 (2000): 1–24.

Lopes, Henri. *Le lys et le flamboyant*. Paris: Éditions du Seuil, 1997.

Lyons, John. *Semantics*. Vol. 1. Cambridge: Cambridge University Press, 1977.

Maran, René. *Batouala*. Paris: Albin Michel, 1938.

Matateyou, Emmanuel. "Calixthe Beyala entre l'oral et l'écrit-cercueil: Essai d'analyse du nouveau discours féminin francophone en Afrique noire." In Jean Cléo Godin, ed., *Nouvelles écritures francophones: Vers un nouveau baroque?* 372–82. Montreal: Presses de l'Université de Montréal, 2001.

Mathuray, Mark. "Realizing the Sacred: Power and Meaning in Chinua Achebe's *Arrow of God.*" *Research in African Literatures* 34.3 (2003): 46–65.

Mbembe, Achille. *On the Postcolony*. Berkely: University of California Press, 2001.

Mbiti, John S. *African Religions and Philosophy*. 2nd edition. Oxford: Heinemann, 1990.

Memmi, Albert. *Portait du colonisé*. Montreal: L'Etincelle, 1972.

Mey, Jacob. *Pragmatics: An Introduction*. Oxford: Blackwell, 1993.

Miller, Christopher. *Blank Darkness: Africanist Discourse in French*. Chicago and London: University of Chicago Press, 1985.

Moi, Toril. *Sexual/Textual Politics: Feminist Literary Theory*. London and New York: Routledge, 1985.

Mokeddem, Malika. *La transe des insoumis*. Paris: Grasset, 2003.

Mongo Beti. *Branle-bas en noir et blanc*. Paris: Julliard, 2000.

———. *Le pauvre Christ de Bomba*. Paris: Laffont, 1956.

———. *Perpétue et l'habitude du malheur*. Paris: Buchet Chastel, 1974.

———. *Trop de soleil tue l'amour*. Paris: Julliard, 1999.

Morris, Charles. *Foundations of a Theory of Signs*. Chicago: University of Chicago Press, 1938.

Mortimer, Mildred. *Writing from the Hearth: Public, Domestic, and Imaginative Space in Francophone Women's Fiction of Africa and the Caribbean*. Lanham, Md.: Lexington Books, 2007.

Mudimbe, V. Y. *The Invention of Africa: Gnosis, Philosophy and Order of Knowledge*. Bloomington and Indianapolis, Ind.: James Currey, 1988.

Muecke, D. C. *The Compass of Irony*. London: Methuen, 1969.

———. *Irony*. London: Methuen, 1970.

Nfah-Abbenyi, Juliana Makuchi. *Gender in African Women's Writing: Identity, Sexuality, and Difference*. Bloomington: Indiana University Press, 1997.

Ngugi wa Thiong'o. *A Grain of Wheat*. London: Heinemann, 1967.

———. *Petals of Blood*. London: Heinemann, 1977.

Niane, D. T. *Soundjata ou l'épopée mandingue*. Paris: Présence Africaine, 1960.

Norrick, Neal. *How Proverbs Mean: Semantic Studies in English Proverbs*. Berlin, New York, and Amsterdam: Mouton, 1985.

Noumssi, Gérard, and Rodolphine Sylive Wamba. "Créativité esthétique et enrichissement du français dans la prose romanesque d'Ahmadou Kourouma." *Présence francophone* 59 (2002): 28–51.

Ogunjimi, Bayo, and Abdul-Rasheed Na'Allah. *Introduction to African Oral Literature and Performance*. Trenton, N.J.: Africa World Press, 2005.

Okechukwu, Chinwe Christiana. *Achebe the Orator: The Art of Persuasion in Chinua Achebe's Novels*. Westport, Conn.: Greenwood Press, 2001.

Okpewho, Isidore. *African Oral Literature: Backgrounds, Character and Community*. Bloomington and Indianapolis: Indiana University Press, 1992.

Ola, Virginia. "Grappling with Irony in the Feminist Text." In E. Emenyonu, ed., *Goatskin Bags and Wisdom: New Critical Perspectives on African Literature*, 129–42. Trenton, N.J.: Africa World Press, 2000.

Olaogun, Modupe. "Irony and Schizophrenia in Bessie Head's *Maru*." *Research in African Literatures* 25.4 (1994): 69–87.

Onyeoziri, Gloria. "Le labyrinthe sémantique du signifiant culturel: le 'monnè' d'Ahmadou Kourouma." *Actes de langue française et de linguistique* 6 (1993): 123–34.

———. "Les petits princes de Beyala." *Études francophones* 16.2 (2001): 183–208.

———. "Revisiting the 'Roman de la Désillusion': A Semiotic and Cultural Reading of Ousmane Sembène's *Xala*." In K. Salhi, ed., *Francophone Post-Colonial Cultures*, 102–113. Lanham, Md.: Lexington Books, 2003.

Ouologuem, Yambo. *Le devoir de violence*. Paris: Éditions du Seuil, 1968.

Oyono, Ferdinand. *Une vie de boy*. Paris: Julliard, 1956.

Paillet-Guth, Anne-Marie. *Ironie et paradoxe: Les discours amoureux romanesques*. Paris: H. Champion, 1998.

Perrin, Laurent. *L'ironie mise en trope*. Paris: Kimé, 1996.

Pexman, Penny. "Social Factors in the Interpretation of Verbal Irony: The Roles of Speaker and Listener Characteristics." In H. Colston and A. Katz, eds., *Figurative Language Comprehension: Social and Cultural Influences*, 209–32. Mahwah, N.J.: Lawrence Erlbaum Associates, 2005.

Ramazani, Vaheed. *The Free Indirect Mode: Flaubert and the Poetics of Irony*. Charlottesville: University Press of Virginia, 1988.

Ricard, Alain. *Littératures d'Afrique noire: Des langues aux livres*. Paris: CNRS/Karthala, 1995.

Rice, Laura. *Of Irony and Empire: Islam, the West and the Transcultural Invention of Africa*. Albany: State University of New York Press, 2007.

Rivkin, Julie, and Michael Ryan, eds. *Literary Theory: An Anthology*. Oxford: Blackwell, 1998.

Rosaldo, Michelle. *Woman, Culture, and Society*. Stanford, Calif.: Stanford University Press, 1974.

Rose, Margaret. *Parody: Ancient, Modern, and Post-Modern*. Cambridge: Cambridge University Press, 1993.

Ryan, Michael. *Literary Theory: A Practical Introduction*. Oxford: Blackwell, 1999.

Salmon, Nathan. "Two Conceptions of Semantics." In Z. Szabó, ed., *Semantics versus Pragmatics*, 317–28. Oxford: Clarendon Press, 2005.

Schiappa, Edward. *Defining Reality: Definitions and the Politics of Meaning*. Carbondale and Edwardsville: Southern Illinois University Press, 2003.

Scott, James C. *Domination and the Arts of Resistance: Hidden Transcripts*. New Haven, Conn.: Yale University Press, 1990.

Selden, Raman, et al. *A Reader's Guide to Contemporary Literary Theory*. 4th edition. London: Prentice Hall, Harvester Wheatsheaf, 1997.

Sembène, Ousmane. *Les bouts de bois de Dieu*. Paris: Le Livre contemporain, 1960.

———. *Xala*. Paris: Présence Africaine, 1974.

Sollors, Werner. *Beyond Ethnicity: Consent and Descent in American Culture*. Oxford and New York: Oxford University Press, 1986.

Sougou, Omar. "Language, Foregrounding and Intertextuality in *Anthills of the Savannah*." In Ehling, ed., *Critical Approaches to "Anthills of the Savannah*," 35–55.

Sow Fall, Aminata. *Le revenant*. Dakar, Senegal: Nouvelles Éditions Africaines, 1976.

Sperber, Daniel, and Deidre Wilson. "Les ironies comme mention." *Poétique* 36 (1978): 399–412.

———. "Irony and the Use-Mention Distinction." In P. Cole, ed., *Radical pragmatics*, 296–318. New York: Academic, 1981.

Szabó, Zoltán Gendler, ed. *Semantics versus Pragmatics*. Oxford: Clarendon Press, 2005.

Tobner, Odile. "La vie et l'oeuvre de Mongo Beti." in O. Pfouma, ed., *Mongo Beti : Le proscrit admirable*, 11–18. Paris: Menaibuc, 2003.

Toplak, Maggie, and A. N. Katz. "On the Uses of Sarcastic Irony." *Journal of Pragmatics* 32 (2000):1467–88.

Trigger, Bruce. *History of Archaelogical Thought*. New York: Cambridge University Press, 2006.

Utsumi, Akira. "Verbal Irony as Implicit Display of Ironic Environment: Distinguishing Ironic Utterances from Nonirony." *Journal of Pragmatics* 32 (2000): 1777–1806.

Warner-Lewis, Maureen. "The Oral Tradition in the African Diaspora." In F. A. Irele and S. Gikandi, eds., *The Cambridge History of African and Caribbean Literature*. Vol. 1, 117–36. Cambridge: Cambridge University Press, 2004.

INDEX